OHIO

GETTING STARTED GARDEN GUIDE

Grow the Best Flowers, Shrubs, Trees, Vines & Groundcovers

Published in 2015 by Cool Springs Press, an imprint of the Quarto Publishing Group USA Inc., 400 First Avenue North, Suite 400, Minneapolis, MN 55401

Cool Springs Press titles are also available at discounts in bulk quantity for industrial or sales-promotional use. For details write to Special Sales Manager at Quarto Publishing Group USA Inc., 400 First Avenue North, Suite 400, Minneapolis, MN 55401 USA. To find out more about our books, visit us online at www.coolspringspress.com.

Library of Congress Cataloging-in-Publication Data

McKeown, Denny, author.
  Ohio getting started garden guide : grow the best flowers, shrubs, trees, vines & groundcovers / Denny McKeown.
     pages cm
  Includes bibliographical references and index.
  ISBN 978-1-59186-911-5 (sc)
  1. Gardening--Ohio. I. Title.

  SB453.2.O3M387 2015
  635.09771--dc23

                          2014044861

Acquisitions Editor: Billie Brownell
Design Manager: Brad Springer
Layout: S.E. Anglin
Cover photo: George Weigel

Printed in China
10 9 8 7 6 5 4 3 2 1

OHIO

GETTING STARTED GARDEN GUIDE

Grow the Best Flowers, Shrubs, Trees, Vines & Groundcovers

Denny McKeown

COOL
SPRINGS
PRESS

Home and Garden Experts™

MINNEAPOLIS, MINNESOTA

Dedication

I would like to dedicate this book to my beautiful wife, Pat, for her support in all that I try to accomplish. She is always there for me as well as our whole family. Patrish, I love you.

Acknowledgments

A big thank you to all of my industry peers, both past and present, who have shared and continue to share their knowledge and expertise with me. This group includes the Ohio State University Extension Service, the Conard-Pyle Company, Lee Larson with Monrovia Nurseries, Dick Posey of Buckeye Resources, and all the Master Gardeners of Ohio.

I would also like to give a big thank you to editor Billie Brownell and all the others at Cool Springs Press, especially Tracy Stanley, and last but not least, to Debbie Scott and Diana Lerch for all their work in putting this book together.

A special thank you to my son, Chris, along with a big hug to you not only for fulfilling your responsibilities as President and co-owner of Denny McKeown, Inc. and Denny Mac Land, but also for taking on some of my responsibilities to free up my time to write this book.

A thank you to all the fine people at Bloomin Garden Centre and Denny McKeown Landscape for keeping yourselves informed and for passing along that information to our customers, as well as for keeping *me* informed as to their wants and needs so that I may take that information and pass it on to others.

Now I save the best and biggest thank you for *you*—the reader—for showing your confidence in me by choosing this book to help you create and maintain your best landscape ever.

CONTENTS

WELCOME TO GARDENING

IN OHIO

Hi! Welcome to *Ohio Getting Started Garden Guide*. The purpose of this book is to help you expand your gardening and landscape knowledge. First, let me introduce myself. I've been a part of the nursery industry for more than fifty years. During that time, I've tried to serve the needs of the gardening public. I've worked in garden centers both in sales and in management. I've been involved with landscape design and installation, and I have also been involved with the growing operations of nursery stock. Before you say, "Gee, Denny, you must have had a hard time keeping a job," let me explain.

My first twenty-nine years in the nursery industry were spent with one company, Natorp's, in Cincinnati, Ohio. There I had the opportunity to learn and grow through working with the many professionals associated with the company. In 1992, I started my own garden center and landscape company that I now operate with my son, Chris, who is the backbone of our operation. I've learned over the years that my success as a nurseryman depends solely on the success of the landscapes that belong to the customers I serve. This book contains over 150 plant varieties that I have worked with personally. Many of the plants are in my own home landscape, and others have been sold to customers and installed in their landscapes. But rest assured, I have personally experienced every plant in this book to see how it grows in all parts of Ohio, with all of Ohio's challenging growing conditions.

When it comes to outdoor plants of all types, I personally am a low-maintenance, high-performance, high-color kind of guy. I like to enjoy a nice-looking landscape with my eyes and not my blood and sweat—and I believe that most homeowners feel the same way. Our busy schedules don't often allow hours of time every week to work in the landscape all season long. This book shares with you those plants that will give you the best in landscape appearance with the least amount of maintenance. But those of you who enjoy yard work won't be disappointed either. Many of these plant varieties will do well without you, but they will do even better than you could imagine if you provide some assistance.

Successful gardening at any level needs you to do one important thing: use common sense. Over the years, I have witnessed many more plants that have been killed with kindness rather than with neglect.

Be Honest with Yourself

Most of us go to buy plants at the garden store with the idea of, *"I'll buy whatever strikes my eye,"* giving no consideration to the location in which that plant will be expected to grow. We may tell ourselves and the nursery staff that we have the right location for a plant, hoping that our poor planting site will be the exception and not the rule. Canadian hemlock and white pine are perfect examples of plants that homeowners often fall in love with at first sight, but both of these plants need special growing conditions to thrive. Roses are another great example of plants that often wind up in too much shade because we have convinced ourselves that two hours of sun are as good as five. When buying plants, if you will be willing to substitute a plant that will be happier in your particular planting site, you will be a happier homeowner. You can learn to love any plant that performs well for you.

The USDA cold-hardiness zone map on page 17 will help you understand your growing environment a little better. A cold-hardiness zone is defined by the northernmost boundary in which plants can grow when the weather is at its coldest. Ohio is divided into two cold-hardiness zones, 5 and 6. Although most of the cold-hardy plants in this book will be hardy in both zones, it is useful to know the zone in which you garden. Much gardening information is specific to one zone or the other.

To Amend or Not to Amend: That's the Question

There are parts of northern Ohio that have very good soil; other parts of northern Ohio have sandy soil. The majority of us, however, have clay soil of varying thickness. There is some good soil in southern and eastern Ohio, but again, most of us have clay soil. For years, it was standard practice to tell homeowners to amend the soil when installing new plants—by that I mean adding peat moss, compost, manure, or all of the above to the soil you dug out while digging the planting hole. Common sense is now convincing the industry to tell you that it is possible to overamend your soil. Think about it. What kind of soil is the plant going to grow in once the roots grow beyond the hole you have dug?

Overimproving the existing soil or, worse yet, replacing the old soil with nice fresh topsoil creates what I call *bathtubbing*. When it rains, or when we water, the moisture goes through the overamended soil very quickly, hitting the hard clay bottom and filling up like a bathtub. Too much water equals a dead plant. I recommend using organic peat, pine bark chips, or even pea gravel to amend soil when needed, but do not add more than 30 percent amendments to the existing soil. And always break up your clay soil so that no particle is bigger than a golf ball.

How Big Will My Plant Grow?

Ohio landscapes are full of sweetbay magnolias and Japanese weeping cherries that we bought as cute little trees and planted against the foundation of a home. Now the

Pick a tree whose mature size won't overwhelm the space given to it.

house looks like it is being swallowed by those trees. Your only recourse is to trim the trees—but then it will look like they have had a bad haircut. Such a situation is not all your fault. When you visited your favorite nursery store, the plant sign that identified the plants for sale probably said something like "Magnolia 'Sweetbay', grows to 10 feet high and 6 feet wide." But no plant—with the exception of annuals, perennials, and ornamental grasses—ever stops growing until the day it dies. A cute little Alberta spruce that's considered a dwarf will grow a couple of inches a year. That growth adds up over a ten-year period. Find out how much growth you can expect from a particular tree, shrub, or evergreen every year, and how much trimming is going to be needed to maintain the plant at the finished size you need. This book will help you determine the growth rate, but your pruning shears will ultimately keep a particular plant within your bounds.

Let's Mulch, It's So Pretty!

We hear that mulch discourages weeds, mulch retains moisture in our planting beds, and mulch gives our landscape beds that finished professional look. But it is reason number three that is the true motivation for most mulching. Although all of the above are true, more and more homeowners are unintentionally harming their landscape plants with mulch—that is, too much mulch.

First, what is mulch? It can be any organic or inorganic material that we use to cover the soil, from newspaper, grass clippings, pine straw, shredded used tires, and gravel to the ever-popular wood mulch. Wood mulches basically come just a few ways: actual bark from the tree that was either chipped or shredded, or recycled hardwood from old house lumber and used wood pallets. The best type of wood mulch is the bark. It lasts longer, both in color and in quality. It also is less likely to host various fungal growths that can appear on wood mulch during hot, humid summers. The following are some different types of mulch, along with the pros and cons of each.

- **Pine bark chips:** These come in various sized pieces from ¼-inch to large 3-inch chunks. This type of mulch does not crust. It stays nice and airy, allowing moisture and air down into the soil. It does tend to float when hit with a heavy rain, and large chunks can become flying missiles out of youngster's hands as well as Fido wanting to play.
- **Shredded bark:** This is 100 percent tree bark that goes through a shredder. It is available in different degrees of coarseness. The coarser the shred, the steeper the slope that it will hold and stay in place during very heavy rains. Fine-shredded bark will cover more ground per bag or cubic yard, but you will have to cultivate the mulch monthly to keep a crust from forming, locking out moisture and air from the soil. Cypress bark keeps its color for several seasons.

Shredded cypress bark

- **Shredded hardwood:** Up to 100 percent wood, it can also have extra filler added—such as sawdust—to help the mulch go further. This is the most economical mulch going by raw dollars, but if you factor in perceived value, the processed bark is much better. Keep this mulch cultivated monthly to keep the soil moist and airy.
- **Washed stone and pea gravel:** As a mulch, this works great to cover the bare soil under decks and steps. It can be used around plants, but it does attract kids and summer heat, really warming the soil temperature during the summer. Never use any stone that has sand or gravel dust in it.

Washed stone

Pine straw

- **Recycled tires:** A great mulch for use in play swing areas. It provides a nice soft landing spot. It can, however, be used by the kids as missiles and does attract heat during the summer. It can also burn if a discarded cigarette butt finds it.

- **Pine straw:** Ah, the Masters in Augusta, Georgia. Pine straw, which comes in bales, is the discarded needles of pine trees. It is the mulch of choice for most homeowners in the Southern states. It is applied to your planting beds just as you would apply wheat straw to lawn areas that you're reseeding. It is a mulch that—once down—will not move, even on very steep slopes. I love its look, but if you don't, put down a thin coating of pine straw and place a thin layer of pine chips on top. The chips will be locked in place by the pine straw. You can also use a leaf blower in the fall to remove any fallen leaves that have landed on the pine straw. Pine straw mulch, when applied to a depth of 2 inches, will remain in place for years. You might want to put a light coating of fresh needles down every other spring, but you do not run the risk of over-mulching like you do with every other type of mulch.

What Do You Mean—Too Much Mulch?

I mean all mulches (except pine straw) should never be put down deeper than 2 inches. Mulch that's too deep slows the movement of air and water into the soil below. Deep mulch also encourages plant roots to leave the soil and grow in the mulch, making those plants more vulnerable to drought damage in summer and frozen roots in winter. Add the fact that no plant—from an annual to a shade tree—wants any mulch on its stem or trunk. This part of the plant wants to be aboveground, not below. You say, "I already have 2 inches of old mulch down, and I want to add some new mulch next spring." Then I would say, "Either loosen the existing mulch to make it look better, or remove all the old mulch completely before applying fresh mulch." And

Pull mulch away from the stems of all plants—trees, shrubs, perennials, annuals.

please don't hire the big truck that blows the mulch through a big black hose onto your planting beds. You'll wind up with mulch that's too deep and very uneven, with pieces hanging from your shrubs. Pine straw sounds pretty good, doesn't it?

Before you buy or apply anything, *read the label.*

Following Directions: Is More Better?

There are many products we can use that will help our plants grow happy and healthy, including fertilizer, selective weedkillers, and other herbicides, pesticides, and fungicides. Companies that manufacture and package these products spend large sums of money to get each product approved by the Environmental Protection Agency and labeled. The label includes the very important *how much to use* information, including the amount to mix with water and how large an area the mixture should cover. The label on granular material will tell you how much to use over how many square feet. All labeled products will do the job that's required and remain environmentally friendly when used properly. Please do not expect any product to work faster by using more than the recommended rate.

With pesticides and fungicides, the directions will also state what diseases and insects a particular product will control. Please be sure you are using a product that will treat your specific problem, and that you use it at the right time of day and month. Remember, common sense tells us to do only as the product label states.

Pests: The Good, the Bad, and the Ugly

Now we're talking about the creatures of the world, like insects (commonly called bugs) and other creatures such as moles, rabbits, voles, deer, and anything else with four legs.

Let's start with insects. Fewer than 3 percent of insects are considered risks to our plants. Most harmful insects only attack plants that are already suffering from severe plant stress. Mother

Ladybugs eat large numbers of aphids, making them an effective natural control of this pest.

Deer are here to stay, and they love (to eat!) many of our garden plants.

Nature has succeeded for many years without the help of pesticides; that's why we have to be careful when treating for those bad bugs. We have a greater chance of killing the many more beneficial insects that are out there than we do of killing just the bad bugs. This is especially true if one is spraying for a bad bug at the wrong time of that insect's life cycle. Most insects have only a short lifespan anyway. A few holes in your maple leaves should not cause alarm. Try to fill up your spare time with other projects that don't allow you time to look for holes in your leaves!

Now, as for four-legged critters, a lot of us have to learn to coexist. After all, who was there first? I would say squirrels, raccoons, chipmunks, and mole ancestors were on your property long before the land was cleared for housing. Those of you who still have surrounding woods and open fields have natural breeding grounds for these critters. If you need controls, raccoons, possums, and skunks can be trapped by a licensed exterminator (it's illegal for you to do it yourself). Chipmunks and squirrels can be captured in a Havahart trap and relocated.

Moles are best eliminated by trapping and killing. There are products being sold to run the moles to your neighbors. These are safe products made up of castor oil and soap detergent mixed with water—but none have been known to work very well and if you have woods or an open field near your home, forget it! Besides, moles only do aesthetic damage and no lawn damage. Voles can be trapped and eliminated, using baited (with peanut butter) mousetraps. Groundhogs can be discouraged by placing ammonia-treated rags in areas in which they're known to reside. With squirrels, make friends quickly. They are smarter than you, and if you get in the habit of feeding them, they'll allow you to keep your sanity and good nature.

Deer have become a major problem in many landscapes. The way to discourage them is to alternate a smell product with a taste product. Spray all your plants with Liquid Fence, a taste product, for two months, then apply Milorganite organic plant food, a smell product the deer don't like but you won't mind.

The best answer to all your critter control problems is to learn to share the landscape with them. Remember, their family was there before yours.

Killing with Kindness

I am sometimes asked by people outside our industry how we can afford to guarantee a living plant. They'll go on to say that anybody can buy a plant and not take care of it, and if it dies, we in the industry will have to replace it free of charge. While this scenario is possible, it's the exception, certainly not the rule. I have found over the years that, when it comes to planting, all homeowners want to be successful. From annual flowers to shade trees, homeowners take tremendous pride in seeing their plants grow. If there is a problem getting new plants and plantings established, it's usually not from neglect but its opposite. I call it "killing with kindness." This comes about by trying too hard to assist Mother Nature. We overamend the backfill, placing soil that is too fine around a plant's root clump. We place too much fertilizer around the roots of freshly installed plants, causing their roots to burn. And the number-one way plants are killed with kindness? Overwatering.

Newly installed trees and shrubs, especially those planted in clay soil, usually get watered every day. During hot summers when our meteorologists on television keep telling us how hot and dry it is, we automatically go outside and water. But before watering, you should always check the soil around your plants with a garden trowel, checking down 3 to 5 inches to see if there's moisture. Water only when the soil is dry. All plants can sustain themselves much longer when kept on the dry side rather than too wet.

Is Cheapest Best?

Ever since gardening has become the number-one hobby of the American public, more and more generic retail businesses have added plants to their inventory, especially in the spring. There has also been an increase in the population of landscape installers. Hey, it's America, the home of free enterprise.

But let's start with the garden center. In today's fast-paced world, we've gotten used to shopping by phone. Homeowners often call garden centers to find out the price of a 1-gallon barberry or a 3-gallon redbud. Then they'll call another nursery to get their price. Remember, you're buying the plant, not the pot it's growing in, and the plant's quality is difficult to judge over the phone. The best way to price-shop for any tree or shrub is to visit different garden centers to see just what you are buying. Would you buy a sofa over the phone? Probably not. And the right tree will outlast even the best sofa.

When you need a landscaper, do some checking before you hire. A lot of people think that the only skill required to plant a tree is the strength to dig a hole. "Heck, anybody can dig a hole! Have you got a chainsaw? Okay, then, you're an arborist." But tree arborists come in all sizes of qualifications. Some, and I really don't classify these as arborists, get a chainsaw and a pickup truck and start knocking on doors. They usually do not have liability or workmen's compensation insurance. "So what?" you say. Well, if one of these today-we-do-windows types causes property damage to you or your neighbor or, worse yet, gets hurt on your property, then that chainsaw fellow could wind up owning your home. Then how much do you save? If you need some tree or landscape work, get a couple of estimates. If one looks too good to be true, it probably is. Good, experienced landscape installers have been trained over the years in how to face the plant, how large to dig the hole, how to read plans, how to make good on-the-job changes to an installation, and how to work with others.

Buying living plants and landscape services is no different from any other consumer purchase: you get exactly what you pay for. Don't forget to figure quality and experience into the value column. This includes handling the trees, shrubs, and flowers before you buy them, and the ability of a retailer to give you future advice and assistance. This type of operation may not be the cheapest in terms of dollars alone, but don't forget to factor in all the other values when you are looking for the best deal.

Plants Are Like People

There are many similarities between people and plants. To begin with, both have a beginning and, unfortunately, both have an end. Both groups have the best chance of a long life when living in the best of environmental conditions. The healthier we keep ourselves, the less likely we are to catch a cold, contract the flu, or have heart disease and other problems. Plants are the same way: the better the planting site, the better it will grow. Choosing poor to minimal planting sites can cause plants to attract bad bugs, disease, and overall stress that will greatly reduce their longevity.

This book will greatly increase your success in improving your home landscape if you heed the "likes and dislikes" of the many plants that are listed. Take the book with you as you shop for new trees, shrubs, perennials, and those summer-blooming flowers. It will help you decide what to buy and where to plant.

The Ohio Nursery and Landscape Association (ONLA) has developed a certification program for retailers and for landscape installers in our industry. Look for companies whose employees display ONLA certificates. Feel free to seek out great gardening and landscape installation advice from highly skilled people.

Now, get set to read and discover some great plants that will add beauty and value to your landscape!

Happy gardening!

How to Use This Book

Each entry in this gardening guide will provide you with information about a plant's particular characteristics, its habits, and its basic requirements for vigorous growth, as well as my own personal experience and knowledge of it. I have tried to include the information you will need to help you realize each plant's potential. Only when a plant performs at its best can it be fully appreciated. You will find such pertinent information as mature height and spread, bloom period and seasonal colors (if any), sun and soil preferences, planting tips, water requirements, fertilizing needs, pruning and care, and pest information. Each section is clearly marked for easy reference. Following is an explanation of the information contained in the major sections provided for each entry.

Additional Benefits

Many plants offer benefits that further enhance their appeal. The following symbols indicate some of the more notable additional benefits:

 Native   Fall color

 Drought tolerant   Attracts butterflies and/or bees

 Attracts hummingbirds   Edible for humans and/or animals

 Deer and rabbit resistant

Sun Requirements

For quick reference, I have included symbols representing the range of sunlight suitable for each plant. *Full sun* means a site receiving eight or more hours of direct sun daily. *Part sun/part shade* means a site that receives direct sun part of the day, or partial sun all day. *Full shade* means a site that is in dappled or even deep shade all day. Some plants grow successfully in more than one range of sun, which will be indicated by more than one sun symbol. **Note:** Afternoon sun is stronger than morning sun, and a site with afternoon sun exposure is more apt to stress those plants that are listed as needing part sun/part shade.

Full Sun   Part Sun/Part Shade   Shade

Companion Planting and Design

In this section, I provide suggestions for companion plantings and different ways to showcase your plants. Many people find this to be the most enjoyable part of gardening. Or, I suggest how the featured plant may be featured in the landscape.

Try These

This section describes those specific cultivars or varieties that I have found to be particularly noteworthy. Or, I sometimes suggest another species that is also a good choice. Give these a try . . . or perhaps you'll find your own favorites.

Hardiness Zones

The United States Department of Agriculture (USDA) has developed cold-hardiness zone designations. They are based on minimum average temperatures all over the country. Each variation of 10 degrees Fahrenheit represents a different zone, indicated by colored bands on a zone map. Because perennial plants—whose roots survive through the winter—vary in their tolerance for cold, it is important to choose those plants that are suitable in the zone for your region of Ohio. Consult this map to determine in which zone you live. Most of the plants discussed in this book will perform well throughout the state. Though a plant may grow (and grow well) in zones other than its recommended cold-hardiness zone, it is best to select plants labeled for your zone, or warmer.

Ohio USDA Hardiness Zone Map

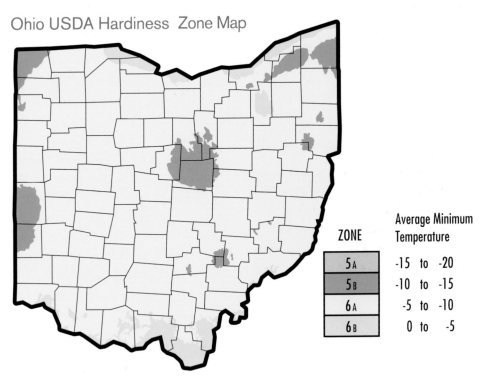

ZONE	Average Minimum Temperature
5A	-15 to -20
5B	-10 to -15
6A	-5 to -10
6B	0 to -5

USDA Plant Hardiness Zone Map, 2012. Agricultural Research Service, U.S. Department of Agriculture. Accessed from http://planthardiness.ars.usda.gov.

ANNUALS
FOR OHIO

Many of us are saddened when the first killing frost of fall appears and wipes out our annuals. Well, before you get out the hanky, remember that all annuals eventually go to seed and die even without a killing frost. The definition of annual is "a plant that grows, flowers, seeds, and then dies, all in one growing season." Annuals bloom, get tired, and go away with or without cold weather. In this chapter, you will read about true annuals as well as tender perennials that are treated as annuals.

Annuals enrich our lives in many ways. Amusement parks in temperate areas, known for their masses of beautifully colored flowers, have to have annuals planted two to three times a year to keep their flowers looking great. So, the next time you visit Disneyland, be sure to appreciate all that the groundskeepers do to keep the park looking colorful.

Calibrachoa planted with other annuals in an urn makes a stunning container.

Buy What Fits Your Landscape Conditions

Most of us make a trip to the greenhouse or nursery in May, and we become like kids in a candy store. We want some of this and some of that, and we take it all home. Then we scratch our heads and say, "Now, *where* am I going to plant all this stuff?"

Before you go and buy, take a walk around your landscape. Make notes about various areas, jotting down the type of soil, the amount of light and sun the area receives, and how much height is needed. Seek out a knowledgeable person and explain your situation. Be open-minded. If what you want won't do well in a particular planting site, be willing to make substitutions.

How to Buy Annuals

Homeowners who start their own seeds can save money (if they don't spend too

Transplanting pansies from a six-pack, which is how they are often sold.

much time and money getting the seeds started, of course). Most "seed-starter home-owners" begin seeds indoors too soon, and the resulting plants grow very weak and "stretchy." Do not start your seeds indoors any sooner than four to six weeks before it's safe to plant seedlings outdoors.

Most homeowners buy their annuals already growing in pots and flats at the garden store or greenhouse. The retailers that sell annual plants have to be experienced enough to take proper care of all those annual bedding plants until they're sold. Poor watering and handling at the retail outlet can have you buying summer-blooming flowers that have one foot in the grave. Make sure all the annuals you buy look fresh and healthy—remember, they won't get any better looking on the drive home.

Another way to further your chance of success is to buy Proven Winners® (PW). What are Proven Winners? They are a select group of plants that are copyrighted by a group of growers who own the rights to those particular varieties. They are hybrids of popular flowering plants, with the undesirable qualities bred out and the desirable qualities bred in. The seed is controlled, so it's not available to homeowners, but you can purchase the plants. These flowers have been tried and tested, and all the descriptions about their benefits are true as written. You will definitely have flowers that are new, colorful, and exciting.

Annual Advice

The best way to plant annuals in your landscape is to buy plants already growing in flats or pots. Planting from seed packets directly into your garden beds can be very disappointing. You'll wind up having to separate, divide, and space your seedlings. That's if they germinate at all. If they do, you could wind up with fifty seedlings in an area that only needs twelve mature plants.

When planting the growing plants, loosen the soil to a depth of 6 to 8 inches. Dig a hole as deep and twice as wide as the root clump. Backfill and water-in well to settle the soil. Water all newly installed annuals as often as needed to keep the soil around them moist, but not wet. This includes those annuals that I'll refer to as drought tolerant. All annuals need to get off to a good growing start. There's a fine line between moist and wet. If you're not sure if the plants need water and the soil still looks moist, err on the side of dry. The worst that will happen is the plants will wilt a little. If plants are kept too wet, the roots will rot—and then it's bye-bye plants!

As far as watering procedures, once annuals start to grow, their moisture needs will vary. Some varieties are listed as drought tolerant, which translates into watering every two weeks if no measurable rain (½ inch or more) has fallen. Some varieties such as periwinkle can go longer, but even they will appreciate an occasional drink every couple of weeks. Impatiens, on the other hand, may need to be watered every day during hot weather. They'll express themselves by drooping when dry. You can water any annual when the soil becomes dry down to 3 to 4 inches. Check soil moisture by digging down with a garden trowel.

Final Tips on Watering

Where and "with whom" you plant your annuals will also affect their moisture needs. For example, if you're planting impatiens in the sun, keep a hose handy. When you are planting impatiens in a bed with deciduous shrubs or evergreens, you'll need to water the impatiens a lot more often than you water those shrubs. That means you'll have to water the impatiens individually so the permanent plants don't get too much water.

Many of the annuals listed in this chapter don't require a lot of water. Read about each variety carefully so you understand the needs of each summer-blooming flower. For example, there are some great petunia varieties. If they need water, don't let a sprinkler ruin the bloom color by getting the flowers wet. Keep the hose on the ground or leave a soaker hose in place.

Fertilizers: Follow Those Instructions

There are many types of fertilizers available. Some are slow in releasing the nutrients, some are fast, and many are in-between. That is why you must read and follow the instructions for the fertilizer of your choice. They will tell you how often to use it and how much to use at a time. Remember, more is not better. A properly applied fertilizer can be a tremendous boost to your annuals, but an improperly applied one can be an early death sentence.

Pinching Off Early Flowers

I know, you're buying your annuals for the color, and it's the color on the annuals for sale that make you want to buy them in the first place. But early blooms on young annual plants slow down initial growth. By pinching off the early blooms, you will cause the plant to grow much more quickly, giving you lots more bloom in less time. Keep the flowers pinched off your young transplants for the first couple of weeks after planting. It will hurt for a moment, but it will pay dividends for months. If my daughter Jenny can do it, so can you!

Mulch with Common Sense

When adding bark mulch, be sure to keep the mulch away from your flower stems; you don't want any mulch piled up 2 to 3 inches on the stems. Many annuals "mulch themselves" with their spreading growth habit, which retains moisture and shades weed seeds, thus reducing weed production. If you do mulch, loosen the mulch monthly

Pinching off flowers of petunias just about to be planted actually helps the roots establish.

during the summer months so it won't become a hardened water barrier. A garden hook and a five-part cultivating tool are two great tools for loosening your mulch. In fact, a cultivating tool will cultivate the mulch very quickly, leaving the mulch looking like it was just freshly applied. If your flower beds are already mulched before planting, remove the existing mulch or dig it into the soil before planting. Annual roots want to be planted in soil, not mulch.

You Get What You Pay For

As with anything in life, the least expensive purchase is not necessarily the best purchase. Buy your summer-blooming annuals from nursery stores, garden centers, and greenhouses where knowledgeable people are on hand to answer all your questions and steer you in the right direction. Seasonal plant stores might have great prices, but if you buy all the wrong stuff or the weather freezes, how much money have you really saved?

Install Compatible Plants

As you read this chapter, you will notice similarities in the water and sunlight needs of some of the different varieties. This is important to note when combining two or more varieties in the same planting bed or container. Select those that have the same needs to plant together. That way, when you water or when the temperature gets hot, all will stay happy together with the same amount of maintenance from you.

The Icing on the Cake

Annuals give the finishing touch to any landscape. Most of the varieties I have listed in this chapter require little to very little maintenance. I believe people should be able to visually enjoy their yards—and not always from behind a hoe or a hose! Annuals (and tender perennials used as annuals) make it easy to be successful with color combinations. These flowers have a way of enhancing all the other plantings and features in your yard, regardless of the variety or varieties that you choose.

Ageratum

Ageratum houstonianum

Botanical Pronunciation
a-jer-AY-tum hoos-tone-ee-AY-num

Other Name
Floss flower

Bloom Period and Seasonal Color
Early summer to frost; blooms in shades of blue, lavender-blue, purple, pink, white

Mature Height x Spread
8 to 24 inches x 8 to 12 inches

Many of you gave up on ageratum several hot summers ago, just as you did with a lot of other older varieties of annuals that performed well only until the hot weather set in. Then they collapsed from the heat, and you probably vowed never to plant them again. But like a lot of old-name annuals, new gutsy ageratum varieties have come along that stand up to the heat. They do well in sun to a half-day of shade and come in shades of blue, purple, and white. Great for borders, many grow only 8 inches tall while producing fuzzy, colorful blooms. Plant them as a mass of color in a mounded bed or as a wonderfully colorful border plant. You really should give ageratum another try.

When, Where, and How to Plant
You can start ageratum from seed indoors four to six weeks before it's safe to plant outdoors. However, I've found it best to plant container-grown or cell-packs of ageratum outdoors after the danger of frost has passed. Choose a location with sun or partial shade. Ageratum will grow in all types of soil with the exception of heavy gumbo clay. See this chapter's introduction for specific planting information. Space plants 6 to 12 inches apart, depending on the variety. With young plants, pinch off any flowers that form for the first two to three weeks after planting. This will be hard to do, but it really works. The results will be faster-growing plants with much quicker and better blooms. If your flowerbeds are already mulched, remove the existing mulch or dig it into the soil before planting. Annual roots want to be planted in soil, not mulch.

Growing Tips
Although somewhat drought tolerant, ageratum should be watered during hot, dry weather. Check the soil about 3 to 4 inches down; if it's dry, water. Fertilize plants with a balanced fertilizer, following the fertilizer container instructions.

Regional Advice and Care
Groom plants by removing spent flowers to keep plants blooming freely. Ageratum is generally free of pests and disease.

Companion Planting and Design
Ageratum is beautiful in its own bed or when used as a low border plant. Many gardeners use it in mixed pots and window boxes with annuals that have similar light and water needs. Alternating light blue and dark blue plants will give you a wonderful look. A similar effect can be had by alternating the white-flowering ageratum with a blue-flowering variety.

Try These
The Hawaii series grows to 8 inches and has flowers of light blue, deep blue, and an improved white. 'Pacific Plus' has the richest purple blooms of any ageratum. 'Blue Horizon' is the height exception; this blue ageratum grows upright to 2½ feet and makes a great cut flower.

Alyssum

Lobularia maritima

Botanical Pronunciation
lob-yew-LAR-ee-ah mah-RIT-ih-mah

Other Name
Sweet alyssum

Bloom Period and Seasonal Color
May to frost; blooms in white, pink, salmon, rosy violet, lavender, purple, apricot

Mature Height x Spread
2 to 6 inches x 10 to 12 inches

Alyssum, often growing just inches tall, is considered an annual groundcover. Like many annuals, it has been around for years. Many of the older varieties left homeowners with second thoughts about choosing alyssum—the old boys stopped blooming when it got hot and just disappeared. Again, the hybridizers have come to our rescue, developing a heat-tolerant hybrid for those of us who want alyssum with continuous summer bloom. And the fresh, new colors are fun too. Now you can choose alyssum with white, pink, rose, salmon, purple, or apricot flowers. The apricot, a light salmon-peach, may fade in hot sunny locations, so plant it in areas of morning sun only. Another benefit of alyssum is its fragrance—hence its common name of "sweet alyssum."

When, Where, and How to Plant
Alyssum does best in a half-day of sun or more. Choose locations with morning or late-afternoon sun for the best results. It will grow in all types of well-drained soil. Just keep it out of heavy gumbo clay. However, even the new varieties of alyssum can suffer from summer heat stroke, so avoid hot, dry locations. I wouldn't bother with starting alyssum from seed; begin with plants already growing in pots or cell-packs. Plant in the ground anytime after the danger of frost is over. Follow the general directions for planting annuals in the chapter introduction. Space plants 6 to 8 inches apart. Keep new plantings moist.

Growing Tips
Don't overfertilize alyssum. I've found the best plant food is a once-a-season, timed-release fertilizer. Make sure your alyssum does not dry out during hot weather. Provide water only as necessary; don't keep the soil damp as the roots will rot. If the soil is dry to a depth of 3 inches, then water. Alyssum "mulches itself," helping to retain moisture and shading weed seeds with its low-growing foliage. Leave the mulch in its bag.

Regional Advice and Care
If your plants "brown-out" in summer's heat, shear them back to promote healthy regrowth. Alyssum often self-sows, returning to your garden the following year. These seedlings won't be the same as the variety you planted, so weed them out in the spring. Pests and disease shouldn't be a concern.

Companion Planting and Design
Alyssum makes a beautiful, trailing flower for hanging baskets. It also works well in pots and window boxes when combined with compatible annuals. Alyssum is a classic edging for flowerbeds.

Try These
'Aphrodite Mix' comes in a combination of red, pink, purple, salmon, apricot, and white with 1-inch flower heads. The Easter Bonnet series is compact and uniform in growth from plant to plant; colors include deep pink, deep rose, lavender, and violet. 'New Carpet of Snow' is an improved white-blooming variety that has a great fragrance.

Angelonia

Angelonia angustifolia

Botanical Pronunciation
an-jel-OH-nee-ah an-gus-tih-FOE-lee-ah

Other Name Summer snapdragon

Bloom Period and Seasonal Color
All summer and fall blooming in pastel pink, purple, white, lavender, bicolor

Mature Height x Spread
1 to 3 feet (depending upon variety) x 12 to 18 inches

Though this plant has been on the market for several years, it still isn't used in flowerbeds. It was introduced in the mid- to late 90s and is an excellent low-maintenance flower that withstands hot, cold, wet, dry and any other condition that's thrown its way. Summer snapdragon is another common name, which is very appropriate as the flowers resemble snapdragon flowers. They bloom on stems that rise slightly above the foilage and make great cut flowers. The flower colors range from pink to bicolors with a lot of other colors in between. Best of all, get them started in the yard and forget the hose. This plant is as hardy and tough as any marigold but with a *lot* more color. If you like to pamper your plants, pretend your angelonia is in your neighbor's yard.

When, Where, and How to Plant

I wouldn't mess with starting these annuals from seed. As inexpensive as they are when sold in growing flats, let someone else do the seed starting part. Plant in mid- to late May when the soil temperature has warmed enough in Ohio. Plant your angelonia on 9- to 12-inch centers in sunny areas of at least six to eight hours or more. It grows well in good old Ohio clay soil per the planting instructions in the beginning of this chapter. If you feel your clay soil is too thick for anything to grow, add some pine bark chips and mix into the soil you'll be putting back in the holes you dig.

Growing Tips

Do not overwater. Angelonia is very drought tolerant. Fertilize one time upon planting with a "start n gro" timed-release plant food, which will slowly feed your plants over the rest of the growing season.

Regional Advice and Care

There isn't any disease or insect that will seriously attack these blooming beauties. Angelonia requires no deadheading, pinching, or pruning. Plant them as a border this year and you'll be doing it every year. Another benefit is the fact that they don't attract deer or bunny rabbits.

Companion Planting and Design

With their upright growing habit makes angelonia perfect in the center of a patio or deck planter. With the different colors offered with this plant, angelonia mixes well with any other varieties of mid-growing annuals that would also be very drought tolerant.

Try These

Angelface® series sport larger blooms of mixed colors to choose from. The Serena™ series is more compact, growing to 10 to 14 inches in all colors.

Asparagus Fern

Asparagus species

Botanical Pronunciation
uh-SPARE-uh-gus

Bloom Period and Seasonal Color
Summer foliage in green

Mature Height x Spread
1½ to 2 feet x 1 to 2 feet

No, this is not about my most despised vegetable. (I had to eat a lot of it from a can as a kid!) I am talking about a group of plants used for their arching stems of fresh fernlike foliage, often called asparagus ferns. No showy flowers here, but asparagus fern adds to a bed of blooming annuals what hot fudge does to vanilla ice cream. When we hear the word "fern," we think of shade. But asparagus fern, which actually is *not* a true fern, will grow in full sun to full shade. Now here's a plant with universal use. Speaking of use, the best uses for asparagus fern are in mixed containers, window boxes, and hanging baskets. *Asparagus sprengeri* is the most popular; it's used the most by the pros.

When, Where, and How to Plant
You'll find asparagus fern in garden centers almost year-round because it can be grown as a houseplant. For seasonal outdoor use, you will find a great selection of container plants in May. Plant anytime after the danger of heavy frost is over. It can also be planted in flowerbeds, especially in shade, although it is very adaptable. Asparagus fern prefers good garden soil, loosened about 6 to 8 inches down. It is a superior container plant. When planting it in a new container, use soilless potting mix. Whether planting in containers or in the ground, dig a hole as deep as the soil clump and twice as wide. If the plant is potbound, first loosen all those wrapped roots so they're dangling freely. Backfill and water-in well.

Growing Tips
Asparagus fern is pretty drought tolerant. Water during hot, dry periods, especially in sunny locations if the soil is dry down to 3 to 4 inches. Feed with an all-purpose fertilizer, following the instructions on the label. See the chapter's introduction for more fertilizing hints.

Regional Advice and Care
There are no bugs or diseases that bother this foliage plant. Occasionally a branch will yellow. This is normal; just prune it off. Speaking of pruning, trim off unwanted growth anytime you want. You can dig up and pot any of the asparagus fern varieties in the fall before a frost. Bring it indoors and the plant will grow all winter; put it back outside in the spring, if you like.

Companion Planting and Design
Asparagus ferns look great in pots or mixed in with blooming annuals. Its soft-looking fronds, when interspersed with flowers, can make an entire planting look like a picture out of a garden book. Combine with dense-growing annuals—such as impatiens, browallia, or periwinkle—for a great effect.

Try These
A. sprengeri has dark green, coarse needles that hang over the sides of pots, giving it a weeping effect. *A. densiflorus* has deep green, tapered needles on foxtail-like spikes. *A. setaceus*, commonly called plumosus fern, grows in layers on multiple branches.

Blue Salvia

Salvia farinacea

Botanical Pronunciation
SAL-vee-uh far-ih-NAY-see-uh

Other Name
Mealy-cup sage

Bloom Period and Seasonal Color
June until hard fall freeze; blooms in medium blue, dark blue, white

Mature Height x Spread
16 to 20 inches x 10 to 12 inches

Blue salvia is near the top of a list of summer-blooming flowers that I call "Denny's Heat Beaters." Give blue salvia some tender loving care for a few weeks after planting, and then let Mother Nature take over—it will tolerate all the hot sun and dry soil she can dish out. This medium-sized annual has blue or white flower spikes that bloom all summer long. It makes a great border plant, or mass it in its own bed. When you shop for blue salvia at the garden store in the spring, you won't see flowers on the plants, just the grayish green leaves. Take my word for it, the flowers will come along shortly, and you'll soon be a fan of this low-maintenance, high-impact performer.

When, Where, and How to Plant

Plant blue salvia in spring after the danger of frost has passed. You will find it available in small pots and cell-packs in mid-May. Many nursery stores and greenhouses offer larger-growing plants in 1-gallon containers in late May to early June. Blue salvia will grow well in all types of soil as long as it has good drainage. It will grow in full sun to areas receiving only four to five hours of sun. To plant, loosen the soil to a depth of 6 to 8 inches. Dig a hole as deep and twice as wide as the soil clump. Loosen any roots wrapped around the soil clump. Backfill and water-in well to settle the soil. Space plants about 8 inches apart.

Growing Tips

Blue salvia should be fed soon after planting with a timed-release fertilizer. Follow label instructions—and remember, more is not better. Mulch will help blue salvia tolerate the summer heat without additional irrigation. Cover with a 2-inch layer of mulch, remembering to keep it off the stems of the plants. Provide extra water during prolonged droughts (two to three weeks without rain) to have the healthiest plants.

Regional Advice and Care

Blue salvia is completely free of bugs and disease. There's no need to deadhead spent flowers, as this plant is self-cleaning. Mild winters, especially in Zone 6, will allow this "annual" to act as a perennial. Blue salvia is an excellent flower for drying and using with other dried flowers. Harvest bunches when the flowers are almost fully open and hang upside down in a well-ventilated location until dry.

Companion Planting and Design

A great combination bed—especially if you like blue and yellow together (and you will!)—is melampodium in the front of the bed and blue salvia in the back. Or try planting a bed of blue-flowering and white-flowering blue salvia; the colors complement each other.

Try These

The Victoria series offers compact-growing, 18- to 20-inch plants that produce medium blue or silvery white flowers.

Browallia

Browallia speciosa

Botanical Pronunciation
broe-AL-ee-uh spee-see-OH-suh

Other Name
Sapphire flower

Bloom Period and Seasonal Color
June to frost; blooms in sky blue, purple-blue, white

Mature Height x Spread
6 to 12 inches x 8 to 12 inches

Have a shade garden but you're tired of impatiens because of their constant need for moisture during dry periods? Give browallia a try. This annual does well in shade or semishade and requires only a little moisture assistance during the hot, dry periods of summer. Although this annual has been around for many years, it has not had much exposure until newer varieties appeared over the last five years. It comes in bloom colors of brilliant sky blue, purple-blue, and white. There is a cascading variety great for hanging baskets, as well as dwarf plants that grow to only 6 inches tall. All browallia are spreading and, when planted 12 inches apart, they will make a solid planting. There's great color and foliage on this one.

When, Where, and How to Plant
Plant browallia from small plants available in pots and cell-packs from your favorite garden center. Wait until all danger of frost has passed. Browallia does not want to be exposed to hot afternoon sun. Plant in shade with good sky light or in any area that gets either morning sun or late afternoon sun. Moist, well-drained soil is preferred. Plant browallia in soil that has been loosened 6 to 8 inches deep. Dig a hole as deep as the soil clump and twice as wide. Loosen any roots that are wrapped around the soil clump, place the plant in the hole, backfill, and water-in well to settle the soil. If plants are lanky, pinch back to promote compact growth.

Growing Tips
Fertilize with a balanced plant food, following the instructions on the container. Help keep browallia watered during the hot, dry periods of summer. Check soil moisture at a depth of 3 to 4 inches. Consider mulching this one to conserve moisture. Mulch no deeper than 2 inches and keep mulch away from plant stems.

Regional Advice and Care
Bugs and disease shouldn't bother browallia. Flowers are self-cleaning, so no deadheading is necessary.

Companion Planting and Design
Plant in solid beds, or use browallia as a low border plant. Combine with other shade-loving annuals, or use as a color accent in areas planted with hostas and ferns. It is also a wonderful plant for a hanging basket where you want color in the shade, and it works well in deck pots and window boxes.

Try These
The Bell series offers cascading plants that grow 10 to 12 inches high and wide. Great for hanging baskets, it is available in dark blue, light blue, and white. 'Amethyst' is a dark purple bloomer that grows to 12 inches and has ¾-inch flowers. This variety is the best of all browallia varieties for tolerating summer heat.

Celosia

Celosia species

Botanical Pronunciation
seh-LOE-see-uh

Other Name
Cockscomb

Bloom Period and Seasonal Color
June to frost; blooms in intense shades of red, orange, pink, yellow, cream

Mature Height x Spread
6 to 40 inches x 8 to 12 inches

This is a tale of two celosias. Plumed celosia (*Celosia plumosa*, sometimes called feathered amaranth) has feathery, plume-type flowers in vibrant shades of red, orange, pink, yellow, and cream. Crested celosia (*C. cristata*, called cockscomb) is rounded in shape with velvety, crested, convoluted flower heads that almost resemble a brain. It is altogether different from plumed celosia, but comes in the same vivid, jewel-like colors. Celosias vary from dwarf types just 6 inches in height to tall plumes of nearly 40 inches high. Cockscomb provides long-lasting color with very little maintenance. Plant in beds or as a border plant; group one solid color or mix a variety of colors for an eye-popping display. Plumed types are great for cut flowers, and they dry well for winter bouquets.

When, Where, and How to Plant
You'll find the best and most popular varieties growing in pots or cell-packs at your garden center or greenhouse in spring. Plant cockscomb in beds after the danger of frost is past. Cockscomb will do well in average soil, but it wants good drainage and at least a half-day of sun. Follow the general planting directions in the introduction to the chapter. Pinch off any flowers at planting—this will make your plants much bigger, much quicker. Plant shorter-growing varieties about 8 inches apart, especially if you want a tight, full border. Space taller varieties 9 to 12 inches apart.

Growing Tips
Fertilize cockscomb as often as recommended on the package of your favorite fertilizer. Keep soil moist until established; thereafter, give cockscomb an occasional drink of water—every two to four weeks during hot, dry periods.

Regional Advice and Care
Pinch off straight branches to encourage side shoots and promote more bloom. This will also create sturdier plants. If not pinched back, the tallest varieties may need staking. Deadhead all spent flowers. To dry flowers, pick and hang upside down in a dark, well-ventilated spot. Celosia has no insect or disease problems.

Companion Planting and Design
Nothing beats celosia for blocks of brilliant color. Stick to one type or the other (feathered or crested) when planting in a mass. Children love the bright colors and unusual shapes, so include celosia in spaces planned for budding gardeners.

Try These
Both the Sparkler and Castle series of feathered types offer many bloom colors on 12- to 14-inch plants. If you go for the crested types, decide how high you want to go. Bred for use as a cut flower, the Chief series tops out at 40 inches. It offers large flowers on sturdy plants with strong stems. 'Jewel Box' only reaches 4 to 5 inches; it usually comes in mixed colors. 'Prestige Scarlet', an All-America Selections winner, grows to 2 feet high and has numerous 3-inch blooms of scarlet red.

Coleus

Solenostemon scutellarioides

Botanical Pronunciation
Sol-en-oh-STEM-on skoot-el-lar-ee-OY-deez

Other Name
Painted nettle

Bloom Period and Seasonal Color
Colorful foliage from June to frost

Mature Height x Spread
6 to 30 inches x 1 to 2 feet

Coleus comes in a amazing array of colors—chartreuse, red, purple, yellow, hot pink, orange, rose, or a mixture of all the above—and I'm not talking about flowers here! The pattern and color combinations of the leaves are endless. The leaves also come in many shapes. Some are heart-shaped, some are oval, and others are fringed or ruffled. Coleus has flowers, but you don't want them. If you let this plant bloom, it will go downhill. Fortunately, you get loads of color from the foliage. Just pinch off the flowers, and you will have a colorful, leafy plant that shows off all summer long. Very shade-tolerant, and with new varieties that even tolerate sun, coleus is one of the best plants for low-maintenance containers.

When, Where, and How to Plant

Plant coleus from containers, either potted or in cell-packs, after all danger of frost is past. You can plant well into summer, as long as coleus is available. Coleus will grow in any soil type as long as there is good drainage. It is one of those tender perennials treated as an annual that will grow well in sun or shade. In sun, it needs plenty of moisture to thrive, so avoid hot dry sites. For planting in the garden, consult the instructions in this chapter's introduction. Space plants 1½ to 2 feet apart.

Growing Tips

Coleus is low-maintenance; just water during dry spells. When planting in hard-to-water areas, mulch the soil with a 2-inch covering, keeping the mulch off the stems. Fertilize with a balanced plant food, following the directions. There are many types of fertilizer available. Some release nutrients slowly, some are very fast, and many are in-between. Be sure to read and follow the instructions on the fertilizer container to see how often you should use it.

Regional Advice and Care

There aren't any bugs or disease to worry coleus. Control plant height by pinching back, keeping it full and bushy. To promote more foliage, pinch out flower stalks as they form. Take stem cuttings from your coleus in early fall and place them in a glass of water to root. After roots form, place each rooted cutting in a 3-inch pot filled with a soilless potting mix. Grow them indoors, and you will have great winter leaf color.

Companion Planting and Design

For finesse in the shade, match the colors on coleus foliage to the blooms of shade-loving annuals, such as impatiens or begonias.

Try These

The compact-growing Wizard series (to 16 inches) is available in a great mix of foliage colors. 'Carefree Mix', which grows to 10 inches, has small, deeply lobed leaves in a multitude of colors. For exciting container options, look for special varieties in 4-inch pots at your local nursery.

Cosmos

Cosmos bipinnatus

Botanical Pronunciation
KOZ-mose bye-pin-ATE-uss

Bloom Period and Seasonal Color
June to fall; blooms in shades of red, pink, magenta, white

Mature Height x Spread
1½ to 5 feet x 1½ to 2 feet

If you want butterflies in your yard, plant cosmos. These daisylike blooming plants have been around for many years, but newer varieties have made them more colorful and bushy. Cosmos' fernlike foliage makes for a graceful plant that looks fantastic in a bed of its own. It also mixes well with other annuals—but after you see it perform, you'll wish that you had planted more cosmos and less of the others. The garnet-red, pink, or white flowers appear on 4- to 5-foot plants. There are shorter varieties that grow to 20 to 24 inches but still bloom freely. Both the bloom and the foliage make a great bouquet. This is an annual that's as beautiful outdoors as it is indoors when displayed in a vase.

When, Where, and How to Plant
You can start seedlings indoors around the middle of April. Plant in a seed tray filled with a soilless potting mix, and keep them moist, but not damp. I prefer to use plants already growing in cell-packs. Plant your own seed starts or store-bought plants outside after the danger of frost is past. Seeds can also be sown directly in the garden, but these plants will get off to a slower start. Cosmos loves as much sun as it can get and will grow well in all types of well-drained soil. Follow the planting directions in this chapter's introduction. To allow the plant to grow bigger more quickly pinch off any early blooms. Do this for two weeks after planting, and then let cosmos do its thing. Plant on 12-inch centers for a full colorful effect.

Growing Tips
Lucky you—no extra watering or fertilization is necessary.

Regional Advice and Care
There are no bugs or diseases that attack cosmos. If the plants start to stretch and grow tall, pinch or prune halfway back to encourage more spread. Cosmos acts like a wildflower—it reseeds itself from year to year. Just space the volunteers the next spring so that each plant has room to grow.

Companion Planting and Design
If mixing with other annuals and perennials, plant the taller-growing varieties toward the back of a mixed bed. The dwarfs look great as a border plant, outlining a bed of taller-growing plants. You can also buy cosmos in mixed flats that have a beautiful blend of harmonizing shades. If you have large bed areas that could use some great summer color, plant cosmos seeds along with tall marigolds and tall zinnia seeds.

Try These
These graceful flowers have been around for years, but new varieties are entering the scene. The Sonata series (20 to 24 inches) is an instant classic with colors of carmine red, pink, and pure white. The 'Versailles' mix is a taller-growing variety (48 inches) that blooms in rose, pink, red, and white.

Dianthus

Dianthus hybrids

Botanical Pronunciation
dye-AN-thus

Other Name
Pinks

Bloom Period and Seasonal Color
Mid-April to frost; blooms in shades of crimson, coral, pink, violet, white

Mature Height x Spread
6 to 10 inches x 8 to 12 inches

Dianthus makes a spectacular full bed of color. For many years, dianthus was offered for sale during the cool weather of spring and fall. Technically a biennial, this plant would bloom in the spring and then go to seed when it started getting hot in the summer (like pansies). Then along came the new hybrids. Much more heat-tolerant, dianthus hybrids (most are crosses between sweet William and the China pink) come in glowing shades, many with a colorful eye zone, and all with the lacy, fringed petals characteristic of pinks. They are available to plant in the spring or, if you miss that season, many growers have them available to plant later in the year. In the fall, look for dianthus sold alongside hardy mums.

When, Where, and How to Plant

Hybrid dianthus is best started from plants already growing in pots or cell-packs in spring. Fall selections will all be potted. They also germinate very quickly from seed indoors. Start your seed around the first of April. Hybrid dianthus is cold hardy, and the plants can be set out and planted in mid-April. Dianthus hybrids can be planted in full sun sites, as well as those that get just a few hours of sun. It tolerates summer heat as long as you water during hot, dry periods. Average soil is okay, but good drainage is important. Turn to this chapter's introduction for planting specifics. Plant hybrid dianthus on 10-inch centers for a full bed.

Growing Tips

Fertilize dianthus hybrids following the instructions on the container; see this chapter's introduction for more details. Check your soil moisture occasionally. When it's dry down 3 to 4 inches, give dianthus a drink.

Regional Advice and Care

Don't worry about bugs and disease—no problems here. Cut off spent flowers with scissors about every two to three weeks to encourage new blooms. Save a few dianthus to bring indoors in pots in early fall, before a frost. They'll continue to give you bloom indoors as the snow flies outdoors.

Companion Planting and Design

Plant in its own bed, or line beds of other flowers with a border planting of dianthus. You can create some great color combinations with hybrid pinks and petunias. Dianthus is also easy to mix with perennials.

Try These

Diamond series is a brand-new dianthus that comes in six colors and is tolerant of heat and cold. Floral Lace series—named for its lacy, serrated flowers that are 1½ inches wide—is the largest of any hybrid. It grows 8 to 10 inches tall, is heat tolerant, and is available in nine colors, including my favorite, 'Violet Picotee'. Ideal series grows 8 inches high and up to 15 inches wide. This variety is like going to the ice cream store—there are sixteen flavors to choose from, including raspberry.

Fuchsia

Fuchsia hybrids

Botanical Pronunciation
FYOO-shuh

Other Name
Lady's eardrops

Bloom Period and Seasonal Color
Late spring until killing fall frost; pink, red, purple, white, bicolor blooms

Mature Height x Spread
8 to 36 inches x 12 to 24 inches

This makes the perfect hanging basket for that shady spot around the home. Place or plant where you can enjoy a view of this beautiful flower from both inside and outside your home. Very oriental in its appearance, the flowers really vary within different varieties. It grows in different combinations of white and either blue, red, purple, or pink. Morning sun is okay but no afternoon hot sun, please. Another caution is to not overwater. This is a shrub down South so you can take it inside before October 1 if it's in a hanging pot or other container. If it starts losing leaves, cut the plant back half way and place in unheated garage against a house wall and water once a month. As new leaves appear in April, place back inside your home and grow until it's safe to plant outdoors in May.

When, Where, and How to Plant
Buy fuchsias already growing in a 4- to 6-inch or larger pot. You can buy one already in a hanging pot or purchase a smaller one and plant in a 10- to 12-inch hanging basket or patio pot. Either way, fuchsias want to hang over the hanging pots if they're a weeping form. Follow the planting instructions in this chapter's introduction. Remember, no hot sun.

Growing Tips
It has no insect or disease problems. If you bought your fuchsia from a not-so-good source, you might find your fuchsia plant has tiny white moths flying around the pot or flower bed. These are whiteflies and a spray of Neem oil, an environmentally safe

pesticide, will take care of the problem. Next time, buy your plants at places known for their quality.

Regional Advice and Care
Deadhead spent flowers once or twice weekly to encourage even more blooms. Fuchsia, like many summer bloomers, will slow down their flower count in really hot summer weather. Many more blooms will come when weather cools down.

Companion Planting and Design
Mix beds with fuchsia, ferns, begonias, and sweet potato vine. Use upright fuchsia in patio planters and the weepers in hanging baskets. Fuchsias come in both upright growing or weeping forms. For a hanging basket that looks like a fuchsia ball of color, take a 12-inch hanging basket and fill with a good soilless potting mix. Take one upright growing type and 3 to 4 weeping types and plant in the hanging basket. You can use plants that are all the same bloom color or mix it up. Both ways make a beautiful basket for that shady spot that needs an lift from color. You can get the same effect in deck or patio pots. Maybe you want to add other shade-loving annuals as asparagus fern, foilage color from caladiums and coleus, tuberous begonia, torennia, and browalia. All of these take the same amount of care and water; when mixing several varieties, get ones that are compatible.

Try These
'Thalia' and 'Gartenmeister' are the most readily available, with tubular orange-red flowers.

Geranium

Pelargonium x hortorum

Botanical Pronunciation
pell-are-GOE-nee-um hor-TOR-um

Other Name
Bedding geranium

Bloom Period and Seasonal Color
May to October; blooms in red, pink, white, rose, lavender, salmon

Mature Height x Spread
1 to 2 feet x 1 to 1½ feet

The geranium is the official flower of the city of Cincinnati, and it's one of the most popular flowers among people throughout Ohio. In fact, geraniums are rated as one of the top summer-blooming plants across the United States. They don't require a lot of attention, and they thrive in sunny, hot, dry areas. Their flowers appear as a ball made up of hundreds of small, individual flowers, forming a globe 5 to 7 inches in diameter. Geraniums have been produced through stem cuttings for years, producing a type called a zonal geranium. Recently, a new type has been developed called seed geraniums, and they also produce lots of bloom. Ivy or vining geraniums are another group; they trail down from a hanging basket.

When, Where, and How to Plant
Geraniums are best planted from pots or cell-packs after the danger of a late frost is over. You can continue to plant geraniums into summer, as long as the plants are available. Most geraniums, zonal and seed type, want at least a half-day of sun. They will still produce good bloom in areas of the garden that get only 3 to 4 hours of sun. Geraniums don't need excellent soil, just soil that has good drainage. Always loosen the soil before you plant any annual. For geraniums, loosen the soil to a depth of 8 to 10 inches. Dig a hole as deep as the soil clump and twice as wide. Free any wrapped roots. Place the plant in the hole, backfill, and water-in well.

Growing Tips
Geraniums like to be on the dry side, at least down to 4 inches, so check before you add more water.

A geranium's worst nightmare is a wet growing season. Fertilize with a balanced fertilizer, following the directions on the container. See this chapter's introduction for more fertilizing hints.

Regional Advice and Care
Remove finished flower stems, especially for the first couple of months after they're planted. There are no bugs or diseases that bother geraniums. Prune back to shape if necessary. Geraniums can tolerate a light frost, which actually keeps them blooming later into fall. The container-grown plants can be brought inside before a fall frost to extend their bloom.

Companion Planting and Design
It's hard to go wrong with geraniums. Geraniums are not only showy when planted in the ground, but they also make excellent flowering plants for patio and deck planters, window boxes, and hanging baskets.

Try These
Red is the classic color, but more and more new colors are hitting the market—from hot pink to lavender-blue. The Pinto series offers many colors on compact-growing plants. The early-flowering Glamour series has lots of 4-inch blooms in many colors. For hanging baskets, look for ivy-leaf geraniums. The Summer Showers series has cascading branches smothered with colorful flowers.

Hypoestes

Hypoestes phyllostachya

Botanical Pronunciation
hy-po-ESS-teez fy-lo-STAK-ee-uh

Other Name
Polka-dot plant

Bloom Period and Seasonal Color
Grown for patterned foliage from spring to frost

Mature Height x Spread
8 to 24 inches x 10 to 12 inches

How do you even pronounce the name of this great annual? Well, it's easier to pronounce the names of its two varieties, Confetti series and Splash series. When you do learn how to pronounce it (hy-po-ESS-teez), then you'll say, "Okay, but what is it?" Hypoestes is a tender perennial, grown as an annual, that is known not for its flower, but for its striking foliage splashed with lively colors—burgundy, red, rose, and white. Even without flowers of its own, it makes quite a statement in the garden when planted as a border plant or when used among other low- to medium-growing annuals. Add it to containers for lively contrast. Looking for a little pizzazz? Treat yourself and your landscape to this colorful foliage plant.

When, Where, and How to Plant

Plant hypoestes from greenhouse-grown plants (pots or cell-packs) that will be available in May. Growing from seed is difficult—don't try it. Do not plant until the danger of a late frost in your area has passed. Hypoestes will grow in areas that have full sun to almost full shade. In shady areas, just make sure there is sky light, so the colors in the leaves will express themselves. Avoid hot, dry sites. Moist, well-drained soil of any type is preferred. To plant, remove hypoestes from its container. Loosen the soil and dig a hole twice as wide as the soil clump. Loosen any wrapped roots growing around the clump, then plant as deep as the clump. Backfill and water-in well to settle the soil.

Growing Tips

Keep hypoestes watered during hot, dry weather. Fertilize with an all-purpose fertilizer, following the instructions on the label. *Always* read the labels—they tell you how much to use and when to use it for best results. More fertilizing tips are in this chapter's introduction.

Regional Advice and Care

These are definitely low-maintenance plants. If your plants get taller than you would like, pinch or prune them back to keep them in line. Pest and disease problems? I've never had any.

Companion Planting and Design

Mix several different colors of the same variety of hypoestes to make a colorful planting. Try it as a border with blooming plants behind it. Polka-dot plants also add a splash of foliage color to patio pots. For a different look in the garden, combine annuals known for their foliage effect. Plant hypoestes with coleus and caladium. Lots of color—no flowers!

Try These

'Confetti' has leaves of burgundy, red, rose, and white, and it looks like an artist dabbled on a little green paint to break up those colors. 'Splash' has less color disruption on its leaves, which also come in pink, red, rose, and white. 'Confetti' grows 18 to 24 inches tall and 'Splash' grows a little shorter, only 8 to 10 inches tall.

Impatiens

Impatiens walleriana

Botanical Pronunciation
im-PAY-shuns wall-er-ee-AH-nuh

Other Name
Busy Lizzie

Bloom Period and Seasonal Color
May to frost; blooms in red, pink, white, orange, lavender, red-violet

Mature Height x Spread
6 to 36 inches x 1 to 2 feet or more

For many years, homeowners were told by those of us in the industry that impatiens would *only* grow in shade. I've put an end to this rumor by growing lots of impatiens in my own yard in full sun. Did they burn up? Heck no, but I have learned to hate them during hot, dry periods. When I just want to rest after coming home from work, instead, I have to water these sun-grown impatiens. Yes, impatiens do well in shade, but they will also do well—with ample water—in sun. Another myth is that various varieties come in different growing heights. Truth of the matter is, the closer you plant them, the taller they grow, and the farther apart you plant them, the shorter they grow.

When, Where, and How to Plant
Growing impatiens from seed is tricky. Buy transplants already growing in pots or cell-packs from your favorite greenhouse or garden store in spring, after the danger of a late killing frost is over. Impatiens grow beautifully in shade to morning sun without much attention. You could choose a sunny spot, but be sure it is close to a water source. They like good, loose garden soil. Follow the planting instructions in this chapter's introduction. Regardless of what the plant label says, impatiens will grow to 3 feet if the individual plants are on 6- to 8-inch centers. These same plants will grow much shorter, 9 to 14 inches, when planted on 18-inch centers. Control the height of your impatiens by varying their spacing.

Growing Tips
Impatiens are over 90 percent water. They need to be watered regularly, especially those planted in sunny locations. Watch for signs of wilting. Fertilize with an all-purpose fertilizer, following the directions on the container. Also refer to this chapter's introduction.

Regional Advice and Care
Impatiens are trouble-free. As long as they don't dry out; pests and disease won't bother your plants. There is no need to groom them either.

Companion Planting and Design
Impatiens are a first-choice annual for bright, glowing color in shady beds and borders. They also do extremely well in hanging baskets, flower pouches, and patio pots. Do not plant water-loving plants such as impatiens in beds with evergreens. Evergreens do not like the daily waterings that impatiens will require in hot weather. You could wind up with beautiful impatiens and dead or weak evergreens.

Try These
There are many great varieties in an almost endless array of colors. The Accent series offers twenty-four different shades of blooms that are not only free flowering, but also glow in the moonlight. The Blitz series comes in many colors with extra-large flowers. The Dazzler series offers twenty-one different shades, including some bicolors. Super Elfin™ series is more compact, blooming in twenty-three different "flavors" (as in colors, that is).

Licorice Vine

Helichrysum petiolare

Botanical Pronunciation
hel-ih-KRY-sum pet-ee-OH-lair-ee

Other Name
Licorice plant

Bloom Period and Seasonal Color
Beautiful silver foilage all growing season

Mature Height x Spread
6 to 10 inches x 24 to 30 inches

If you put together your own hanging basket or patio planter, make sure this beautiful ground-cover plant is included along the edges of your container. Licorice vine is a native to South America and is very tolerant of heat and drought. Butterflies *love* this plant. They can leave some small holes in the silver leaves but who cares? Soon you'll be rewarded with beautiful swallowtail butterflies. Remember, it's the caterpillar stage of the butterfly that puts a few holes in these leaves, but again, let it go and the butterfly show will go on as planned by nature. It will also grow anywhere from a hot, sunny spot to a cool, shady spot.

When, Where, and How to Plant
The best way to buy these plants is in cell packs of four, or you can also buy them in 3- to 4-inch pots. Don't mess around taking cuttings of a neighbor's vine or with planting from seeds. Buy the plants that are growing in pots and ready to make you instantly happy. Plant and grow licorice vine in full sun to a half-day of sun. Space plants out in pots on 8-inch centers. See the planting instructions at this chapter's introduction.

Growing Tips
Soil in containers dries out quicker than the garden beds. Check your patio pots or hanging baskets daily for needed moisture. To see if soil stays moist (but not wet) with containers, make sure there's a drain hole at the bottom of pots. Those plants in a planting bed should need watering *maybe* once a week. Check every couple of days with a garden trowel. Licorice plant doesn't require much plant food, if any.

Regional Advice and Care
The beautiful foilage color mixed in with flower color makes all the colors blend in. Pinch the ends if it's getting a bit too long.

Companion Planting and Design
Fuzzy gray leaves make licorice vine adaptable to many color schemes. With hanging baskets and patio containers, mix in with trailing petunias, verbena, and million bells for a very colorful display. Plant as a groundcover in semi-shaded areas of your landscape.

Try These
'Petite Licorice' and 'Silver Mist' are both compact and full. 'Variegatum' is a strong grower with variegated green-and-silver leaves.

Marigold

Tagetes spp. and hybrids

Botanical Pronunciation
TAG-e-teez

Bloom Period and Seasonal Color
May to frost; blooms in yellow, gold, orange, white

Mature Height x Spread
6 to 36 inches (by variety) x 8 to 18 inches

They say if you can't grow marigolds, you should stay out of the garden. These flowers need very little assistance from us or from the hose during the summer. As is true for many annuals, major improvements have been made to these sunny summer bloomers. Now there are three different types, and all are great performers. The French marigolds (*Tagetes patula*) are neat and compact with single or double flowers. The African marigolds, now called the American or Aztec marigolds (*T. erecta*), have large globe-shaped flowers and grow tall—some up to 3 feet. The sturdy Triploid marigolds (*T. erecta* × *patula*) are a cross between the French and the American types. Their long-lasting flowers don't set seed. If you want bright summer color, look no further than marigolds.

When, Where, and How to Plant

You can successfully plant marigolds from seed or store-bought transplants. Marigolds are hardy and will grow in all types of soil. Although they will grow well in only four to five hours of sun, the more sun they get, the happier they will be. Plant seeds directly into the soil in late May. Place them ½ inch deep and as far apart as the seed packet suggests. Container-grown plants may be set out after any danger of a late spring frost passes. Consult this chapter's introduction for specifics. Space according to variety. To promote growth and sooner, more abundant blooms, pinch off any existing flowers at planting.

Growing Tips

Marigolds appreciate an occasional watering when it gets hot and dry. A 2-inch layer of mulch will help conserve moisture; just keep the mulch off the stems. Too much fertilizer will promote foliage over flowers, so go easy with this one.

Regional Advice and Care

Marigolds are relatively easy to grow. Some American marigolds have large 4-inch flowers on tall plants. Staking with thin bamboo stakes may be necessary, especially during heavy rains and in windy planting sites. Although often listed as self-cleaning, deadhead marigold's spent flowers, especially when the plants are young in late spring. They are pest-free.

Companion Planting and Design

Marigolds offer many benefits to the home landscape, from growing in containers to forming a low barrier hedge. Some homeowners plant marigolds around vegetable gardens to ward off pests and four-legged, night-feeding creatures. Whether this actually works or not has never been scientifically proven . . . but there are those who believe.

Try These

Among the French types, I like both the 'Aurora' and Disco series. They are compact growing and offer a wide range of sunny shades. In the American types, Crush varieties are extra-dwarf, growing from 12 to 18 inches tall with full 4-inch flowers. The Inca series is similar, though a bit larger. In the Triploid F1 hybrids, look for the Zenith series.

Million Bells®

Calibrachoa hybrids

Botanical Pronunciation
kal-ih-bruh-KOE-uh

Bloom Period and Seasonal Color
May to frost; blooms in shades of red, pink,
yellow, apricot, white, red-violet, blue

Mature Height x Spread
3 to 12 inches x 12 to 24 inches

This Proven Winners® is a real proven winner! Million Bells® features hundreds of quarter-sized, petunia-like flowers and is available in many beautiful colors. The plant thrives in bright sun and heat. It is fast growing and, most important, self-cleaning with blooms from spring through fall. It has a low-growing, compact growth habit and thrives in sun to a half-day of shade. Oh! Did I mention that I *like* it? Million Bells® will naturally grow downward 5 to 6 feet when planted in a hanging basket. Many greenhouses and nursery stores will offer these mixed baskets. Select the one that catches your eye. Once you try this charmer, you will always make room for it in the future. Remember, Million Bells® is easy to grow and oh, so beautiful!

When, Where, and How to Plant
Plant Million Bells® growing in pots and cell-packs in spring. It can tolerate some late-spring cool weather. Hurry! Buy plants from the greenhouse or nursery before the fourth week of May or they will all be gone. Choose locations with lots of sun, although some shade is okay. Average, well-drained soil is fine. Use a soilless mix for containers. Follow the general directions for planting in this chapter's introduction, spacing plants 8 to 12 inches apart.

Growing Tips
Maintenance for Million Bells® is a lot like that of petunias. It is a heavy feeder, which means it must be fertilized often, following the package instructions for frequency and amount. It tolerates dry soil, but water anyway during periods of drought. In hanging baskets in full sun, keep it happy by checking daily in hot weather to see if it needs more water.

Regional Advice and Care
The blooms of Million Bells® look like miniature petunias, about the size of a quarter. Fortunately, the many flowers are self-cleaning. No bugs or disease with this one either. It spreads very quickly; keep it in-bounds by pruning away any unwanted growth.

Companion Planting and Design
Million Bells® makes an excellent bed planting all by itself, or use it to edge a bed of larger-blooming flowers. It makes outstanding hanging baskets on its own or when combined with scaevola, browallia, or other colorful annuals. Million Bells® is also great in a 10- to 12-inch hanging basket combined with other clump-type flowers that will fill out the top and provide some height for the arrangement.

Try These
Upright varieties include 'Terra Cotta' (a yellow bloomer—though this hardly describes its beautiful color) and 'Cherry Pink' (bright pink with a yellow throat). Both grow to 12 inches tall, and they do spread. 'Trailing Blue' and 'Trailing Pink' are super choices for baskets—actually, they are *all* fantastic for baskets. There are lots of new ones on the way—as the catalogs say, "incredible flower power" and that's the truth!

Nemesia

Nemesia cultivars

Botanical Pronunciation
ne-MEE-see-uh

Bloom Period and Seasonal Color
June to frost; blooms in blue, white, purple, pink, yellow

Mature Height x Spread
10 to 14 inches x 8 to 10 inches

Well, Denny, here you go again! Writing about another flower that many Ohio gardeners have never heard of. Well, it's not anyone's fault—it's still new! It's a member of the Proven Winners®, a group of plants creating new gardening opportunities. Several selections of nemesia are P.P.A.F. (which means, plant patent applied for). That's an impressive statement to make for any plant. Now why are they P.P.A.F.? To begin with, they are cold hardy to 15 degrees Fahrenheit, yet tolerant of heat into the 90s (not a bad statement). *Nemesia* 'Blue Bird' has blue flowers with yellow centers, and 'Compact Innocence' has pure white flowers with bright yellow centers. When in bloom, which is all summer, 'Compact Innocence' smells just like a lilac. Plant it once, and you'll never forget it!

When, Where, and How to Plant

Plant nemesia from potted plants. You won't be able to obtain seed by mail order—only growers who pay a patent fee can order it. You will have to settle for potted plants, which is the best way to go anyway. Plant in the soil after the danger of frost is over in your part of Ohio. This relatively low-growing plant is best grown in full sun in pretty good, loose soil. If you don't have good soil, and you still want to grow this beautiful annual, add 25 percent organic soil amendments. Nemesia will still grow well in a half-day of sun. To plant, follow the general directions in this chapter's introduction. Space plants about 6 to 8 inches apart.

Growing Tips

Fertilize with a complete plant food, following the instructions on the container. Water nemesia during dry periods of the summer, but don't keep it wet. For healthy containers, always plant flowers in pots with other plants that have the same "wants." Make sure the plants are sun- and water-compatible.

Regional Advice and Care

No bugs or disease bother this great annual. The flowers are plentiful and self-cleaning.

Companion Planting and Design

Nemesia does very well in mass plantings and as a border plant, and it is especially colorful in containers. Mix nemesia with other drought-tolerant flowers to make your patio pots look fantastic. Try it in hanging baskets and mixed planters with 'Summer Wave' torenia, for a great combination of color that will have blooms all summer long.

Try These

Nemesia is no fluke. (You can't be a fluke and be considered for a P.P.A.F.) The Sunsatia series introduced recently has six vibrant colors called pineapple, banana, cranberry, coconut, peach, and lemon. Aromatica has flowers in colors of lavender ice, true blue, and compact white. Nemesia is typical of other Proven Winners® plants. These varieties have gone through vigorous garden trial tests and have proven their worth.

Ornamental Cabbage and Kale

Brassica oleracea

Botanical Pronunciation
BRAS-ee-ka awl-lur-RAY-see-uh

Bloom Period and Seasonal Color
Grown for ornamental foliage from September through late fall in colors of red, rose, pink, white, green

Mature Height x Spread
6 to 12 inches x 1 to 1½ feet

Ornamental cabbage and kale look just like their vegetable cousins in the spring and summer. But as the weather cools in September, all of a sudden the leaves show their true colors. The cooler the weather becomes, the prettier the leaves turn, with shades of pink, red, rose, or white. Cabbage and kale make excellent plants for prime planting spots, making beautiful replacements for tired-looking, summer-blooming annuals. Ornamental cabbage and kale will persist in the fall landscape until the mercury dips to 20 degrees Fahrenheit. That means that in central and southern Ohio, you can expect color through Thanksgiving—even Christmas some years. Oh, yes! What is the difference between cabbage and kale? Ornamental cabbage has round leaves, and ornamental kale has crinkly, wavy leaves.

When, Where, and How to Plant

Plant ornamental cabbage and kale from seed in late spring, if you like, and grow them for the fall season. If you want to start seeds indoors, do it in April and plant outdoors as soon as the seedlings reach 3 inches. Remember, though, they are going to look like veggies until fall. I recommend you buy nursery-grown potted plants in September and October. That way, you only have to care for them while they're pretty. Plant in average, well-drained garden soil in part shade to full sun. The more sun they get, the more intense the fall leaf colors will be. Dig a hole as deep as the soil clump and twice as wide. Loosen any wrapped roots, backfill the soil, and water-in well.

Growing Tips

Fertilize with a water-soluble plant food as often as the label advises. Watering is seldom necessary, but it wouldn't hurt during a dry spell.

Regional Advice and Care

When started from seed in spring, ornamental cabbage and kale are susceptible to green cabbage-worms. Treat with a control such as B.t. (*Bacillus thuringiensis*). This is not a problem for plants that are installed in fall. Remove any nibbled leaves.

Companion Planting and Design

Wondering what to plant with those beautiful pink mums? Here is your answer. Or in the fall, replant your summer containers with ornamental cabbage or kale. They may still be there to greet your holiday company—dusted with snow, of course.

Try These

There are standard-sized plants growing 11- to 12-inch diameter heads, and there are dwarf types that grow 3- to 6-inch diameter heads. For ornamental cabbage, try the Dynasty series. These plants have tight, compact heads in pink, white, or red. Plants in the Pigeon series grow smaller, 4-inch leaves in red or white. For kale, plants in the Emperor series have 3- to 6-inch, heavily fringed leaves of red, rose, or white. The Peacock series offers 10- to 12-inch heads of red, rose, or white.

Pansy

Viola x *wittrockiana*

Botanical Pronunciation
vy-OH-la wit-rok-ee-AH-na

Other Name Ladies delight

Bloom Period and Seasonal Color March to June, and September to winter; blue, purple, yellow, pink, orange, red-violet, bronze, multicolor

Mature Height x Spread
6 to 10 inches x 6 to 8 inches

When asked about pansies I say, "Plant pansies in the fall and get six months of pleasure." If you wait until spring, you may get only six weeks. Which is the better deal? Pansy varieties have been improved so much that now they that can be planted in the fall and overwintered in your garden. In fact, the new, cold-hardy varieties will bloom on sunny winter days when the temperature hits 40 degrees Fahrenheit. These new-fangled pansies (unlike the old-timers that would give up when there was a week of 80 degree weather) will continue to bloom into the early summer, despite the warm weather. Yes, pansies are tough. Check with your local garden center in the fall to see which pansies are best for your landscape.

When, Where, and How to Plant
My, how times have changed. Just a few years ago, pansies were only available in spring. Now, great, cold-hardy varieties are available during all fall months. Plant pansies in early spring or early fall. When planting in fall, plant early in September to give them more time to establish their roots. Pansies grow best in full sun. Some varieties are more heat and cold tolerant than others, and will tolerate a half-day of shade in the afternoon. Shade will keep all pansies blooming later into summer. Plant all varieties in areas that receive morning sun to extend their blooming period in late spring. Buy pansies in pots or cell-packs. Site in any type of well-drained garden soil—including clay. Loosen the garden soil 6 to 8 inches. Dig a hole as deep and twice as wide as the soil clump. Loosen any wrapped roots, backfill, and water-in.

Growing Tips
Fertilize with a high-phosphorus (middle number) fertilizer. Water if your garden runs into a dry spell; pansies like moisture.

Regional Advice and Care
Deadhead spent flowers every couple of weeks. Pests and disease are seldom a problem. When temperatures rise into the 80s, pansies will start to stretch with a few small blooms and become outright ugly—pull them out!

Companion Planting and Design
If you can dream it, you can do it. Pansies come by variety in at least twenty-five colors and combinations of colors. Make sure the variety you want is cold hardy, so you can plant in fall for six months of enjoyment.

Try These
Bingo series is a highly rated pansy with short flower stems and a 3½-inch flower that "looks at you." Baby Bingo series is low growing, with loads of blooms in all colors; it tolerates heat and cold better than most and is a great variety for overwintering. Crystal Bowl series is very heat tolerant and compact. 'Purple Rain F1' has large, purple flowers on well-mounded plants. It's a free-flowering variety ideal for hanging baskets.

Pentas

Pentas lanceolata

Botanical Pronunciation
PEN-tass lan-see-oh-LAY-tuh

Other Name
Star cluster

Bloom Period and Seasonal Color
June to frost; blooms in shades of red, pink, violet, white

Mature Height x Spread
6 to 15 inches x 10 to 12 inches

Pentas lanceolata is another terrific "Heat Beater"—that is, a flower that will perform well all summer through lots of heat and drought. This relatively new plant is a summer-blooming tender perennial (treated as an annual) that you may not have heard of, but don't shy away from it. The pink, red, or violet flowers appear as clusters; each cluster is made up of many star-shaped flowers for a gorgeous starry effect set off by dark green, somewhat glossy foliage. Some years, I've waited too long to secure them for myself and we ran out at my nursery. Get to the nursery early for this one. They might become available before it's safe to plant outdoors. Buy and hold indoors until it's planting time.

When, Where, and How to Plant
You will probably find pentas only in 3- or 4-inch pots, although they may be available in cell-packs. Do not plant outdoors until the danger of frost has passed. Just keep them inside in their pots till it's safe to plant outside. Pentas will grow in full sun, in morning sun, or in afternoon sun. For best bloom results, make sure they get at least four hours of sun. They will grow in all types of soil as long as there is good drainage. If your soil is heavy clay, add some soil amendments to loosen it. Never amend more than 25 to 30 percent. Loosen your garden soil to a depth of 6 to 8 inches. Dig a hole as deep and twice as wide as the soil clump. Loosen any wrapped roots, plant, backfill the soil, and water-in well.

Growing Tips
My pentas enjoyed being fed with a once-a-year, timed-release plant food. Find your favorite fertilizer and follow the instructions carefully (remember, more *is not* better). Pentas are very drought tolerant, but an occasional drink of water during dry periods would be appreciated—just don't keep them moist all the time.

Regional Advice and Care
There are no bugs or diseases that will bother your pentas. The flowers are self-cleaning. Just plant and enjoy!

Companion Planting and Design
Pentas make a wonderful display in a mass planting, or use them as my daughter Molly does in a border planting. Colors of pentas are very fluorescent and will show off in the sunlight and also by the moonlight. Plant them in a spot that can be viewed from both inside and outside your home.

Try These
I like the New Look series. It offers pink, red, or violet flower clusters that bloom all summer on plants that grow 6 to 12 inches tall. The Butterfly series promises to be even better. Butterflies love it, of course.

Petunia

Petunia x *hybrida*

Botanical Pronunciation
peh-TEWN-ya hy-BRID-uh

Bloom Period and Seasonal Color
Early May to late fall; red, pink, purple, blue, white, lavender, yellow flowers; may be zoned or striped

Mature Height x Spread
6 to 16 inches x 12 to 36 inches

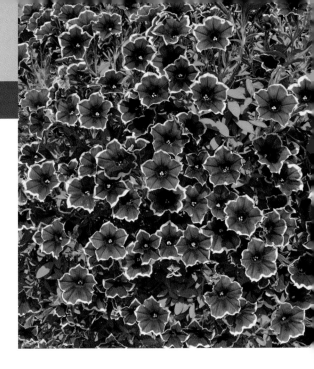

To be honest, until a few years ago, I hated petunias. The older varieties had to be deadheaded, which meant sticky green fingers from removing all those spent flowers so the petunias would stay looking good. Then, when hot summer weather came along, forget it. Those flowers went away. But hey, this is the new millennium, and new varieties have come to the rescue. First the 'Wave' petunias were introduced with 'Purple Wave' and 'Pink Wave'. Then there were the 'Supertunias'. Next came the 'Surfinia' petunias, then the 'Hulahoop' and Picotee series. All of these new petunias have several things in common—they're colorful, love hot weather, are very drought tolerant, and are self-cleaning. Petunias are back in a big way, and I *love* them!

When, Where, and How to Plant

Most of the new petunia varieties are not available from seeds, but you shouldn't have any problem locating the plants in hanging baskets, pots of all sizes, and cell-packs. Petunias are cold hardy, and you can plant them as early as the first week of May. Petunia hybrids will grow in any type of soil that has good drainage. Give your petunia hybrids at least a half-day of sun; all-day sun is best. Petunias will also produce nice color in areas of good sky light with little direct sun. For planting in the garden, follow the instructions in this chapter's introduction. Space plants according to their variety.

Growing Tips

Hybrid petunias are cold hardy and will also tolerate lots of summer heat. They are heavy feeders. Keep them on a steady diet of fertilizer, following the instructions on the fertilizer package. Hybrid petunias do not want frequent watering during the summer. Put the hose away, and let Mother Nature take care of them.

Regional Advice and Care

These new varieties are also self-cleaning—no green fingers from pinching off spent flowers. However, any petunia that is getting scraggly can be cut back. Pests and diseases? You will find no problems here.

Companion Planting and Design

Use petunias anywhere you have enough light; their wide range of colors gives you the opportunity to mix and match. Many of these newer varieties— 'Surfinia', 'Supertunia', and 'Wave', for example— have a naturally cascading habit. These are amazing hanging-basket plants! Remember to plant your petunias in a soilless potting mix when filling a hanging basket.

Try These

'Wave' petunias are awesome. They are easy to grow, have large 3-inch blooms, spread up to 4 feet per plant, and take both hot and cold weather. The four colors to choose from are 'Purple Wave', 'Pink Wave', 'Misty Lilac Wave', and 'Rose Wave'. 'Madness' is a floribunda petunia that really performs. It has loads of 3-inch blooms in twenty-one beautiful colors.

Portulaca

Portulaca grandiflora

Botanical Pronunciation
por-tew-LAK-uh gran-dih-FLOR-uh

Other Name
Moss rose

Bloom Period and Seasonal Color
Late May to frost; pink, magenta, fuschia, yellow, white, cream, orange, peach blooms

Mature Height x Spread
4 to 6 inches x 6 to 8 inches

"Would you like a portulaca?" My mom used to say this when I was seven years old and helped her plant our summer flowers. She always planted portulaca as a border plant across the front of our home. Maybe it's an old-fashioned flower, but old or new, portulaca is tough as nails. The flowers come in a wide range of bright glowing colors—pink, fuchsia, yellow, white, cream, orange, and a trendy shade of peach. A succulent-looking plant with leaves that resemble evergreen needles, it is low-growing with a mature height of only 4 to 6 inches. Portulaca is very drought tolerant; the hotter and drier the summer weather becomes, the prettier your portulaca will be. Now, I ask you again, "Would you like a portulaca?"

When, Where, and How to Plant

Portulaca is easy to start from seed. Start indoors four to six weeks before seedlings are safe to plant outdoors. Plant transplants or nursery-grown cell-packs in mid- to late May after the danger of a late spring frost has passed. It does well in any hot, sunny spot where nothing else seems to want to grow. It will grow in a half-day of sun, but remember, the more sun it gets, the more flowers it will give. Any well-draining soil is fine. Pinch off early flowers on your freshly installed plants—this will promote quicker growth and sooner, more abundant blooms. Refer to this chapter's introduction for more planting tips.

Growing Tips

For the first month after planting, water when the soil is dry. After that, let Mother Nature take over. Moss rose likes it on the dry side. Start off your transplant with a little water-soluble plant food when you plant it, and then put the fertilizer away.

Regional Advice and Care

There are no bugs or diseases to worry about with portulaca. Self-sown seedlings may appear the following year. They will be colorful, but they may not resemble the parent plant. Keep them or weed them out—it's up to you.

Companion Planting and Design

Portulaca is a good border plant and is great for rock garden color or anywhere the hose won't reach. It's a wonderful annual to plant around perennial creeping phlox, which tends to go away with summer heat. Portulaca also makes a beautiful hanging basket for hot, sunny areas and a nice addition to a combination container planting.

Try These

The Sundial series offers free-blooming, 1½- to 2-inch flowers that love the heat and bloom in ten different flavors. Check out 'Peppermint' (striped like a peppermint candy) and 'Mango', a delicious peachy orange. If you like orange—and the style-makers say it's "in"—look for 'Tutti Frutti', an upbeat mix of orange, apricot, and white. 'Calypso Mix', another great heat beater, offers 1- to 2-inch double blooms in many colors.

Salvia

Salvia splendens

Botanical Pronunciation
SAL-vee-uh SPLEN-denz

Other Name
Scarlet sage

Bloom Period and Seasonal Color
June to frost; red, white, purple, lavender, salmon, bicolor flowers

Mature Height x Spread
10 to 30 inches x 8 to 12 inches

Salvia is another old-timer among the summer-blooming annuals. For years, salvia was available only as a red-blooming plant with just a few varieties, most in the tall 20- to 30-inch size. But plant breeders never sleep, and over the last twenty-five years new varieties have been developed, offering a range of colors. Many are still red, but now you also have a choice of a deep burgundy red to bright red, rose, salmon, white, purple, orchid, and bicolors of scarlet, salmon, and rose. Wow, what choices! One thing salvia plants—new and old—have in common is that they are heat and drought tolerant. The foliage of all salvia is dark green and very attractive, making a wonderful contrast to the blooms. Finally, this plant attracts hummingbirds.

When, Where, and How to Plant
You can start salvia seeds indoors four to six weeks before it's safe to plant outdoors (based on the last frost date). Plant garden center or greenhouse transplants in mid- to late May after the danger of a late frost is over. Full sun will give you the best flower count, although I've been very successful with my salvia that gets only a half-day of sun. Salvia will grow in all types of soil as long as there is good drainage. Follow the directions in this chapter's introduction for more specifics. Pinching off all the flowers for the first couple of weeks allows plants to grow a lot more stems and will quickly give you a lot more bloom.

Growing Tips
Feed regularly with an all-purpose fertilizer, following the instructions. Even though salvia is drought tolerant, an occasional drink of water is appreciated during hot, dry weather. They are tough, so if you forget to water them today, just water them tomorrow.

Regional Advice and Care
Once a week, pinch off old, spent flowers as they appear. This is most important for the first four weeks after they're planted. Taller-growing salvia might require staking when planted in windy areas. No pest or disease problems here.

Companion Planting and Design
Depending on the variety, these terrific low-maintenance flowers look great mixed or planted in solid colors in large beds, as borders, or as background blooms. Salvia does well in patio or deck pots as well as planter boxes. The new colors, such as grape-purple and rich salmon, leave lots of room for creativity. For a patriotic display, you couldn't ask for a redder red.

Try These
The Empire series has uniform-growing plants (broadly growing to 12 to 15 inches high and wide) that are available in all the new colors. The Salsa series also has all the new colors, including bicolors. The Sizzler series is another great choice. If you go for classic red, try 'Early Bonfire'. It's tall (28 to 30 inches) with large, showy flower spikes.

Scaevola 'New Wonder'

Scaevola aemula 'New Wonder'

Botanical Pronunciation
skee-VO-luh EM-yoo-luh

Other Name Fan flower

Bloom Period and Seasonal Color
Late May to frost; blooms in lavender-blue

Mature Height x Spread
1 foot x 1 to 2 feet (or more)

Bring on summer—you may run inside for the air-conditioning, but scaevola beats the heat with cool blue flowers. It actually *thrives* on heat and humidity. Also called fan flower, scaevola is a weeping annual that trails over the soil like a groundcover in the garden or cascades over a pot's edge when planted in a container or hanging basket. Each well-branched plant is covered with hundreds of blue fan-shaped flowers. 'New Wonder' is a superior selection of scaevola, and it is one of the summer-blooming annuals marketed by Proven Winners®. To earn this designation, these plants have to be both beautiful and tough; many are unusual compared to what you are accustomed to seeing. Scaevola is a great one on this list; it won't be unusual for long.

When, Where, and How to Plant

Plant scaevola from plants growing in pots or cell-packs in spring after the danger of frost has passed. Buy before June, as this is one of the first flowers sold out in spring. Plant scaevola in full sun to half-day sun. It will grow in any garden soil as long as there's good drainage. Loosen your garden soil to 6 to 8 inches deep. Dig a hole as deep and twice as wide as the soil clump. Loosen any wrapped roots before placing it in the hole. Backfill, and water-in well. For a mass display, space plants about 8 to 12 inches apart. Use a soilless potting mix when planting scaevola in a 10- to 12-inch hanging basket.

Growing Tips

Dry weather isn't a concern if scaevola is planted in the ground. Water *only* when it's extremely dry, such as no rain for two to three weeks. I've had three in hanging baskets on my front porch facing south, and the only work for me was to water every other day if they were dry. Fertilize with a timed-release fertilizer, which is applied just once for the entire growing season.

Regional Advice and Care

Scaevola is very low maintenance. The plant self-cleans, and pests and disease are insignificant.

Companion Planting and Design

You can mix scaevola and another Proven Winners®, Million Bells®, in the same hanging pot. It makes a beautiful combination that will have your basket very full on top and weeping down 4 to 5 feet.

Try These

'New Wonder' is the best cultivar because it's very floriferous. In hanging baskets, it weeps over the pot, while still remaining full. Planted in a bed, it forms a full bed of color. These new varieties of Proven Winners® don't last long at your favorite flower shop for two reasons: shoppers fall in love with them, and many storeowners who aren't familiar with them don't buy enough. Get 'em fast!

Snapdragon

Antirrhinum majus

Botanical Pronunciation an-ter-REE-num MAY-jus

Other Name Snaps

Bloom Period and Seasonal Color
Mid-May to killing frost; blooms in red, pink, mauve, bronze, white, yellow, orange, bicolors

Mature Height x Spread
6 to 36 inches x 8 to 12 inches

Snapdragons have been around for quite a few years. Like other short-lived perennials treated as annuals, improvements have been made so that the plants you buy at your favorite nursery, greenhouse, or garden store are the best they can be. They come in many colors, with individual blooms consisting of two upper petals and three lower petals, forming a claw-type flower that looks as if it wants to pinch you. Snapdragons are easy to maintain in the garden. The tallest varieties make great cut flowers, while the dwarf varieties make excellent border plants. Snaps also look great when planted with other summer bloomers in mixed patio pots and window boxes. They are cold hardy, producing blooms in the fall even after a few light frosts.

When, Where, and How to Plant
Start seeds indoors four to six weeks before it's safe to plant outdoors (based on the last frost date). You can cheat a little because of snapdragon's cold hardiness. Plant bedding plants around May 1 in Zone 6 and mid-May in Zone 5. Snaps grow in almost any type of well-draining soil. Site them in full sun to all-morning sun. Consult this chapter's introduction for more planting details. Space dwarf snaps on 12-inch centers and tall varieties on 15-inch centers. Pinch off blooms for the first couple of weeks after planting.

Growing Tips
Fertilize with a balanced plant food, following container directions. For the first month, water transplanted snaps when the soil is dry. With timely summer rains, that may be all the water you'll have to provide.

Regional Advice and Care
A few diseases can hamper snapdragons. To reduce the risk, follow my mulching instructions in this chapter's introduction and *avoid overhead watering*. Planting in a breezy area dries the morning dew, helping ward off disease. Stake tall snaps if they start to lean. Deadhead to keep your snaps blooming.

Companion Planting and Design
Snaps come in various blooming heights, from 12 to 36 inches. Dwarfs look great in their own bed. Snapdragons are one of the flowers I remember most as a young child. Get your children started in gardening by giving them a small spot to plant with flowers and vegetables, such as snapdragons and green beans.

Try These
For dwarf snapdragons, I recommend Floral Showers series; it grows 6 to 8 inches tall with uniform plants and blooms in thirteen colors. Tahiti series offers loads of bloom on 7- to 9-inch plants; it comes in fourteen colors. For medium snapdragons, I highly recommend the Ribbon Rose and Sonnet series. The Rocket series of tall snapdragons has plants growing 30 to 36 inches tall; it's great for cut flowers.

Spider Plant

Cleome hassleriana

Botanical Pronunciation
klee-OH-me hass-ler-ee-AY-nah

Other Name
Cleome

Bloom Period and Seasonal Color
June to killing frost; blooms in pink, purple, white

Mature Height x Spread
3 to 4 feet x 1½ to 2 feet

Spider plant gets its common name from its appearance; when in bloom, the flowers look like actual spiders weaving their webs of silken threads. Spider plant, also called spider flower as well as cleome, is an annual that's been around for many years. Like so many annuals that have the same name today that they did thirty years ago, it has been improved by those wonderful people known as hybridizers. The flowers, which start appearing on the plant when it's 12 inches tall, continue to bloom on the top 25 percent of the stems, which grow until they reach a fall height of up to 4 feet. A variety known as Queen is a series whose plants come in four colors; all are strong all-summer bloomers, and are fragrant too.

When, Where, and How to Plant
Plant spider plants from plants already growing in pots or cell-packs, after the danger of frost has passed. You can start plants from seed if you can find it; start indoors around the middle of April or start outdoors in late May. Spider plant is one of those summer-blooming annuals that will bloom in all types of soil as long as there is good drainage. Plant in full sun to a half-day of shade, and it will give you lots of color. Follow the planting directions in this chapter's introduction. If your plants have blooms at planting time, pinch them off to promote stronger growth. Continue to pinch flowers off for a couple of weeks after planting. Space plants on 12-inch centers.

Growing Tips
Spider plants grow well regardless of the care you give them. Watering is rarely needed. Fertilize spider plants following the directions on your favorite plant food. See this chapter's introduction for more tips.

Regional Advice and Care
Pinch back the stems if they get tall and leggy. In exposed locations, tall varieties may need staking. Spider plants produce *a lot* of seed, which volunteers quite readily the next season. If you want loads of free plants, you'll be happy. If you don't, and you want to keep these plants from taking over your flower bed, be sure to use a high yield turf and ornamental grass-type weed killer using a preemergent herbicide in mid-March and again in mid-June. Spider plants also have prickly spines on the stems; don't get stuck. They suffer no pests.

Companion Planting and Design
Spider plants make quite a statement when planted in their own bed. They are also a dramatic tall center for a circular bed. Use them as an annual hedge or to soften the look of a fence.

Try These
Queen series plants grow 3 to 5 feet tall. They bloom all summer and produce fragrant flowers in colors of 'Cherry Rose', 'Rose Queen', 'Violet', and 'Helen Campbell', white. This is truly a carefree, low-maintenance group of summer-blooming flowers.

Spike

Cordyline species

Botanical Pronunciation
kor-dih-LYE-nee

Other Name
Dracaena

Bloom Period and Seasonal Color
Season-long green foilage that will winter over indoor your home

Mature Height x Spread
24 inches x 15 inches

Considered a tropical plant, native to South America and southernmost parts of this country, spike—also called dracaena—can make quite a statement here in Ohio with its ability to set off any planter. Regardless of a planter's theme, spike always fits in. All planted combinations can use some vertical accent. Dracaena also makes a great plant to repot into a 4-inch pot and place indoors in a room with good natural light. Keep on the dry side in the spring; you can decide whether to use this spike in a mixed planter or leave indoors. Repot into a 6-inch pot and grow on as an indoor plant.

When, Where, and How to Plant
Plant your spike (or spikes, because who can plant just one?) outdoors after all danger of frost here in Ohio has passed. You can cheat if you plant in a container with soilless planting mix, keeping the container light enough to carry inside on a frosty night. In a mixed container combine with other flowers that are also drought compatible so you don't overwater your spike keeping other flowers happy. Spikes can be purchased growing in 3- and 4-inch pots from a greenhouse or garden center in spring.

Growing Tips
It doesn't get any easier than growing spikes. Just don't kill them with kindness by giving them too much water and plant food. Forget them, and they'll love you for it.

Regional Advice and Care
Spike is pest–free. If your spikes start to get brown tips to the outer part of the leaves, they are getting too much water. I've had a dracaena in my office that goes without water a month at a time.

Companion Planting and Design
The usual container planting includes a spike in the middle of the container surrounded by three geraniums some dusty miller, vinca vine, million bells, and anything else that catches your eyes. Some gardeners use spikes throughout their annual planting area for a scattering of vertical interest.

Try These
Some fun cultivars include 'Burgundy', Festival®, 'Electric Pink', and Centerpiece™, which has green, creamy white, and pink leaves.

Sunflower

Helianthus hybrids and cultivars

Botanical Pronunciation
hee-lee-AN-thus

Bloom Period and Seasonal Color
Midsummer to frost; blooms in yellow, orange,
crimson-red, bronze

Mature Height x Spread
2 to 7 feet (by variety) x 1 to 2 feet

Who would have thought years ago that we would talk about sunflowers as an annual for the home landscape? Back then they were judged by how high they grew. Can you imagine a 12-foot-high border plant? I don't think so. But flower hybridizers have been busy civilizing sunflowers. They have reduced those big, heavily seeded flowers on sky-high plants to new petite varieties—some topping out at just 2 feet. The flowers themselves have changed, ranging in size from 3 to 7 inches in diameter. And they come in a range of hot colors—some with no center seed disk at all, just a globe of golden petals. All of the new hybrid sunflowers make great cut flowers and provide natural bird food for our feathered friends.

When, Where, and How to Plant
Many of the newest varieties are available only as plants in pots or sometimes in cell-packs. But seeds are easy to plant directly in the soil. Plant outdoors from plants or seeds after the danger of a late-spring frost is over. These plants do well in any type of Ohio soil as long as the drainage is good. They want lots of sunshine, but they will still bloom well in morning-only sun. Loosen your garden soil to a depth of 6 to 8 inches. Plant seeds directly into the soil ¼ inch deep and 12 inches apart. For potted plants, follow the directions in this chapter's introduction. Space plants according to variety.

Growing Tips
Sunflowers are big eaters. Be sure to fertilize as often as your favorite plant food container says to do so, particularly if your soil is infertile. Although drought tolerant, they appreciate an occasional drink of water when it's hot and dry.

Regional Advice and Care
Pests and disease are rarely a problem. Some of the tall selections may profit from a stout stake to keep them upright. All sunflowers produce seeds, and some varieties provide more than others. Cut off and save the spent flowers. When they've completely dried, peel out the seeds to use in your birdfeeder during the winter or enjoy a few yourself.

Companion Planting and Design
These newly refined sunflowers can be used in containers, in a mass display, or grown for cut flowers. Tall varieties look great growing against a wall or fence.

Try These
A few of my favorites follow; I can't list them all! 'Big Smile' has large, 6-inch, golden yellow flowers on 2½-foot-tall plants; it's great for containers. 'Sundance Kid' is a new variety that has several long-lasting, 4- to 6-inch, yellow flowers on the same stem; the plants grow 2½ feet tall and are great for bedding. 'Teddy Bear', a true double, has golden yellow, 3- to 5-inch flowers on a 2½- to 3-foot plant.

Sweet Potato Vine

Ipomoea batatas

Botanical Pronunciation
eye-poe-MEE-ah bah-TAH-tass

Bloom Period and Seasonal Color
All growing season; lime green, purple, or variegated green, cream, and pink leaves

Mature Height x Spread
Branches grow out 30 to 36 inches in length

This is actually a variety of the edible sweet potato. It's also a cousin to the morning glory. The heart-shaped or lobed leaves make a nice trailing plant for any container or use as a groundcover. If you have never planted sweet potato, plant one. Plants cover a lot of ground; you only need one sweet potato per pot and it will give you all the weeping color you need. You can overwinter sweet potato vine by leaving the pot in an unheated garage or by digging a hole the size of your pot and placing the pot and all in the soil until spring. The potato tubers are edible but based on my experience—even though the tuber has lavender insides—it's not very tasty.

When, Where, and How to Plant
Buy your sweet potato vines at nurseries or garden centers. They'll be available in flats, and in 3- or 4-inch pots as well. Place outdoors after danger of frost is over. They grow well in full to part sun. When planting in a pot, make sure that pot has drainage holes on the lower sides of the bottom of the pot. When using as a groundcover, plant sweet potato vines 24 inches apart. Trim anytime to keep your sweet potato within the boundaries you've assigned. Remember, *you* own the shears. Plant according to the instructions in this chapter's introduction.

Growing Tips
Water if your soil starts to dry during hot summer weather. Fertilize with a "start and grow" timed-release plant food when you first plant; this will feed your plants the entire season.

Regional Advice and Care
Sweet potato vines are low maintenance and free of any plant pests. A few night-feeding beetles may eat a few holes in leaves. It's no big deal; they have to eat too. You can wait until a killing frost knocks out the leaves; then just dig up the tubers and let them dry on the kitchen sink. Place them in a netted bag and store in the basement until the following spring, when you can replant them.

Companion Planting and Design
This vining plant will look beautiful when used in a mixed pot of annuals with similar needs. 'Wave' petunias and million bells or even the larger growing cannas would be *excellent* companions.

Try These
The most common and easy-to-find sweet potato vine is 'Marguerite'. 'Blackie' is another great one with leaves of dark purple, which look black to the naked eye.

Verbena

Verbena hybrids

Botanical Pronunciation
ver-BEE-nah

Other Name
Garden verbena

Bloom Period and Seasonal Color
May to frost; blooms in shades of red, pink,
purple, blue, peach

Mature Height x Spread
8 to 12 inches x 8 to 12 inches

Verbena, a summer-blooming plant known for its heat and drought tolerance, has been around for quite a few years. Older varieties flowered in colors of purple to pink and could be lanky; they often succumbed to powdery mildew. Then along came a new group called Temari—what an improvement! This group of plants literally blooms and blooms, and there are many new colors—bright red, bright pink, burgundy, cherry blossom pink, blue, and all other shades of pink. Beyond the candy store of color, Temari is also known for its larger flower clusters, bushy growth habit, disease resistance, and, of course, it's still just as heat and drought tolerant. All verbenas are attractive to butterflies and bees, adding even more interest to the plantings.

When, Where, and How to Plant
Verbena is best planted from pots or cell-packs in spring. Install after the danger of frost has passed. Old-fashioned verbena prefers decent soil in a location with full sun to a half-day of sun. Decent soil means good, loose garden soil. Amend average to poor soil with organic peat or compost at a ratio of 30 percent amendments to 70 percent native soil. Just make sure the area has good drainage. Loosen the soil to a depth of 6 to 8 inches. Dig a hole as deep as the soil clump and twice as wide. Free any roots wrapped around the soil clump. Place the plant into the hole, backfill, and water-in well. If planting verbenas in a hanging basket, make sure the basket is 10 to 12 inches in diameter and use a soilless potting mix.

Growing Tips
Verbena likes to be fertilized regularly. Choose your plant food and apply according to the instructions on the container. Although plants are heat tolerant, water during drought conditions. When planting verbena in a landscape bed, apply 2 inches of shredded bark mulch, keeping it off the stems.

Regional Advice and Care
Older varieties often succumbed to foliar disease. With the newer types, pests and diseases are of no concern. Pinch their tips to keep verbenas bushy.

Companion Planting and Design
'Temari' patio verbena is a prime choice for gardens as well as patio containers and hanging baskets. It grows close to the ground in sunny areas and is great for hanging baskets where you need color to really weep over the pots.

Try These
Gorgeous red, burgundy, violet, blue, pink, and magenta colors, as well as disease resistance—can I mention 'Temari' verbenas again? Their low-growing growth habit makes them weep over hanging baskets or patio pots. They stay fuller than their predecessors when planted in similar situations. I'm partial to the ones with "patio" in their name: 'Patio Red', 'Patio Blue', and 'Patio Pink'. 'Peaches and Cream', an All-America Selections winner, has lots of flowers.

Vinca

Catharanthus roseus

Botanical Pronunciation
kat-uh-RANTH-us RO-zee-us

Other Name
Periwinkle

Bloom Period and Seasonal Color
Late May to frost; blooms in magenta, pink, white; some with a contrasting eye

Mature Height x Spread
12 inches x 12 inches

To be or not to be? But the real question is, "Is this plant called periwinkle?" Well, I usually go with vinca—that's how it's identified by the major seed companies. The confusion doesn't end with its name. When I started working in a garden center in the early 1960s (child labor, of course!), this plant was sold as a shade lover with the warning, "Don't give vinca any more than morning sun." Then it was discovered that vinca was a tremendous heat beater, literally growing on its own with no water or shade. The original came in purple-pink or white. There are new varieties now, and your choices of colors are many. All vinca varieties—old and new—have glossy green leaves to add to their overall beauty.

When, Where, and How to Plant

Vinca should be planted in spring after the danger of frost is over. If growing from seed, start it indoors six to eight weeks before it is safe to plant outdoors. Site in any type of well-drained soil, in sun to shade. It blooms less in less sunlight, so a half- to full-day of sun is best. The less summer water, the better these plants perform. So avoid the grass zone of a sprinkler system. If you have bedding plants, follow the specific directions for planting annuals in this chapter's introduction. Space plants on 12-inch centers regardless of their starting size.

Growing Tips

Vinca almost never needs watering; in fact, too much water will result in stunted plants with yellow leaves. In infertile soils, apply a fertilizer following the directions on the package.

Regional Advice and Care

I want to emphasize that vinca—with its glossy green leaves, many growth sizes, and beautiful 2-inch flowers of many colors—is very, *very* low-maintenance. No bugs, no disease (unless it's overwatered!), and no pruning. It is a great plant to dig up before a killing fall frost, pot up, and bring indoors to place by a sunny window for great indoor winter color.

Companion Planting and Design

This great flower resembles impatiens in bloom. With its many new colors and all kinds of blooming forms, it is becoming my favorite. Don't miss the opportunity to plant vinca's 1-foot-tall and -wide plants in a hot spot, especially if that spot is difficult to water. It's great for edging and low borders.

Try These

Wow! I have a lot. Little series is a dwarf variety that grows 6 to 8 inches tall; it's available in five different colors. Cooler series has large over-lapping flower petals and dark green leaves; it grows 10 to 14 inches and blooms in ten different colors. The Heat Wave series is very drought tolerant. Unique 'Apricot Delight' blooms in a soft apricot with red eyes. 'Sterling Star' is a lavender-blue variety that grows taller than most, each plant growing to 14 to 16 inches high.

Wax-Leaf Begonia

Begonia x *semperflorens-cultorum*

Botanical Pronunciation
be-GON-yuh sem-per-FLOR-enz kul-TOR-um

Other Name Fibrous begonia

Bloom Period and Seasonal Color
May to frost; bronze or green foliage; blooms in red, white, pink, coral

Mature Height x Spread
6 to 12 inches x 6 to 10 inches

If your thumb doesn't feel green, plant begonias and you'll feel practically Irish. Wax begonia is a flower for all occasions, blooming well in sun or shade and withstanding serious summer heat and drought. Best of all, it is just beautiful. Let's start with the leaves—there are varieties that have greenish red leaves, narrow leaves, shiny green leaves, or leaves that are green with a tinge of red on the edges. The flowers come in different shades of pink, white, white-edged pink, rose with a white center, and bright red. Salmon-and-white, edged with pink, also works its way into the color mix. Wax-leaf begonias make a great statement when planted in a solid bed; they also make great border plants. Wow, what a wonderful summer-blooming plant!

When, Where, and How to Plant
Don't bother trying to start your own plants from seed. You'll spend at least ten dollars, and you might not end up with anything. Plant wax begonias from nursery-grown plants in pots or cell-packs; plant after the danger of frost has passed. Wax begonia will grow in sun or shade. When planting in sun, both green-leafed and red-leafed varieties will work well. If you have mostly shaded areas, stick with the green-leafed varieties. Begonias do well in all types of soil as long as there's good drainage. Consult this chapter's introduction for planting details.

Growing Tips
Begonias are very heat and drought tolerant. If you notice they are not as colorful during heat-stressed

weather, give them a drink of water. Fertilize with a timed-release plant food for the best results.

Regional Advice and Care
There is no need to deadhead the old blooms, as these plants are self-cleaning. If the stems start to stretch in shady locations in August, cut them back halfway to encourage new, compact growth that will produce more blooms. Pests or diseases? Forget about it!

Companion Planting and Design
Plant wax-leaf begonias in areas that are hard to water during the hot periods of summer. They will grow in any landscape with very little work on your part. My favorite way to use these plants is to alternate white-flowering ones with either pink or red ones—be sure to always use the same variety so you will have standard leaf color along with the alternating blooms.

Try These
The Cocktail series offers flowers in light pink, rose, white edged with red, red, and white on 8- to 10-inch, bronze-leafed plants. Plants in the Super Olympia series are early bloomers with beautiful, broad, green leaves and large flowers. The Encore series has both green and bronze leaves and very large flowers; it offers many colors and is bushy and upright, growing 10 to 12 inches.

Zinnia 'Profusion'

Zinnia angustifolia x *elegans* 'Profusion'

Botanical Pronunciation
ZIN-ya an-gus-tee-FOH-lee-uh ELL-eh-ganz

Bloom Period and Seasonal Color
June to frost; blooms in cherry pink, light pink, orange, creamy white

Mature Height x Spread
6 to 24 inches x 1 to 2 feet

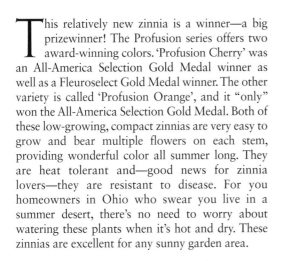

This relatively new zinnia is a winner—a big prizewinner! The Profusion series offers two award-winning colors. 'Profusion Cherry' was an All-America Selection Gold Medal winner as well as a Fleuroselect Gold Medal winner. The other variety is called 'Profusion Orange', and it "only" won the All-America Selection Gold Medal. Both of these low-growing, compact zinnias are very easy to grow and bear multiple flowers on each stem, providing wonderful color all summer long. They are heat tolerant and—good news for zinnia lovers—they are resistant to disease. For you homeowners in Ohio who swear you live in a summer desert, there's no need to worry about watering these plants when it's hot and dry. These zinnias are excellent for any sunny garden area.

When, Where, and How to Plant
'Profusion' zinnias can be planted directly into the ground from seed. Do not plant seeds outdoors until the soil temperature warms in mid- to late-May. The seeds are large enough that you can place and space them without having to transplant later. They don't mind transplanting, but they dislike cold soil. Install growing plants from the garden center or greenhouse after the danger of late frost is over. 'Profusion' zinnias do best in full sun in fertile, well-drained soil. When planting from seed, follow the instructions on the seed packet. When planting zinnias from cell-packs, follow the general directions in this chapter's introduction. Space plants 8 to 18 inches apart, depending on the variety.

Growing Tips
For the first three to four weeks, water young plants and seedlings when it's dry. Then let Mother Nature take care of their moisture needs. Fertilize with an all-purpose plant food, following the directions on the container.

Regional Advice and Care
Pinch off old blooms for four to five weeks after planting—this will help your 'Profusion' zinnias develop faster. (If you grow giant or tall-growing zinnias, continue to deadhead all season.) In general, most zinnias are susceptible to mildew; to avoid problems, choose disease-resistant varieties. Avoid wetting the foliage and space plants generously for better air circulation. **Remember:** The Profusion series is very resistant to mildew.

Companion Planting and Design
'Profusion' zinnias are great in beds and borders, wherever you have sun and need a splash of color. A great cut flower, plant a row in your vegetable garden so you have plenty of blooms for inside.

Try These
It's hard to choose favorites; there are so many great ones. I also like *Zinnia elegans* 'Peter Pan' and Thumbelina series for bright colors on compact plants. *Z. angustifolia* is a disease-resistant zinnia with a spreading habit. The Star series, available in gold, orange, and white, has 2-inch blooms; it grows 10 to 12 inches high. 'Crystal White' is an All-America Selection winner and grows to 15 inches.

BULBS, CORMS, RHIZOMES & TUBERS

FOR OHIO

B ulbs are a whole group of plants put on this earth to bring us color. The term "bulb" can refer not only to true bulbs, but also to bulbous plants, such as those that come from corms, rhizomes, and tubers.

Bulb Definitions

True **bulbs** (daffodil, tulip, or hyacinth) are complete plants wrapped in a skin. Inside the fleshy mass are the roots, stems, leaves, and flowers of the plant, which is very cold hardy and remains in the ground year-round. Most true bulbs have pointed tops. Buy only firm bulbs with no mushy spots. **Corms** (gladiolus) are squatty, saucerlike bulbs whose tops/bottoms are sometimes hard to distinguish. Most corms have one sunken side (top) and one flat side (bottom). Corms are not considered cold hardy; they must be dug up after a frost and overwintered indoors. **Rhizomes** are fleshy underground stems that grow horizontally under the ground. Canna is a popular rhizome. Most rhizomes are not considered cold hardy and must be dug up every fall. Bearded iris is an example of a cold-hardy rhizome however. **Tubers** are plant stems that grow underground. Some popular tubers are dahlias and caladiums—even potatoes! The "eyes" on tubers are the flowers and growth buds. Always buy tubers that have two or more eyes, and plant them with the eyes facing up. Tubers are not considered cold hardy and must be dug up in fall and properly stored.

Buy only firm, unblemished bulbs.

Bulb Dos and Don'ts

Bulbs that are not cold hardy are called tender. Tender bulbs must be dug up in fall, overwintered inside, and replanted the following spring. Or, treat them as annuals and let them die in the ground.

To overwinter tender bulbs, wait until a killing frost starts to wilt the leaves. Then, using a spade or spading fork, loosen the tubers or rhizomes. Hand-pull the plants out of the ground by their stems to lift them up. Lay the entire plants, including roots and stems, on newspaper. Leave them until the foliage and stems dry completely (possibly a week); then remove the foliage and stems from the tubers or rhizomes. (If the temperature drops really low, dry them inside the house or garage.) Store bulbs in an open container, packing them in sphagnum peat moss, in a dark, cool place.

If you are growing cold-hardy bulbs (tulips, daffodils, and hyacinths) plant new bulbs in fall. The best months to fall-plant are October and November. By this time, a lot of seasonal color has dwindled, and you won't feel so bad pulling annuals out to plant spring-flowering bulbs. These months also provide a better chance of soil moisture from rains, making digging easier. All spring-flowering bulbs want sunny locations. Remember, early-flowering bulbs (snowdrops, crocus, daffodils, and early tulips) bloom before the leaves emerge on the trees. That means you can plant these and other early-flowering bulbs under shade trees, since they will grow and bloom before any shade.

Piggyback Planting

Plant bulbs in soldier-like rows or five to seven bulbs to a hole, called bouquet planting. Bouquet planting leaves some space between clusters, allowing you to install other plants to camouflage fading bulb foliage. Most bulbs bloom for one to two weeks. You can double the bloom time by digging a hole as deep as the variety should be planted, and then digging 2 inches deeper. Plant four bulbs in the hole. Add 2 inches of soil and plant three more. The shallower bulbs will bloom first, and the deeper ones bloom through the others a week later. This "piggyback planting" doubles bloom times, and allows you to use different colors in the same bouquet. It will drive your neighbors nuts when they see white daffodils one week and yellow the next!

Dividing Bulbs

Divide cold-hardy bulbs in spring as the leaves dwindle, approximately six weeks after flowering. Carefully dig down around the outside of the buried bulbs with a shovel or gardening fork. Lift up the bulbs. Remove any dried leaves and smaller attached bulbs (bulblets). You can relocate the freshly dug bulbs and, if you like, plant the smaller bulblets in their new growing bed. The smaller bulblets will probably not bloom for the next two years, but eventually they will. Some gardeners say to wait until fall to replant dug-up bulbs, but don't listen to them. You'll just wind up forgetting about them after football starts in August. You'll find them next spring while you are looking for that misplaced paintbrush.

Tender bulbs, rhizomes, and tubers can be divided in spring when you're ready to replant. Divide your tubers and rhizomes with a sharp knife, leaving at least two eyes on each divided tuber. Let divided tubers and rhizomes air-dry for forty-eight hours or longer to let the fresh cuts heal before planting them.

Allium

Allium species

Botanical Pronunciation
AL-lee-um

Other Name
Flowering onion

Bloom Period and Seasonal Color
Late spring to midsummer; blooms in purple, blue, pink, white, yellow

Mature Height x Spread
6 to 60 inches (by variety) x 6 to 15 inches

There are over four hundred species in the *Allium* family, including herbs, veggies, and ornamental plants. This family features such well-known players as onion, garlic, leek, chives, and shallot. It makes one hungry just thinking about it! Tastiness aside, there are lots of colorful alliums as well. Giant onion (*Allium giganteum*) is a beautiful late-spring bloomer with a 5- to 6-inch flower that sits atop a 3- to 4-foot stem, much like a large purple-lavender burst of fireworks—a real showstopper. On the other side of the height spectrum is lily leek, *A. moly*, just 6 to 12 inches high with starry yellow flowers. Allium comes in large, small, and all sizes in between, so you're sure to find one for your garden.

When, Where, and How to Plant
Plant alliums from mid-September until early November or later, but before the ground freezes. Alliums will grow in full sun to all-morning sun. They will grow in any type of soil as long as the drainage is decent. Plant allium bulbs according to the general instructions listed in this chapter's introduction. As a rule, plant allium two to three times deeper than the thickness of the bulb. Space smaller bulbs 4 to 6 inches apart and larger bulbs 10 to 12 inches apart. After planting, always water-in well. No extra water should be necessary through winter.

Growing Tips
The most important thing you can do for all bulbs is to fertilize them in spring as they start to grow. Use a fertilizer high in the middle number (for example, a 5-10-5 analysis), and follow the instructions on the container to determine how much to use. Water during dry spells when the bulbs are in active growth. Do not water after the leaves start to yellow. All bulbs want to rest in dry soil during summer and fall.

Regional Advice and Care
When the flowers finish blooming, cut off the spent flower heads and allow the leaves to remain. When the leaves yellow naturally, cut them back to the ground. Until then, leave them. The leaves rebuild the bulbs with the food they make so that the bulbs will bloom again next year. Alliums are free of pests and disease.

Companion Planting and Design
Large alliums make striking accents in perennial beds, while smaller ones can be planted in drifts. When buying bulbs in fall, be sure to check the label for the growing height of that particular variety. This information will help you plant them in the best site.

Try These
It's hard to upstage the giant onion, but try these on for size: *A. cyaneum* has purple-blue flowers on 6- to 10-inch stems. *A. roseum* has ½-inch, pinkish white flowers on 2-foot stems. *A. senescens* has rose-purple flowers on 2-foot stems.

Caladium

Caladium x *hortulanum*

Botanical Pronunciation
kuh-LAY-dee-um hor-too-LAY-num

Other Name
Angel wings

Bloom Period and Seasonal Color
June to frost; foliage in shades of green, pink, magenta, white; blooms are insignificant

Mature Height x Spread
1 to 2 feet x 2 feet

Now here is a tender bulb that produces *great* shade color. Caladium does have a flower, but it's insignificant compared to the beautiful color mixes provided by the leaves. The leaves come in exotic color combinations and fantastic patterns, and they grow in shade—yes, even tree shade. Caladiums thrive in heat and humidity because they are native to the tropics. What could be better for containers on a shady patio in the dog days of summer? Add some impatiens to pick up the flamboyant colors and create a knockout! If you leave your individual caladiums potted all summer, you can bring them indoors in September and treat them as a houseplant all winter. When growing them indoors, only water the pot when the soil is dry.

When, Where, and How to Plant

Start caladium bulbs indoors in April by planting each bulb 1 inch below the surface in a 5-inch pot filled with soilless potting mix. Place in a warm, bright room, but not in direct sun. Keep the soil moist, but not wet. Plant outdoors after the last frost date. Bulbs can be planted directly in the garden after the danger of frost is over at 1 inch below the soil. Container-grown caladiums are available in May; plant at the same depth as the caladium was growing in the pot. Caladiums are shade lovers; they tolerate morning sun, but *not* hot afternoon sun. They like decent soil that's kept moist, but not wet.

Growing Tips

Keep the soil moist, but not wet. Caladiums planted under trees must compete for moisture, so check their soil moisture every few days, especially during hot weather. When they're too dry, the leaf stems will bend toward the ground. Caladiums appreciate fertilizer. Use a water-soluble fertilizer to keep them big and beautiful. Follow the directions on the label.

Regional Advice and Care

Caladiums are not winter hardy. After a killing frost has burned the leaves, dig up tubers and dry them in the sun. Overwinter in an open container, covered with sphagnum peat moss, located in a cool, dark place. Replant next spring. You can bring individual potted caladiums indoors in September and treat them as an indoor plant all winter. Keep them away from any cool drafts. There are no disease problems, but slugs can a problem if your area experiences lots of late spring rains. If you see holes in the leaves, apply slug bait to the area.

Companion Planting and Design

Use drifts of the same variety for the best effect. Don't forget caladium when planning containers for shady locations.

Try These

There are many great choices. 'Lord Derby' has deep rose leaves with green veins. 'Pink Beauty' has tricolored leaves of pink, rose, and green. 'Candidum' has snowy white leaves with green veins and borders.

Canna

Canna x *generalis*

Botanical Pronunciation
KAN-uh jen-nur-RAL-liss

Other Name
Hybrid canna

Bloom Period and Seasonal Color
Midsummer through fall; blooms in red, pink, salmon, yellow, orange, some bicolors

Mature Height x Spread
1 to 6 feet x 1 to 3 feet

Hey, what's that blooming in the park with the impressive leaves and enormous red (or yellow or pink) flowers? Those flowers are cannas, tropical-looking plants that grow from rhizomatous rootstocks. Their leaves are big, stately, and sometimes colored or striped. Cannas show off best when planted in a bed all to themselves, making quite a statement whether that bed is a formal one or just out in the middle of a big yard. You can also use cannas as a dramatic centerpiece for a large container. They are available packaged as rhizomes in plastic bags that you can plant directly into the soil in late May, or you can buy them already growing in containers from your favorite nursery. Use cannas to add an exotic look to your garden.

When, Where, and How to Plant
Plant rhizomes directly into the garden in late spring, or start them in pots indoors in late April. Canna rhizomes need a soil temperature of at least 65 degrees Fahrenheit, which means late-May planting in Zone 6 and mid-June in Zone 5. Lots of hot sun and moist, well-drained soil produce the best results, but cannas also do well in a half-day of sun. To plant, loosen the soil down 6 to 8 inches. Make sure each rhizome has at least one—but not more than two—eyes (the pointed swellings on what looks like a root). Plant so the eyes are 3 to 4 inches deep in the soil on 18- to 24-inch centers. Plant container-grown cannas at the same level they were in the pot.

Growing Tips
Cannas want water during dry periods in summer. Don't let them get bone dry. Cannas are heavy feeders. A good plan is to fertilize once when planting, again when they just come above the surface, and then continue to feed following the instructions on your favorite fertilizer container. Or use a timed-release fertilizer that is applied only once a growing season.

Regional Advice and Care
Cannas are not troubled by bugs or diseases. They need little grooming; just remove flowering stalks before seedpods form. To overwinter, dig up plants after the first hard frost with the rhizomes attached. Lay them out on a newspaper in the sun to dry. Store canna rhizomes like dahlias: Separate stems and dried leaves from rhizomes, and store rhizomes in a dark, cool place. Lightly cover them in moist, but not wet, peat moss. Check monthly so they don't dry out.

Companion Planting and Design
Give cannas their own bed. If planting different varieties, make sure the taller-growing ones go toward the center or back of the bed.

Try These
'Tropicana' has striped leaves of burgundy and yellow veins turning to red, pink, yellow, and gold. Flowers are bright orange. 'Black Knight' has bright red flowers with deep mahogany to purple leaves.

Crocus

Crocus vernus

Botanical Pronunciation
KROE-kuss VUR-nuss

Other Name
Dutch crocus

Bloom Period and Seasonal Color
March to April; blooms in white, blue, purple, lavender, yellow, yellow-orange, striped

Mature Height x Spread
5 to 6 inches x 1 to 3 inches

A blooming crocus is often considered the first sign of spring. Other bulbs may bloom earlier, but nothing says "spring is here" like crocus. Although considered a hardy minor bulb, it is actually a corm. The leaves of crocus are grasslike, and the rainbow of cup-shaped flowers offers blooms that are all about 2 to 3 inches wide. Year after year, crocus will continue to spread, becoming showier over time. Because crocus blooms early and wants at least a half-day of sun, the bulbs can be planted under any deciduous tree, as the blooms will appear before any tree puts on its leaves. Dutch crocus come in blooms of white, purple, lavender, yellow, and striped flowers. With crocus, you can afford to be lavish—plant them by the hundreds.

When, Where, and How to Plant
Buy crocus corms as early in fall as possible to allow sufficient time for the roots to establish. Plant the corms in sunny locations, at least a half-day or more. They grow well among competing tree roots. Always plant in groups of at least ten bulbs per planting hole to make a first-year statement. Plant crocus bulbs in any type of well-draining soil. Set them in a hole that is 4 inches deep and large enough to accommodate at least ten bulbs spaced 4 inches apart.

Growing Tips
Fertilize crocus bulbs as new growth appears in spring, following the instructions on your favorite fertilizer. Watering isn't an issue with crocus.

Regional Advice and Care
Crocus require little, if any, care. If you decide to plant crocus in lawn areas, don't mow the leaves until at least four weeks after the blooms finish. Ohio in spring can be warm, cold, and then warm again. When changeable weather occurs, crocus can start poking leaves out of the ground early. We have a natural, caring tendency to go out and cover those green leaves. Don't—the bulbs know what they are doing. Crocus can be forced in pots for late-winter bloom indoors.

Companion Planting and Design
You can never have too many crocus, so my best advice is plant a lot. Avoid areas where you plan to plant summer-blooming flowers that will need summer watering. Crocus bulbs want to stay dry during their summer resting period.

Try These
I love the cheerful mix of Dutch crocus in shades of purple, white, and yellow-orange. For even earlier bloom, plant snow crocus, *Crocus chrysanthus*. They are smaller than the Dutch types and are better for planting in lawns. Try 'Blue Bird', 'Cream Beauty', or 'Ladykiller' for the earliest garden color.

Crown Imperial

Fritillaria imperialis

Botanical Pronunciation
frit-i-LAIR-ree-uh im-per-e-AL-is

Bloom Period and Seasonal Color
Mid-April to mid-May; blooms in red, orange, yellow

Mature Height x Spread
2 to 3 feet x 1 foot

Oh boy, when you buy this bulb, you might ask yourself, "What is that *smell*?" Crown imperial has a bad-smelling bulb, kind of a musky-skunk odor. But the flower is more than beautiful—it's spectacular! Once you see it in bloom, you will want one in your garden. The flower stem grows about 3 feet tall before it starts to bloom, with either red, orange, or yellow trumpet-shaped flowers that hang toward the ground and are topped by a tuft of green foliage. These are specialty flowers that should be planted where their true beauty can be appreciated and observed. Crown imperial has one of the largest bulbs. Don't worry about the smell—once you get the bulb in the ground, you won't smell it anyway.

When, Where, and How to Plant
Buy locally so you can see that you're buying firm, healthy bulbs. Plant as soon as you can in fall before the soil freezes, as they can dry out while waiting to be bought and planted. Site *Fritillaria* in well-draining, fairly decent soil, in a sunny location with at least a half-day of sun. Don't cheat, or you'll be disappointed. Dig a hole 12 inches wide and 8 inches deep. Place the bulb pointed-end-up and backfill with the existing soil, first breaking up all soil clumps to the size of golf balls. Water-in well. A 2-inch layer of mulch is a nice insulator for bulbs. When planting in a row, space crown imperials on 16-inch centers.

Growing Tips
Fertilize in spring as new foliage starts growing, using an all-purpose fertilizer. Follow the instructions on the container of your favorite plant food, which will tell you how much to use and how often. Supply ample moisture during spring to early summer. If a week goes by without rain, give bulbs a drink.

Regional Advice and Care
Crown imperial is care-free if sited correctly. There are no bugs or diseases that bother this plant. When blooms have finished, cut off spent flowers and allow the foliage to yellow (about four weeks). There's no need to lift bulbs in fall; they are cold hardy.

Companion Planting and Design
Plant crown imperial where you want to draw attention. Like most bulbs, the foliage will die back, so combine it with other plants that will mask the dying foliage. Crown imperial blooms on stems 3 feet tall. They don't take up a lot of room, but if you're planting with other plants, place them toward the rear of the bed.

Try These
Though not as showy as crown imperial, for something different give checkered lily (*Fritillaria meleagris*) a try. A partially shaded, less than well-drained spot is perfect for this one—few other bulbs thrive in such conditions. It has nodding flowers in maroon-purple, distinctively marked with a checkerboard pattern.

Daffodil

Narcissus species and hybrids

Botanical Pronunciation
nar-SIS-us

Other Name
Narcissus

Bloom Period and Seasonal Color
Early April to early May; blooms in yellow,
orange, white, pink, bicolors

Mature Height x Spread
4 to 20 inches (by variety) x 4 to 6 inches

What a terrific family of hardy bulbs! To begin with, daffodils aren't bothered by rodents. That's saying a lot for a bulb. Also they are considered very perennial—even when planted in bed areas in which you've planted other summer-blooming flowers, they won't rebel and refuse to bloom again the following year. They always bloom! There are many sizes, shapes, and colors. The *Narcissus* family includes both the daffodil and jonquil narcissus. Daffodils are known for their elongated trumpets, while narcissus has a short trumpet. Daffodils make excellent bulbs for early forcing indoors during late winter. How much room do you provide for daffodils? Plenty, because they are dependable bloomers for many years.

When, Where, and How to Plant
To allow good root development, plant daffodil bulbs at least six weeks before the ground normally freezes, about November 15 in Zone 5, December 15 in Zone 6. Daffodils like full sun to at least a half-day of sun. Daffodils bloom before trees leaf out, so they can be planted in what's considered summer shade under large trees and still be unaffected by the subsequent shade. They tolerate any type of soil as long as it drains well, but they need moisture during spring. I prefer to plant daffodils bouquet-style. That means digging a hole 6 to 8 inches deep and wide enough to accommodate three to five bulbs. Since individual bulbs need to be planted 6 inches apart, dig an area wide enough to accommodate them. Backfill, and water-in well. Remember; buy the largest bulbs to get the largest flowers.

Growing Tips
Feed your daffodils when their foliage first appears in spring. Use a fertilizer higher in the middle number (for example, 5-10-5), and follow the package instructions. Daffodils like spring moisture, which is usually provided by rain. If less than 1 inch of rain falls weekly in early spring, give daffodils a good watering during each dry week.

Regional Advice and Care
Daffodils are resistant to pests and disease. Cut off spent flower stems and leave the foliage undisturbed until it naturally turns yellow and then brown. Daffodils are the only bulbs that deer will not bother. Deer know that daffodils are poisonous—for them and for us.

Companion Planting and Design
Daffodils are great for naturalizing where the foliage will not be in the way of lawn grass. A great companion plant in a daffodil bed is daylilies. Daylilies are just getting perky as the daffodils are starting to fade, and the daylily leaves will hide daffodils' yellowing foliage.

Try These
I have many favorites, from 'Tête-à-Tête', which grows only 6 inches tall, to many of the taller-growing common daffodils that give you great color, from yellow to white and some bicolors.

Dahlia

Dahlia hybrids

Botanical Pronunciation
DAH-lee-ah

Bloom Period and Seasonal Color
Mid-June to frost; blooms in yellow, orange, red, purple, pink, white, bicolors

Mature Height x Spread
1 to 8 feet (by variety) x 1 to 3 feet

I bet you would be surprised to know that there are hundreds of different dahlias available—some with small, exquisite, pompon blooms and others with enormous, plate-sized flowers—all in dazzling colors. They are a specialty plant, and the people who grow them are crazy for them. Dahlias have tuberous roots that you plant in the spring in any sunny landscape with a half-day of sun or more. They are available in packages from your garden centers. Smaller-blooming, seed-grown dahlias are often sold in cell-packs. Dahlias are available in dozens of shapes—cactus, anemone, peony, daisy—and in many sizes. What are the most important things to know about dahlias? They are easy to grow and beautiful. Try a few and see what all the fuss is about.

When, Where, and How to Plant

Plant dahlias in late May to early June after soil temperatures reach 65 degrees Fahrenheit. Site in lots of sun. Dahlias do best in soil that is well drained, fertile, and high in organic matter. Now this won't be the natural soil for many of you, so add a fertilizer high in the last two numbers (for example, 5-10-10) and mix organic material into the soil, such as peat humus. To plant, dig a hole 1 foot by 1 foot. Place tubers (eye pointing up) about 6 inches deep and partially fill to cover the tubers with 2 to 3 inches of soil. Don't water until shoots appear. As the shoots grow, add more soil gradually until the hole is filled. Space 2 to 3 feet apart.

Growing Tips

Water dahlias regularly with 1 inch of water per week if no rain occurs that week. Fertilize every three to four weeks with a general garden fertilizer, following the instructions on the container.

Regional Advice and Care

If dahlia is well sited, pests and disease won't be a concern. Pinch out the center shoot after three sets of leaves form to create bushier plants and more flowers. Tie plants to stakes or a tomato cage so they grow through the center. Deadhead spent flowers. To overwinter, let a killing frost kill the tops of your dahlias. Carefully dig up the roots, removing any soil. Allow the roots to dry for several days in the sun. Cut away the rest and store roots in an open container, covering them with moist, but not wet, sphagnum peat. Store at 40 to 45 degrees Fahrenheit.

Companion Planting and Design

Dwarf dahlias make superb border plants, while their larger cousins are excellent for making a tall statement in any sunny garden.

My Personal Favorite

The package or plant stake that comes with a dahlia will show its color, blooming height, and size of bloom. Check out 'Barbarossa', a showy "dinner-plate" dahlia with enormous, 11-inch red blooms.

Gladiolus

Gladiolus x hortulanus

Botanical Pronunciation
GLAD-ee-oh-lus hor-tew-LAY-nus

Other Name
Glads

Bloom Period and Seasonal Color
July to October (depending on when you plant); blooms in all colors of the rainbow

Mature Height x Spread
2 to 5 feet (by variety) x 6 to 12 inches

Want great blooms to show off in your yard and in a bud vase? The solution is easy: plant gladiolus. Commonly called glads, these bulbous plants are available in miniature (growing just 2 to 3 feet tall) to giant varieties (growing 3 to 5 feet tall). Glads have one flower spike per bulb. To extend the blooming period, buy three times as many as you think you need, and plant one-third in early June, one-third in late June, and one-third in mid-July. This staggered planting will ensure that you will have colorful glads most of the summer. Glads are usually frost tender; however, new cold-hardy glads have come along. Recent mild Ohio winters have not really tested these newer ones, so the jury is still out.

When, Where, and How to Plant
Start planting glads in mid- to late-spring after you've planted your summer-blooming annuals. Glads need good soil drainage; avoid areas of heavy gumbo clay. Glads would love sun all day; give them at least all-morning sun. For miniature corms (½ inch), plant them 3 inches deep. For medium corms (½ to 1 inch), plant 4 to 5 inches deep. If you have large corms (1¼ inches or larger), plant 6 to 8 inches deep. Space corms 4 to 6 inches apart. Dig a 6-inch wide hole as deep as you're going to plant the glad. Break up the soil to pieces no bigger than a golf ball. Backfill and water-in well.

Growing Tips
Glads don't want too much fertilizer; a liquid feed applied once when growth begins and again after cutting the stalk should be ideal. Water during dry spells, about 1 inch per week, from the time shoots emerge until blooming ends. After that, watering isn't a concern.

Regional Advice and Care
In good garden conditions, pests and disease shouldn't be troublesome. Blooming glads can become top-heavy. Some options: Plant your corms deep. This allows the soil to support top-heavy blooms. Or use a bamboo stake for large gladiolas. Finally, some growers mound several inches of soil around the stalk to keep it upright. Dig up corms six weeks after blooms finish—you don't have to wait until fall. Use their space in the garden for fall-blooming plants. Store glads in mesh bags in a dark, cool place (45 to 55 degrees Fahrenheit) until spring.

Companion Planting and Design
Glads produce dramatic flower spikes. For the best effect, use them in groups (not straight lines) among other perennials. But if it's straight lines you want, the vegetable garden is a great place to grow glads for cutting.

Try These
'Homecoming' is a two-toned creamy white bloom with a purple throat. 'Priscilla' has tricolored flowers consisting of a white background, bright pink on the wavy petals, and a yellow throat.

Grape Hyacinth

Muscari species

Botanical Pronunciation
mus-KAR-ee

Bloom Period and Seasonal Color
April into May; blooms in blue-violet, blue, white

Mature Height x Spread
6 to 12 inches x 3 to 6 inches

How did a bulb named *Muscari* become known as "grape hyacinth"? Take a look at each individual flower cluster; it looks just like a bunch of grapes. Grape hyacinths look best planted in large masses of twenty-five to fifty bulbs. When you buy large quantities, you can often get a price break. Over time, they continue to spread. The bloom colors are light blue, dark purplish blue, or white, making a wonderful contrast when planted with daffodils. And oh, yes—they have a very pleasant fragrance too. Grape hyacinths are enjoyable to behold and trouble-free to grow. They grow best in sunny areas in loose, rich, somewhat sandy soil. That's what they want—but I've seen grape hyacinths bloom and thrive in clay. They also do well when planted around small flowering trees.

When, Where, and How to Plant
Plant in mid- to late fall before the ground freezes. Grape hyacinths prefer good, loamy, somewhat sandy soil; however, they will tolerate light clay. Just make sure the area you've selected has good drainage. Grape hyacinths do well in full sun to a half-day of sun. In fact, afternoon shade will extend their blooming time. Dig up and loosen the soil to 6 to 8 inches deep. Plant bulbs 3 inches deep and 4 inches apart. You can plant them singly or use the bouquet method described in the bulb chapter introduction. Cover with soil and water-in well.

Growing Tips
Fertilize in early spring as the bulbs start to grow. A slow-release bulb fertilizer is ideal; follow the label's directions. Watering is seldom a concern with grape hyacinth.

Regional Advice and Care
No pest or disease problems here. After grape hyacinth blooms, allow the leaves to remain until they turn brown on their own. Refrain from planting in lawn areas as you'll be tempted to mow off the *Muscari* foliage permanently. Clumps can be lifted and divided to increase your planting. Do this just after blooming. Drifts increase by both seed and offsets. Don't be alarmed by the appearance of foliage in fall. This is normal with some species.

Companion Planting and Design
Grape hyacinth is another "minor" bulb (less than 2 inches in diameter), like scilla, that makes a major display if planted in mass. Plant plenty, forty to fifty to an area, to make a great showing the first spring. The bright blue flowers look great with tulips and daffodils or in sweeps under small flowering trees, such as magnolias and cherries. Because *Muscari* sprouts in fall, plant a few with each clump of daffodils. Often, they will bloom together and the fall *Muscari* foliage will "mark" your daffodil clumps when they are dormant so you don't disturb them.

Try These
Muscari armeniacum is the most common grape hyacinth. For something different, 'Blue Spike' is a double form with full, rich blue flowers. If you prefer a softer blue, plant 'Cantab'.

Hyacinth

Hyacinthus orientalis

Botanical Pronunciation
hy-ah-SIN-thus or-ee-en-TAL-iss

Other Name
Dutch hyacinth

Bloom Period and Seasonal Color
April to May; blooms in blue, purple, pink, red, yellow, white

Mature Height x Spread
6 to 12 inches x 4 to 6 inches

Hyacinth! Talk about an aromatic flower! These richly fragrant flowers are actually a series of hundreds of small, bell-shaped flowers growing on the same stem. They come in shades of blue, purple, white, yellow, pink, and red. Hyacinths force well in pots; this process is explained in the bulb chapter introduction. They also can be grown in water in a hyacinth glass. Make sure the bulb was "pre-cooled" at the nursery. Place the bulb in water in a special glass made for this purpose. Place the glass in the dark, and wait until the bottom of the glass is filled with white roots. Then place the glass in a bright room. It's great fun for a young child to watch the bulb grow and bloom—fun for grandmas and grandpas too.

When, Where, and How to Plant
Hyacinths should be planted as early in fall as possible. They form all their root growth, necessary for a healthy plant, within six weeks after planting. Select nice, firm bulbs. Hyacinths, like all hardy bulbs, need well-drained soil. Avoid heavy clay that tends to stay wet. They perform best in lots of sun, at least a half-day. Plant 6 to 8 inches apart and deep. Use a spade, bulb planters just won't cut it. I prefer to plant hyacinths in groups of five bulbs to a hole, spacing the groupings 2 feet apart. Backfill the hole and water-in well. **Note:** Hyacinth bulbs have a dust on them that can cause skin irritation. Wear gloves, and wash your hands with soap and water after you handle the bulbs.

Growing Tips
Fertilize hyacinths with an all-purpose fertilizer in spring as new growth starts. Hyacinth bulbs are cultivated to produce a large bloom the first year they flower. Chances are they will not bloom as large the following year. Fertilize as mentioned, and they should produce large flowers again their third year. Water if a spring dry spell occurs, but watering won't be necessary later. Ohio usually doesn't have dry early springs but if we should, water newly planted hyacinths 1 inch a week.

Regional Advice and Care
Cut away the spent flowers. Leave the foliage on until it naturally browns off. Plant hyacinths in a bed where you won't be planting summer-blooming annuals later in the season. Hyacinths want to stay dry during their summer sleeping season. They have no disease or insect problems.

Companion Planting and Design
Hyacinths make a statement when planted in clusters. Line a bed with all of the same or mixed colors to make a great border planting. Just avoid a single line approach where hyacinths can look like a line of soldiers.

Try These
'City of Haarlem' has soft yellow flowers on 8-inch stems. 'Delft Blue' has pale lilac-blue flowers and is especially good for forcing indoors.

Iris

Iris germanica hybrids

Botanical Pronunciation
EYE-riss jer-MAN-ih-kuh

Other Name
Bearded Iris

Bloom Period and Seasonal Color
May to June; blooms in blue, purple, pink, peach, yellow, bronze, orange, white; some bicolors

Mature Height x Spread
1½ to 3 feet x 1½ feet

Iris is one of the prettiest flowers of spring. A common expression heard when people view an iris flower is, "It almost looks artificial." I guess some people think manufacturers can make something more beautiful than Mother Nature. I myself don't think so. The tall stems bearing the gorgeous flowers grow from the base of the plant. Each flower has six petals. Three of these petals are called "standards." The other three droop downward and are referred to as "falls." Iris rhizomes continue to expand (growing from existing rhizomes), giving you more and more blooms over time. They have a few drawbacks—the swordlike foliage can be unappealing late in the season and iris borer can be a concern. But all in all, they are *more* than worth it.

When, Where, and How to Plant
Plant bare-root rhizomes in August to early September. Bearded irises are available as container-grown plants; plant these anytime. Choose a site with good drainage; they will grow in clay soil as long as that soil does not stay wet. Amend clay soil to improve drainage. Irises prefer full sun, but will bloom in areas just of all-morning sun. When planting bare-root rhizomes, loosen the soil 6 to 8 inches deep. Dig a hole as deep as the rhizome is thick. (Make sure the top of the rhizome is even with the top of the soil!) Water-in well. With potted iris, dig a hole as deep and twice as wide as the soil clump. Plant it at the same level it was growing in the pot. Irises resent being planted too deeply. Backfill and water-in well. Space according to variety.

Growing Tips
Feed iris in spring with an all-purpose fertilizer. Read the fertilizer instructions to determine the amount and frequency. Once established, bearded irises are drought tolerant. Keep soil moist but not wet for the first three months after planting.

Regional Advice and Care
Cut off spent flowers. If the foliage looks shabby, cut back all leaves to 2 to 3 inches from the ground in August. Divide rhizomes every four or five years in August. Dig up the rhizomes, separate, throw away any soft ones, and replant right away. Iris borer can be a problem. The borer enters the tops of young leaves in spring and eats down toward the rhizomes. Look for what appears to be a lighter green line that continues to get longer. Soil-drenching systemic pesticides will eliminate the problem.

Companion Planting and Design
Combine irises with daylilies and other summer-blooming plants to help conceal the iris foliage later in the season.

My Personal Favorite
Who can pick a favorite? If I must, I would choose an American Iris Society Dykes Memorial Medal winner. 'Beverly Sills', a coral-pink bloomer, is unsurpassed as a pink iris in form, color, performance, and all-around beauty.

Lily

Lilium cultivars

Botanical Pronunciation
LIL-ee-um

Other Name
Hybrid lily

Bloom Period and Seasonal Color
Late spring to midsummer (by variety); blooms
in yellow, white, orange, pink, red, and speckled

Mature Height x Spread
2 to 7 feet (by variety) x 6 to 12 inches

Hybrid lily flowers are extremely showy and surprisingly easy to manage. They are also cold hardy and grow well in Ohio. Their funnel- or trumpet-shaped flowers come in many colors, some solid and some speckled. The hybrids are divided into several classes. American hybrids have large, 4- to 6-inch flowers on 4- to 6-feet tall plants and bloom in summer. Asiatic hybrids grow 2 to 5 feet tall and produce 4- to 6-inch flowers. Aurelian hybrid lilies flower 6 to 7 inches wide. Oriental hybrids bloom in summer with fragrant flowers that range from 2½ to 10 inches wide on stems that grow from 2½ to 7 feet tall. Lilies are native to the United States as well as to Europe and temperate Asia.

When, Where, and How to Plant
Plant hybrid lily bulbs in fall or spring, but fall is preferred. Get them in the ground fast because they shouldn't be allowed to dry out. Container-grown lilies are often available in spring. If you buy potted lilies in spring, plant them in the ground—pot and all. Plant in lots of sun, or at least all-morning sun. Lilies want decent or better garden soil; good drainage is important. Loosen the soil to 10 to 12 inches deep. Incorporate organic matter to improve drainage. Plant bulbs pointed side up at a depth three times the height of the bulb (e.g., if your lily bulb is 2 inches high, plant it 6 inches deep). Space 12 to 18 inches apart. The Easter lily (*Lilium longiflorum*), commonly given at Easter, is also a hardy lily. If you receive an Easter lily, let it bloom and leave it in the pot until the leaves die. Then remove the bulb from the pot, and plant it three times deeper than the height of the bulb.

Growing Tips
Fertilize each spring with an all-purpose granular fertilizer as new growth appears. Keep your garden soil moist, but not wet, until flowering finishes. Then cut back the water and allow the lily to dry out.

Regional Advice and Care
When planted in a happy home, lilies require little maintenance and are generally pest- and disease-free. Tall types may need staking. Do not remove leaves until they naturally brown. Lily clumps can be divided in fall if they become crowded. Lift the bulbs, separate, and replant. This is a great method of propagation.

Companion Planting and Design
Adding lilies is an easy way to add more color and bloom to perennial beds. Hybrid lilies like to have their roots shaded; there are many groundcovers and low-growing perennials that fit that bill.

Try These
'America' is my favorite Asiatic lily with large crimson blooms on a 30- to 40-inch stem. Aurelian hybrids (trumpet hybrids) are fragrant and easy to naturalize.

Scilla

Scilla sibirica

Botanical Pronunciation
SIL-a sih-BEER-ih-kah

Other Name
Siberian squill

Bloom Period and Seasonal Color
February to March; blooms in dark blue, white

Mature Height x Spread
4 to 6 inches x 2 to 3 inches

This is a great little hardy bulb that produces a very-early-blooming, blue, bell-shaped flower. Did I say flower? I meant to say flowers—lots of flowers. This is another bulb you'll want to use in masses. Scillas are very inexpensive to buy and look best in groups of twenty-five to fifty. Before you say, "Hey, I'm not digging all those holes!"— remember, these bulbs can be planted in a large shallow-dug hole. Place each bulb a couple of inches from the others and then cover all at once. Scillas give you lots of late-winter bloom and are out of the way before your spring color arrives. They will also reseed themselves, and that's good. They are not invasive, and you will get even more blue color for free.

When, Where, and How to Plant
Scillas are early risers, so try to plant by mid-October to give them ample time to root. *Scilla sibirica* prefers full sun to part shade in areas with decent soil. Remember, all bulbs want to stay on the dry side after they bloom. Do not plant in lawn areas if you have an irrigation system. Plant bulbs 3 inches deep in well-drained soil. Dig a hole 18 inches wide. Place twenty-five scilla bulbs in the hole, 2 inches apart. Move over 4 to 5 feet and repeat. You can also plant smaller clumps, but make each clump a minimum of five bulbs. Backfill and water-in well.

Growing Tips
Feed your scillas along with all your other spring-flowering bulbs as the leaves start to grow in February. Use an all-purpose plant food, following the instructions on the container. Watering isn't a concern with scilla.

Regional Advice and Care
I've never seen any pest or disease problems with scilla. Let the foliage mature; it goes away before your other landscape plants start growing. You can assist in spreading your scillas by collecting and scattering the seed yourself. New seedlings take several years to flower.

Companion Planting and Design
These are small bulbs producing small flowers; the secret to success is planting a lot of them in several drifts. Talk about a show of color! **Note:** When planting around young shrubs, plant them far enough away that the scillas won't be engulfed by the shrubs later. Try planting in unirrigated lawn areas—everything will be gone before the lawn needs to be mowed.

Try These
'Spring Beauty' is a bigger and more robust selection in the same shade of deep blue as the species. There is a *S. sibirica* called 'Alba' that is a pure white variety. If you like white flowers this one is for you. The species, *S. sibirica*, has electric blue flowers that multiply annually and provide tons of late winter to early spring color.

Snowdrops

Galanthus nivalis

Botanical Pronunciation
guh-LAN-thus niv-VAL-us

Bloom Period and Seasonal Color
Mid to late February; blooms in white

Mature Height x Spread
4 to 6 inches x 2 to 3 inches

Wonder how this bulb got its name? Could it be that it blooms in Ohio in mid-February to early March, depending on the severity of the winter? I think so. Snowdrops are among the earliest spring bulb flowers to appear, producing lots of charming blooms in late winter to early spring. Plant them in a sunny location, especially in the midst of groundcover, and they'll bloom in mid-February. Considered a minor bulb, snowdrops should be planted in masses of twenty-five to fifty bulbs to a planting site. They also mix well when planted among other early bulbs, such as winter aconite and scilla. Snowdrops are great for naturalizing under deciduous shrubs and trees. When planted in rich soil, they will continue to spread in large numbers through the years.

When, Where, and How to Plant

Plant these small bulbs anytime in fall before the soil freezes. Try to plant before mid-October to give the roots time to establish before winter. Choose a mostly sunny location with light to partial shade and moist, well-drained soil. Snowdrops want decent soil. It can be clay, but not the heavy gumbo clay. Plant the bulbs in groups of twenty-five to fifty. Dig a hole 3 inches deep and 18 inches wide. Place the bulbs in the hole, spacing them 2 to 3 inches apart. Backfill and water-in well. Space drifts at least 4 to 5 feet apart, allowing them room to spread each year by themselves. Plant snowdrops where you won't be doing any future cultivation.

Growing Tips

Fertilize snowdrops as new growth starts to appear in late winter. Use an all-purpose fertilizer, following the instructions on the container. When sited correctly, snowdrops won't need watering. Spring rains and melting snow usually do the trick.

Regional Advice and Care

There are few, if any, pest and disease problems with snowdrops. Let the leaves dry naturally after the flowers have finished blooming. The old leaves will be gone before most of your landscape wakes up. Did you know that you can divide and spread snowdrops "in the green"? After flowering, but before the foliage matures, dig clumps, separate, and replant them in the garden or share with friends.

Companion Planting and Design

For snowdrops, choose areas where you can view them from inside the house—remember that they'll bloom when the snow is coming down. They bloom early enough that their foliage is not in the way of other spring-growing plants. Try snowdrops and crocus coming up through low groundcover planted under trees or shrubs.

Try These

The double form is a spring surprise—'Flore Pleno' has a ruff of inner petals tinged with green. For something a bit bigger, try the giant snowdrop, *Galanthus elwesii*. It grows to about 8 inches tall and has gray-green leaves.

Tuberous Begonia

Begonia x tuberhybrida

Botanical Pronunciation
be-GON-yuh too-ber-HY-brid-uh

Bloom Period and Seasonal Color
Early summer to early fall; blooms in pink, orange, red, yellow, white, and picotee

Mature Height x Spread
12 to 16 inches x 8 to 16 inches

Tuberous begonias are a group of frost tender-blooming bulbs so spectacular that when you first see blooming ones for sale in the spring at your favorite garden store or greenhouse, you will undoubtedly say to yourself, "I've *got* to have that flower in my yard!" These are the begonias with large—up to 4 inches wide—tissue paper-type blooms. They are absolutely beautiful. The flowers resemble double peonies, roses, or camellias and their color range is the rainbow. But the biggest mistake a homeowner makes is not realizing that these plants are shade lovers. They'll be okay in morning sun, but absolutely no hot sun! Regardless of which way you go, begonias are a beautiful summer-blooming plant that I'm sure you will enjoy. More color in the shade is a good thing!

When, Where, and How to Plant

Tuberous begonia bulbs, which is the most economical way to buy them, are available in early spring—though you will have to care for them a while indoors. They transplant well from pots or hanging baskets; in fact, they are better when planted as transplants. Start bulbs indoors in mid-April by placing each one in a 5-inch pot of soilless potting mix. Plant 1 inch below the soil line. (Always make the soil line 1 inch below the top of the pot to allow for a water reservoir.) Keep them moist until it is safe to plant outside in mid- to late May. Choose locations with light shade to morning sun—no hot sun. Good air circulation is important. Tuberous begonias prefer moist, well-drained, decent soil. Don't let your new transplants dry out.

Growing Tips

Feed tuberous begonias regularly with a liquid fertilizer, following the instructions on the container. They can be tricky to water, especially in containers such as hanging baskets, because it's easy to overwater begonias. Always check the soil to be sure it feels dry down a couple of inches. Do not water begonias with overhead irrigation; water at ground level.

Regional Advice and Care

For optimum blooms, remove spent flowers. Pests and disease shouldn't be a problem, especially if you have good drainage and avoid overhead watering. If you want to save the bulbs for next year, dig them up after a killing frost and store the bulbs in a cool dry place for winter, covered with moist, but not wet, peat moss.

Companion Planting and Design

I like them in containers, planters, and hanging baskets for shaded locations. They are beautiful and bright massed on their own in a border. You could design some crazy color schemes in the shade garden by adding caladiums or coleus.

My Personal Favorite

The 'Non Stop®' begonia group of hybrids is vigorous, compact, heat tolerant, and produces masses of colorful double and semidouble flowers. Oh! Did I mention that 'Non Stop®' begonias never seem to stop blooming?

Tulip

Tulipa cultivars

Botanical Pronunciation
TEW-lih-pah

Bloom Period and Seasonal Color
Early April to late May (by variety); blooms in every color but blue

Mature Height x Spread
4 to 36 inches x 4 to 6 inches

Mass displays of tulips offer a wider range of colors earlier than any other flower. Tulips, a huge bulb group that produces flowers of different shapes and plants of different heights, often have a common problem: great blooms the first year and then few, if any, the following years. There are some reasons for this. Let me begin by saying many of us plant tulips in bed areas in which we later plant summer-blooming flowers. What do we primarily do with summer-blooming flowers? We water them—and tulips, even more than most other bulbs, are very intolerant of moisture during their summer rest period. There are also some tulips that are more naturally perennial than others. Darwin hybrid tulips, emperor, and species tulips are among the best repeat-bloomers.

When, Where, and How to Plant
You can buy tulip bulbs in early fall, but don't rush to plant. Refrigerate them and plant in October after the soil has started to cool down. Plant tulips where they will get at least a half-day of sun. Tulips need well-draining soil, and please, no heavy clay. If Alvin and his chipmunk buddies tend to visit, dust the bulbs with sulfur to disguise their good taste. Throw away the bulb planter and get out the spade. To plant, dig a hole 8 inches deep and 12 inches or more in diameter. Place three to five bulbs in the hole. Break up the backfill to pieces no bigger than golf balls. Water-in well.

Growing Tips
Fertilize your tulip bulbs in mid-November with an all-purpose fertilizer high in phosphorus, such as 5-10-5. Follow the package directions to determine how much to use. Feed again as the leaves poke their heads out of the soil in spring. Watering tulips is generally not necessary, and they prefer to be on the dry side while dormant.

Regional Advice and Care
After the flowers finish, deadhead to prevent tulips from forming seedheads, but leave the foliage to supply the bulb with food. Tulips can be a great dessert for deer. Instead of fencing, use a proven deer repellent as tulips start to grow. Use as often as recommended on the container, spray the flower petals as they start to open and continue treating until the flowers have finished.

Companion Planting and Design
I suggest bouquet planting. Since tulips don't want a lot of irrigation after flowering, this allows you to interplant with drought-tolerant annuals, such as periwinkle. This method also allows for lots of color all summer and gives your tulips a fighting chance.

Try These
Darwin hybrids have large flowers in May on tall stems; lots of color choices here. Fosterianas (which include the emperor tulips) are early flowering with large flowers on shorter stems.

GROUNDCOVERS
FOR OHIO

W hat's the number-one groundcover? It's *grass!* Grass greens up the landscape and it's the easiest groundcover to maintain—even if a lawn is full of weeds, just mow it and the lawn looks good. But what about areas where grass (and sometimes even weeds) won't grow? Try a groundcover. A low-growing groundcover can beautify a landscape *and* provide many benefits of mulch as well. You might consider a low-growing groundcover *instead* of bagged mulch.

The ABCs of Planting

Most groundcovers are purchased in spring in cell-packs or as rooted cuttings growing in a flat of soil (which is the most cost-effective). Groundcover plants are available in 3-inch, 4-inch, and 1-gallon containers. If the area you wish to convert into groundcover currently has vegetation, remove that with an application of total vegetation killer. If it's a lawn that you're converting to a groundcover, say grass growing on a steep bank that's hard to mow, remove the grass by using a total vegetation killer made of glyphosate. Once the vegetation starts to turn yellow, apply coarse, shredded bark mulch or pine needle straw to a depth of 2 inches. Then install groundcovers, planting *through* the mulch and into the soil. It's a lot easier doing this than planting first and then trying to mulch. Dig each hole as deep and twice as wide as the soil clump, spacing on 12-inch centers. If you're planting groundcovers in 3-inch pots, follow the same instructions. For 4-inch pots, follow the same instructions, but space on 18-inch centers. Space 1-gallon containers on 36-inch centers.

Loosen all roots when planting potted groundcovers so that they are no longer wrapped around the outside of the root clump. Groundcover cuttings growing in a solid flat of soil should be removed by cutting the plant's roots much as you would cut a piece of fudge from a pan.

Lily of the valley makes a beautiful underplanting to trees.

After planting, water-in for an hour on each area. Water at a rate of 1 inch of water per week, minus any rainfall. You'll have a solid bed of groundcover by the end of its second growing season. The only mulch that you will need is at planting. Get into the habit of applying a weed seed preventer to your groundcover beds in mid-March and again in mid-May, following the container's instructions. This will prevent unsightly weeds from poking up in the midst of your groundcover.

Do not plant any groundcover (except 1-gallon size) later than the end of August. Groundcover roots need 2 to 3 months to establish in their new home. If sufficient time isn't allowed, the roots could heave out of the ground during their first winter, causing both the roots and plants to die. The 1-gallon groundcovers have a large enough soil clump that they don't run the risk of winter heaving. Plant these big boys anytime the ground isn't frozen.

In order to contain a groundcover's height and spread, you have to discipline it. Use a lawn mower, string trimmer, hedge shears, or any other means to keep it within *your* bounds. You're the boss—you control your space. Some groundcovers travel lower and slower than others. Some grow taller and need more trimming. Pick the right one for you.

The Weed Problem

One of the biggest headaches are *weeds*. If you have weeds in turfgrass, just mow and they're gone (for now). You can't do that with other groundcovers. There are products that are weed seed germination preventers. Sixty to seventy percent of the weeds in planting beds come from wind-blown or bird-carried seed from last year's weeds. These products kill weed seed as it germinates. Because different weed seeds germinate at different soil temperatures, apply in mid-March and again in mid-June. If you experience a very wet spring, apply again in mid-May.

If you already have weeds, try a vegetation killer product, which can be sprayed on English ivy, myrtle, or purple wintercreeper, but be careful—these products damage or kill new groundcover growth along with weeds. Don't apply when plants are putting on new leaves.

If you have weeds in other types of groundcovers, use the wick system.

1. Put a plastic surgical glove on your right hand and place a cotton glove over the plastic glove.
2. Follow the mixing instructions on a package to combine vegetation killer and water in a bucket.
3. Place your gloved hand in the solution, pull out your hand, squeeze out the excess solution, and carefully wipe weeds with your gloved hand. If you just have grassy weeds in your groundcovers, spray grass killer to kill them.

There are lots of options. Check the Perennials chapter for more great low-growing, blooming plants too.

Ajuga

Ajuga reptans

Botanical Pronunciation
a-JOO-guh REP-tanz

Other Name
Bugleweed

Bloom Period and Seasonal Color
Late April to early May blooms in blue, pink, white; foliage in green, bronze, multicolored

Mature Height x Spread
3 to 8 inches x 12 to 14 inches (or more)

Ajuga is a low and colorful groundcover. Although it is available with plain green leaves, its foliage can also be purplish bronze; green, pink, and white; coppery; or green and white. With all that color, a sweep of ajuga creates a textured carpet of foliage. It's one groundcover plant whose bronze-leaf variety keeps its leaf color even in shade. In spring, ajuga also flowers in shades of blue, white, or pink. The show lasts for several weeks, and it is a nice addition to the foliage, which is ajuga's greatest asset. Ajuga needs good soil to spread and thrive. Just remember, where it thrives, it spreads quickly. However, ajuga and tree roots do not go well together; the tree roots will win this contest.

When, Where, and How to Plant

Plant ajuga beginning in spring up until mid-August. Later planting won't allow time for the roots to establish before winter. Ajuga wants good, well-drained soil. If you don't have that type of soil, look for other groundcover options. Ajuga does best in a fairly shady location, which means shade to morning sun. Use a rototiller or spade to loosen the soil for planting. To amend light clay soil, add organic amendments. Plant ajuga on 12-inch centers, following the general directions in this chapter's introduction. A layer of mulch will help conserve moisture and deter weeds. Keep new plantings watered.

Growing Tips

Ajuga requires little care if sited correctly. Watering during drought (about ½ to 1 inch of water minus any rainfall) every two weeks will keep plants healthy, especially those planted in sun. Ajuga doesn't need frequent fertilizer applications.

Regional Advice and Care

Ajuga is susceptible to a disease called crown rot. An ounce of prevention is the best solution here—site in well-drained soil to avoid problems. Otherwise, your plants should be trouble-free. You may need to occasionally restrain ajuga's growth; it spreads fast. Remove surface runners to contain it, or remove any unwanted plants. Ajuga bordering turf is a bad scenario; site ajuga where it can be contained by a concrete sidewalk or edging. Ajuga is easy to dig and divide in mid-May. If your colored ajuga reverts back to a plain green form; dig and remove the green-leafed sections to maintain the desired color.

Companion Planting and Design

Ajuga grows low and full, forming a carpet of foliage. Use it in a sweep under shrubs or on a shaded slope. Be sure you have the right growing conditions, and site it where it can be contained.

Try These

There are lots of pretty foliage options. 'Burgundy Glow' offers shades of purple, cream, pink, and green on the same leaf. 'Gaiety' is a popular form with dark purple foliage. Some types are selected for flowers such as 'Pink Beauty', which has—you guessed it—pink flowers.

Creeping Juniper

Juniperus spp. and cultivars

Botanical Pronunciation
jew-NIP-er-us

Other Name Groundcover juniper

Bloom Period and Seasonal Color
Evergreen foliage in shades of green, blue-gray,
steely blue

Mature Height x Spread
4 to 8 inches x 5 to 10 feet (depending on
species)

Creeping or low-growing junipers are among the best and fastest-growing groundcovers you can plant. This group of plants will do well in any type of soil as long as it has good drainage. Some of you may hear the name juniper and think of sticky, prickly evergreens; but the varieties listed here are soft to the touch and grow into each other, forming a wonderful evergreen groundcover. Best of all, junipers perform quite well in conditions of heat, drought, and not-so-great soil. Some varieties have good foliage color as well. Junipers have a lot to offer for places where you need an evergreen that stays low and colorful. There are many varieties from which to choose; I've listed my favorites here.

When, Where, and How to Plant
Junipers are available in 1-, 2-, 3-, and 5-gallon containers and as balled-and-burlapped plants. You can plant juniper anytime the ground is not frozen. Any soil type is fine; just make sure it has good drainage. Junipers are drought tolerant. For most of them, the more sun they receive, the better they grow. Refer to this chapter's introduction for specifics on planting. Space plants based on the mature size of the variety you select.

Growing Tips
Junipers are drought tolerant and won't require watering once established. Water when the soil is dry during the first growing season. Fertilization is generally unnecessary.

Regional Advice and Care
Twig blight is a disease that is prevalent in wet spring seasons. You can't control the weather, so remove any brown tips when they appear. Prune infected branches back to healthy growth. To steer clear of twig blight, choose well-drained locations and avoid overhead watering. To retain juniper's form, tip-prune any unwanted growth as it appears. Use handpruners, not hedge shears, and the result will be junipers with an attractive, natural-looking form.

Companion Planting and Design
Junipers make good accent plantings under high-branched trees, whether they are in the lawn area or the foundation planting. Creeping juniper does well in difficult soil. It's great massed along driveways, on banks, and in other tough sites.

Try These
Shore juniper, *Juniperus conferta*, is a good choice. 'Blue Pacific' has soft, silver-blue needles and grows to 6 inches. It is more tolerant of partial shade and is considered disease resistant. 'Silver Mist' has wonderful needle color; the more sun it receives, the prettier it will be. Excellent for slopes and banks, *J. hortizontalis* is very low growing. 'Blue Chip' has a great blue color; it does best in the sun, growing to 6 inches. One more great choice: *J. procumbens* 'Nana' grows to 18 inches tall with mounds of bluish green foliage.

Creeping Phlox

Phlox subulata

Botanical Pronunciation
FLOCKS sub-yoo-LAH-tuh

Other Name
Moss phlox

Bloom Period and Seasonal Color
April to May; blooms in pink, blue-purple, lavender, white, bicolors

Mature Height x Spread
3 to 6 inches x 3 feet or more

Talk about a groundcover that makes a spring bloom statement—creeping phlox produces thousands of flowers that smother the foliage in shades of magenta, pink, blue, or white. It gets noticed in the spring! Creeping phlox grows very flat, its foliage is like a mat—thick, fine textured, and mosslike. The flowers, which appear in spring, bloom for an average of two weeks. The foliage stays perkier if the phlox stays out of hot afternoon sun in the summer. Creeping phlox works well in rock gardens, on top of stone walls, or anywhere else you can take advantage of its low, creeping growth habit. Phlox is considered an evergreen perennial, but don't be disappointed if the foliage turns bronze in winter and tries to hide. It's a perennial—it will be back.

When, Where, and How to Plant
Creeping phlox is most often available from garden centers in spring. You can plant it before it blooms or while it's in bloom. Plant creeping phlox in partial sun. It blooms best in full sun, but it's likely to cook in southern Ohio; it seems to disappear in summer heat. Keep it away from shade, or you'll be disappointed in the amount of blooms. Though moist, well-drained soil is best, it tolerates sandy dry soil well. Creeping phlox is available in 3- to 6-inch pots and often in half and full flats or large clumps. You can divide the clumps into several plants. Dig a hole as deep as the soil clump and half again as wide. Backfill and water-in well. Keep new plantings moist to encourage strong root growth.

Growing Tips
Water phlox when the soil gets dry. Creeping phlox tolerates poor soils and doesn't need excessive fertilization; however, a little slow-release fertilizer boost in spring is advisable.

Regional Advice and Care
Creeping phlox is free of bugs and diseases. Prune or remove any unwanted growth. Some gardeners shear their plants back by about one-third after flowering to promote vigor and a neater appearance. After flowering is also the best time to divide plants. Division may occasionally be necessary to invigorate old plantings.

Companion Planting and Design
Phlox is very low growing and colorful when in bloom. It's a great plant for walls, along paths, or in rock gardens. It makes a beautiful appearance when planted between steppingstones. Always plant it in an area large enough to allow for summer-blooming annuals to fill in when the phlox stops blooming.

Try These
When creeping phlox is in bloom, you can't help but notice the dazzling patches of pink, purple, and white. One I really like is 'Candy Stripe'. It has delicate white flowers with a pink stripe that completely covers the ground-hugging mat of foliage. Though just 6 inches tall, the plants can grow as much as 3 feet wide.

English Ivy

Hedera helix

Botanical Pronunciation
HED-er-uh HEE-licks

Bloom Period and Seasonal Color
Attractive foliage year-round

Mature Height x Spread
6 to 8 inches x indefinite spread

Need a reliable, maintenance-free ground-cover with attractive, glossy green leaves? English ivy makes one of the best ground-covers, especially under trees. Not only is it evergreen, covering the ground with lush foliage year-round, but it will also grow well in many different areas and will even tolerate more year-round sun than most people think. English ivy will not interfere with trees and shrubs in the landscape; it just makes a fresh, green covering of the planting bed. Remember that ivy functions much as mulch does: both cover the roots of our plants to keep weeds out and moisture in. And both do another important thing for landscape beds: they simply look good. Forget ivy-covered walls—use ivy to cover the ground!

When, Where, and How to Plant
English ivy is available in spring in three forms: potted plants, cell-packs, and rooted cuttings. Rooted cuttings and cell-packs are best planted in spring and summer, no later than mid-August. Larger potted plants can be planted anytime. Ivy grows great in full shade, partial sun, and even full sun and in all types of soil as long as it has good drainage. Amend heavy clay soil with a soil conditioner. Dig a hole as deep as the root or soil clump and a little wider. Mulch after planting to help retain soil moisture. Plant cuttings, cell-packs, or small pots on 12-inch centers. One-gallon plants can be planted on 3-foot centers. Either type will fill in by the end of its second year.

Growing Tips
Keep new plantings of ivy moist to allow for healthy root development. Watering during periods of drought will promote lush growth. Extra fertilizer is unnecessary.

Regional Advice and Care
Pests and disease are rarely a concern. Trim anytime to keep the ivy contained and as short as you would like. I personally like to see ivy kept at 6 to 8 inches. Weeds are easy to contain in an English ivy bed—you can spray a product containing glyphosate at the normal rate without any fear of damage to the ivy. Just don't spray when the ivy is producing new, young leaves, or they could burn. Cuttings are easy to root if you want to propagate your own plants.

Companion Planting and Design
For an elegant groundcover to define bed lines, this one can't be beat. Choose English ivy when planting underneath trees with competing tree roots. Ivy has a central root system that allows it to compete well with tree roots.

Try These
There are lots of fancy types of ivy and specialty growers, but in Ohio, cold-hardy selections are what you want. 'Baltica' has blue-green leaves and is winter hardy. 'Thorndale' is similar to 'Baltica', it is quite hardy as well and has leaves with creamy white veins.

Lamium

Lamium maculatum

Botanical Pronunciation
LAY-mee-um mak-yew-LAY-tum

Other Name
Deadnettle

Bloom Period and Seasonal Color
Attractive foliage year-round

Mature Height x Spread
8 to 12 inches (prune to desired height) x
2½ to 3 feet

Lamium is a very pretty plant that makes an excellent groundcover with its low growing height and variegated foliage of white and green and beautiful pinkish purple summer flowers. Many think the flowers resemble snapdragons. Those that have been planted for two seasons or more will sustain dry soils and shade, even under a shade tree. This is a very low-maintenance plant that's at its best when covering the ground with lots of room to grow. It attracts beneficials, hummingbirds, and has great fall foliage—what more could you want from a plant whose other name is deadnettle?

When, Where, and How to Plant
Lamium is mostly available from your local garden center or nursery store growing in pots of various sizes; smaller 3-inch potted plants seem a lot less expensive, while 1-gallon size seems like a government loan. But it works out pretty evenly as it takes a lot more of the smaller ones versus one larger plant to establish an area. Lamium is best kept out of the hot afternoon sun locations; plant in a bed consisting of moist soil. Follow the planting instructions including spacing and other planting tips in this chapter's introduction.

Growing Tips
Keep your lamium mulched with a good bark mulch or pine straw, keeping it 2 inches deep. Check the moisture in the soil religiously the first summer after planting. Keep plant beds moist, but not wet. Use common sense, please! Fertilize all groundcovers with an application of a start-and-grow product once a year in the spring.

Regional Advice and Care
Keep weeds under control with two applications of a weed seed killer. There are no bugs to keep an eye out for. If you wish to spread the wealth (taking from Peter and giving to Paul), do your dividing in early spring as the new growth starts to appear. Take a clump at least 6 inches in diameter.

Companion Planting and Design
Lamium is a great groundcover for shady areas. It performs well under very shady trees such as maples and oaks. Remember, when it's too shady for grass to grow, lamium will come to your rescue and you won't have to mow!

Try These
'Pink Chablis' has long-lasting true pink flowers. 'Purple Dragon' has spectacular flowers that outshine its variegated leaves. 'White Nancy' has silver edges on its leaves; they're so attractive, you wouldn't miss the flowers if they didn't appear, but they do!

Lily-of-the-Valley

Convallaria majalis

Botanical Pronunciation
kon-vuh-LAIR-ee-uh maj-AY-liss

Bloom Period and Seasonal Color
April to May; blooms in white or, rarely, pink

Mature Height x Spread
6 to 8 inches x 12 to 18 inches (or more)

Lily-of-the-valley is an old-time favorite that's becoming new again. A grandmother can get teary-eyed thinking back to her childhood and this fragrant beauty that graced her parents' home. It remained popular until the 70s, and then for some reason nobody seemed to want it anymore. Because of decreased demand, garden centers quit stocking it. Now it is back in style, and homeowners are rediscovering it as a shade-loving groundcover. Lily-of-the-valley produces glossy leaves each spring and then, in May, they share the spotlight with perfumed, bell-shaped flowers. In late summer, you might find orange berries where the flowers once were. **Note:** It is important to remember the berries are poisonous. The plant loves shade, especially consistent shade on the north side of a house. Plants die back to the ground in late fall but return in spring.

When, Where, and How to Plant
Buy lily-of-the-valley in spring as pips, which are bulblike stems; plant these by the end of April. Pots of lily-of-the-valley can be planted anytime the ground is not frozen. Choose locations in natural shade, or tree shade. Lily-of-the-valley does not compete well when planted in the root areas of shallow-rooted shade trees, but it will grow in beds shaded by those trees. Any type of well-drained soil is fine. When planting from pips, loosen the entire soil area to a depth of 6 to 8 inches. Plant each pip 1 inch deep and space 6 inches apart. Water-in to settle the soil. For potted or container-grown plants, dig a hole as deep as the container and twice as wide. Loosen any wrapped roots, plant, and backfill with existing soil. Water-in well and keep moist

until established. Mulch new plantings to conserve moisture and reduce weeds.

Growing Tips
Lily-of-the-valley is low-maintenance. Except for an occasional watering during hot, dry summers, this groundcover is on its own. The foliage lasts longer when soil moisture is constant. Feed with a 10-10-10 or similar formula granular, slow-release product every three months during its growing season.

Regional Advice and Care
Lily-of-the-valley is resistant to bugs and disease. Keep it contained by pruning or cutting away excess with a spade. If you find that your plants get crowded and stop flowering, it is time to divide your planting. Dig it up in spring, separate, and replant, spacing about 6 inches apart. Before replanting, enrich your soil with organic amendments.

Companion Planting and Design
Lily-of-the-valley can be described as invasive under certain conditions. To keep it controlled, plant it in those narrow shady areas between the sidewalk and a wall. Other good places for this groundcover are those areas of the landscape where grass won't grow, especially near the house or on a shaded slope. Note that lily-of-the-valley does *not* compete well with tree roots.

Try These
'Flore Pleno' has beautiful foliage and large, double flowers. 'Fortin's Giant' has healthy, large leaves and beautiful, large, fragrant flowers with many blooms on each stem.

Lily Turf

Liriope muscari

Botanical Pronunciation
lir-RYE-oh-pee mus-KAR-ee

Other Name
Liriope

Bloom Period and Seasonal Color
August through September; evergreen foliage;
blooms in blue, blue-violet, white

Mature Height x Spread
1½ to 2 feet x 1 to 1½ feet

L ily turf, or liriope (which is how I will refer to it), is a member of a wonderful group of plants. However, it is not your typical groundcover. It does not spread by creeping aboveground growth or by underground stems. Instead, it grows in clump form, with those clumps getting a little larger each year. The foliage is slender and grasslike—the "turf" part. The flowers are blue, grape-hyacinth-type flowers—the "lily" part. From the flower comes black fruit, which is borne on the old flower stems. Lily turf is tough and adaptable to almost any well-drained soil. Though considered evergreen, liriope's leaves will be windburned back towards the ground during very cold winters. It makes an incomparable understory planting for larger trees.

When, Where, and How to Plant
Plant liriope anytime the ground is not frozen. It's available mostly in 1-gallon containers, although some garden stores sell it in 2¼-inch pots. If you have good soil drainage, plant liriope anywhere in sun to shade. The plant adapts to heavy clay soil, but it will spread faster in rich, fertile soil. Follow the general planting directions in this chapter's introduction. Keep new plantings moist but not wet the first year. A layer of mulch will conserve moisture and reduce weeds.

Growing Tips
Lily turf is amazingly drought tolerant, but give the plants an occasional drink during hot, dry weather, especially new plantings. Feed with an all-purpose or slow-release garden fertilizer in the spring, as directed on the package.

Regional Advice and Care
Liriope is *tough*; it withstands heat and humidity as well as bugs and disease. After a cold winter, some leaves may be windburned. Remove the old damaged foliage using flower or pruning shears before new growth begins. Plants can be divided in spring to increase your groundcover plantings.

Companion Planting and Design
This plant has many options in your landscape. It makes a beautiful accent plant, can border a bed, can substitute for turfgrass in small areas, and makes a fine edger for walks. It complements any other plant growing in its vicinity. Contrast lily turf's grassy texture with bold-textured hostas and lacy ferns. Liriope does not have to be so thick that it completely covers a bed area. If it does, that's great, but if there's space in-between plants, that looks good too.

Try These
Plain-foliaged forms allow you to appreciate the flowers. One good choice, 'Majestic', has dark green leaves and deep lilac flowers beginning in August. On the other hand, variegated forms add interest to the landscape all year. The standard *Liriope muscari* 'Variegata' has creamy yellow, variegated foliage; it's wonderful. 'Silver Dragon' adds sparkle to shady areas with foliage edged in white.

Myrtle

Vinca minor

Botanical Pronunciation
VIN-kuh MY-nor

Other Name
Vinca

Bloom Period and Seasonal Color
April to May; evergreen foliage; blooms in blue,
lavender-pink, white

Mature Height x Spread
6 to 8 inches x 24 to 36 inches

In recent years, the name vinca makes us think of that wonderful, summer-blooming annual: periwinkle (*Catharanthus roseus*). But way before anyone heard of the annual periwinkle, *Vinca minor*, or myrtle, which is also sometimes called periwinkle, was leading the pack of popular groundcovers. Myrtle is an evergreen groundcover that has waxy, dark green leaves forming an attractive green carpet. The lilac-blue—or dare I say, periwinkle blue—flowers create an admirable show. When myrtle is blooming in the landscape, neighbors are sure to want some in their own yards. Myrtle will seldom grow more than 8 inches tall. It gives an excellent small evergreen effect in winter when planted under deciduous shrubs. Vinca spreads quickly and can choke out wildflowers, so keep it away from woodland gardens and natural areas.

When, Where, and How to Plant
Plant potted flats or bare-root myrtle in spring to early summer. Larger, 1-gallon containers can be planted anytime the ground is not frozen. Plant myrtle in average to good soil in an area that gets morning sun to total shade; avoid hot sun. Make sure the planting site is well drained. Follow the general directions for planting and mulching groundcovers in this chapter's introduction. Plant small myrtle plants on 12-inch centers. Larger, container-grown plants can be spaced at 3 feet.

Growing Tips
Water newly planted myrtle during any hot, dry periods the first year. A slow-release fertilizer applied in the spring is beneficial, especially if your soil is less than fertile.

Regional Advice and Care
During wet springs, especially in clay soil, myrtle can get vinca stem blight, which causes leaves and stems to turn black. This is not fatal, but good drainage will help prevent this unsightly problem. Be sure to apply a weed seed germination preventative in mid-March and again in mid-June. It's a great way to keep down weeds. If you already have weeds, the only way to remove them is by pulling or by using the wick method mentioned in the introduction of this chapter. Mature plantings are thick enough to keep out weeds. Plants are easy to divide in spring.

Companion Planting and Design
Use vinca under trees and shrubs, as an edger, to fill raised planters, or to replace struggling turfgrass in shady locations. I like creating drifts of myrtle with contrasting flower colors; combining blue and white creates a cheerful mixture. If your property borders native woodland, choose a less invasive groundcover, such as pachysandra.

Try These
Perhaps the best and most popular selection is 'Bowles Variety' (also called 'Bowlesii') with its larger, darker blue flowers in the spring that repeat throughout the season. It tends to spread less rapidly, forming mounds of foliage. 'Alba', which also blooms in the spring, has white flowers.

Pachysandra

Pachysandra terminalis

Botanical Pronunciation
pak-ih-SAN-druh term-in-AL-iss

Other Name
Japanese spurge

Bloom Period and Seasonal Color
April to May; evergreen foliage; blooms in
creamy white

Mature Height x Spread
6 to 10 inches x 8 to 12 inches

For a lush swath of green, few groundcovers can beat pachysandra. Its glossy evergreen foliage is a treat even in the winter. To achieve this description, it must be sited correctly. It needs shade and decent soil, and by that I mean well drained and preferably loamy. Choose an exposure that protects its evergreen leaves from the prevailing winter winds. A slow grower, it will take several years to fill in, but after that you've got a low-maintenance groundcover with real eye appeal. Cold winters can produce yellowish leaves if the plant is in an unprotected location. Don't worry, though, because pachysandra recovers just fine. It also produces fragrant, white, spiked flowers in the spring, adding much to its beauty.

When, Where, and How to Plant
Plant pachysandra from small pots, cell-packs, or rooted cuttings in spring to early summer. Don't plant cuttings in late summer to fall; it won't have enough time to establish before winter. Plant from 1-gallon containers anytime the ground is not frozen. Pachysandra prefers shade with some good natural light or areas of morning sun. Choose a location protected from prevailing winter winds. The soil should be fertile and well drained. Loosen soil to a depth of 6 inches. If you are going to mulch the planting area, do it now. Then plant the rooted cutting or soil clump through the mulch into a hole as deep as the roots and a little wider. Keep the mulch off the stems, and water-in well after backfilling with existing soil. Plantings take about three years to fill in.

Growing Tips
Pachysandra appreciates water during dry spells. Placing a soaker hose in the bed (before planting) is a good idea for large plantings. Water until moisture reaches 4 to 5 inches deep. Fertilize new and existing plantings in early spring with a general all-purpose fertilizer or a fertilizer for acid-loving plants.

Regional Advice and Care
If sited correctly, pachysandra shouldn't fall prey to pests and disease. Be sure to use a weed seed preventer in mid-March and again in mid-June. Weeds don't look pretty in a bed of pachysandra. Mature plantings are dense enough to prevent weeds. If your plants grow too tall, shear them back to the desired height. A time-saving method is to set a rotary lawn mower to 3 inches and mow in mid- to late-April. Collect and remove the cut-off foliage. Keep tree leaves off the pachysandra in the fall; a leaf blower is best for this chore as a metal rake can damage your plants.

Companion Planting and Design
Pachysandra makes a great "living mulch" when planted under flowering trees and shrubs—plus it looks fantastic!

Try These
'Green Carpet', the most popular cultivar, has dark green leaves. It's cold hardy and compact. 'Green Sheen' has glossy, green leaves.

Wintercreeper

Euonymus fortunei 'Coloratus'

Botanical Pronunciation
yoo-ON-ih-mus for-TOO-nee-eye

Other Name
Purple wintercreeper

Bloom Period and Seasonal Color
Attractive green foliage turns purplish red in fall

Mature Height x Spread
10 to 12 inches x indefinite spread

Another popular plant to blanket the ground with foliage is wintercreeper. There are many cultivated varieties of the low-growing *Euonymus fortunei*, and 'Coloratus' is especially hardy and attractive. 'Coloratus' is commonly referred to as purple wintercreeper because of its beautiful purplish leaf color in the fall that remains on the plant during most, if not all, of the winter. It is a vigorous-growing groundcover that has deep green, glossy leaves during the summer. In spring, the old leaves fall and are replaced by shiny, new, green ones. This groundcover does well in all types of soil that drain and it grows well in shade to full sun. It is great for steep banks that are difficult to mow, competes successfully with tree roots, and fills in quickly.

When, Where, and How to Plant
Plant young plants in cell-packs or rooted cuttings in spring to early summer to allow enough time for roots to establish before winter. If you wait until fall, the plants could heave out of the ground during freeze-and-thaw periods. Plant 1-gallon containers anytime. Choose locations in sun or shade and in loamy, sandy, or clay soil—as long as the drainage is good, it will grow. Follow the general directions for planting groundcovers in this chapter's introduction. Mulch new plantings and keep them moist until established.

Growing Tips
Although wintercreeper tolerates drought, a deep soaking (to a depth of about 5 inches) during drought is beneficial. Feed to encourage strong growth with an all-purpose fertilizer following the package directions.

Regional Advice and Care
Wintercreeper is susceptible to attack by scale, especially in mass plantings. If your plants lose vigor, look for yellow spots on the foliage and white specks on the stems. For control options, consult the fact sheets published by Ohio State University. Check their website for information. You can spray for weeds with the herbicide containing glyphosate, which is the only herbicide that will kill unwanted growth while not harming 'Coloratus'. However, don't spray when the plant is putting on new growth. To control height, set your rotary lawn mower at a 3-inch cutting height, and mow the groundcover in April for fast, effective pruning. You can also prune with a grass string-trimmer. To deter deer, use a good deer repellent product.

Companion Planting and Design
Summer tree shade that gives way to harsh sun in winter does not bother wintercreeper as it does ivy. Use it to solve a vegetation problem on steep slopes that are dangerous to mow.

Try These
The Emerald series is made of low-growing evergreens that have colorful leaves during the growing season; some are gold and some are white with green leaves.

HERBS

FOR OHIO

It is said that a smart man realizes his own limitations. Well, I must finally be getting smart. I will admit that it is impossible for me to know everything when it comes to gardening. At the same time, herbs are very popular. Homeowners are using herbs for their flavor as well as their ornamental beauty, but they are not my area of expertise. Because I want to make this book as informative and up-to-date as possible, I asked Carol Mundy, whom I consider one of the best experts with herbs, to write the following chapter. Carol's background is as a naturalist in the Cincinnati area, where she works for a large, regional park district. She possesses great expertise not only with herbs, but also with wildflowers, naturalized landscaping, and critters. It is with great pleasure that I introduce you to Carol. —Denny

Herb can be a vague term. In some dictionaries, it is defined as any plant used for culinary or medicinal purposes. *Any plant.* I would agree with this definition, as you

Herbs grow well in the garden, but they can also be potted up and grown indoors during the colder months.

will find that even the lowly ground ivy creeping into your lawn has some marvelous medicinal properties. When you do a little research about the way plants have been used throughout history and then inspect your own yard, you will find you have a full pharmacopoeia growing. Sour grass, dandelion, clovers, and purslane—all plants that most people detest today—were brought here with the pioneers as part of their "medicine chest." We humans are constantly moving, and when we go we take our valued and prized possessions with us. We pack seeds and sometimes dig up whole plants to travel to our new home. Today, herbs can enhance our lives by giving us good taste, good medicine, or just simply good looks about our yards.

Remember Natives

In this day and time, we tend to place less value on herbs found growing in the wild than those we manage and manicure in our gardens. While the descriptions I've included here stay with the "managed and manicure" line, I want you to be aware of the natural value of all plants. I especially want you to consider our native species, and how they enrich our lives. While they may not all be used in our kitchens, native species provide us with clean air, quieter neighborhoods, and precious habitats for wildlife. We tend to judge plants by their immediate beauty rather than their intrinsic value to the world that we share with them.

I tend to "preach" native species, but I would never want you to take these plants from the wild. The only exception to this rule would be a bonafide plant rescue, where you have permission to collect seed or dig plants from an area about to be destroyed. If you want to grow natives, contact your local park naturalist, the Division of Natural Resources, or the local wildflower society to find out about reputable native plant nurseries in your area.

Use Common Sense

While herbs are used medicinally, it is not my intention to encourage you to do so, unless you embark on a journey including the dedicated study of herbs. Research their former uses and work with an experienced herbalist, someone who has years of training and a true understanding of the medicinal uses of herbs. The way herbs are prepared for culinary use can be very different from the infusions and decoctions an herbalist prepares. So, while I am vigorously interested in and extremely curious about the various ways herbs are used, I will address their uses here in a strictly culinary sense.

Growing Wild Elegance

I am a reluctant gardener at best. Most gardeners would probably shake their heads at my yard and give me a good scolding. Because I am so curious about nature, I'm likely to leave a "volunteer" in a bed when I know it will have a nice bloom. The majority of what grows in my yard are native species; I call that "wild elegance." Oh well, so much for my managed and manicured yard!

Anise

Pimpinella anisum

Botanical Pronunciation
pim-pi-NEL-uh uh-NISS-um

Bloom Period and Seasonal Color
Midsummer; umbels of tiny white blooms

Mature Height x Spread
2 feet x 2 feet

The delicate look of mature anise adds grace to any garden. Growing about 2 feet tall, its leaves have a wispy, fernlike appearance. You can enjoy its beauty as well as its edibility, since the flowers, leaves, and seeds are all edible. Anise will also attract butterflies, such as the black swallowtail, to your garden. In the kitchen, you can add a few fresh flowers or leaves to your favorite salad, or allow them to steep in sauces and stews. Collect only the mature seeds for culinary uses. You will know the seeds are mature when they appear gray and dry. The dried seeds can be added to baked goods for a mild licorice flavor, or nibble a few seeds to calm an upset stomach.

When, Where, and How to Plant
Anise seeds require a constant soil temperature of 70 degrees Fahrenheit or more to germinate, so plant them in late spring or early summer. Space seeds 2 to 3 feet apart to allow plenty of growing room. Select a sunny site that offers some protection from wind. Anise doesn't require fancy enriched soil. It will do well in poorer soil as long as it is well drained. If the soil is too moist or rich, amend it with a little sand or pea gravel. This annual does not transplant well, so select a site where anise can be "at home." If you are installing a young plant, be careful not to damage the taproot when removing it from the starter pots. Lightly mulch to hold in moisture and reduce weed invasion.

Growing Tips
Lightly water seedlings every other day (with ½ inch of water) until they reach about 8 inches tall. Take into account any rainfall so as not to overwater. Do not use chemical fertilizers on anise as they can cause the plant to mature and die off too rapidly.

Regional Advice and Care
You could stake anise as wind protection, but I think staking detracts from its beauty. Weeding becomes difficult around mature plants as they are top-heavy; weed young plants. Use the tender leaves of thinned plants to flavor salads, sauces, or stews. Anise seeds are tricky to collect. When you notice a few ripened seeds, clip the whole seedhead and allow it to drop into a paper sack or other container. Outside of a few butterfly caterpillars, there are few pests to bother anise and none to take action against.

Companion Planting and Design
You can group anise with similar, lacy-looking plants (such as dill), but it is easier to discern these herbs from one another when they are given their own spot. Don't forget your garden markers!

Try These
The old world variety, *Pimpinella anisum*, is most handsome.

Chervil

Anthriscus cerefolium

Botanical Pronunciation
an-THRIS-kus ker-ee-FOH-lee-um

Bloom Period and Seasonal Color
Early to midsummer; umbels of tiny white blooms

Mature Height x Spread
2 feet x 2 feet

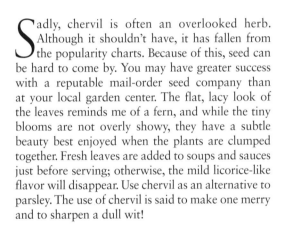

Sadly, chervil is often an overlooked herb. Although it shouldn't have, it has fallen from the popularity charts. Because of this, seed can be hard to come by. You may have greater success with a reputable mail-order seed company than at your local garden center. The flat, lacy look of the leaves reminds me of a fern, and while the tiny blooms are not overly showy, they have a subtle beauty best enjoyed when the plants are clumped together. Fresh leaves are added to soups and sauces just before serving; otherwise, the mild licorice-like flavor will disappear. Use chervil as an alternative to parsley. The use of chervil is said to make one merry and to sharpen a dull wit!

When, Where, and How to Plant
Sow this lovely annual as seed in well-worked, rich, moist soil after the danger of frost has passed. If needed, amend the soil with leaf compost and a little seasoned (composted) manure. Cover seeds with no more than ½ inch of soil. Tiny seedlings emerge in ten to twenty days. Site in partial shade to avoid scorch on the emerging plants. Stagger planting every two weeks throughout the growing season to keep you in fresh chervil until frost. When the plants are 2 to 3 inches tall, thin them to 10 inches apart. Indoors, choose a container offering good drainage and start with good quality soil. Keep potted chervil out of direct sunlight. Pinch back the flower stalk when it starts to form so the plant will continue to grow fresh young leaves to use in cooking.

Growing Tips
Keep newly planted seeds moist with a light spray or misting every other day. Continue until the plants are at least 6 inches tall, then you can move to about 1 inch of moisture per week (this includes rainfall). No fertilization is necessary.

Regional Advice and Care
Chervil is largely "self-reliant," as it requires little care once it's past the tender seedling stage. Outside of a few aphids, there just isn't much that bothers chervil. Trim leaves for use at about six weeks. After that, regular trimming will help keep chervil from blooming. Once it flowers and goes to seed, chervil is at the end of its season. It will look scraggly and unkempt, and produce few usable leaves. Chervil prefers cooler temperatures. When temperatures rise quickly, it may react with wild growth—termed *bolt and grow*—in preparation for flowering.

Companion Planting and Design
Chervil can be grouped with parsley or basil. Because it looks similar to some parsleys, add a plant marker to distinguish the two.

Try These
'Brussels Winter' is said to be less likely to bolt and grow, meaning you'll get more chervil leaves to use.

Chives

Allium schoenoprasum

Botanical Pronunciation
AL-ee-um skee-no-PRAY-zum

Bloom Period and Seasonal Color
Early summer; blooms form a showy, pale purple globe

Mature Height x Spread
1 ½ feet x 6 inches

Why is it that when you plant chives in your garden they please you, but when they pop up in your lawn you're disgruntled? Chives are quite happy in any sunny, well-drained area—whether that is the herb garden or your lawn! Be sure to look for the odd leafless stalk that will shoot up just above the blades. In early summer, this stalk has a funny looking capsule at its end. When the capsule breaks open, you are rewarded with a small globe of pale purple flowers. Add the separate flowers to your summer salad, they'll add color and a mild onion flavor. There is no comparison for fresh chives; while you can easily dry chives for winter use, they "lose a lot in the translation."

When, Where, and How to Plant
Chives are one of the easiest herbs to grow, if you start with bulbs. They are slow to germinate, so if you are as impatient as I am, buy plants in spring or check with local garden clubs for plant sales. Since chive clumps should be thinned every few years, bulbs are easy to come by. Select a sunny spot, and plant in showy clumps of six or more bulbs. Plant them in early spring after the danger of frost has passed, or in early autumn, well in advance of the first frost. Work some compost into the soil before planting; this will enrich new plants and keep heavy soil from compacting around the bulbs. You can also dig a clump, pot it, and bring it inside for winter use.

Growing Tips
Watering can be a little tricky with young plants, they do not do well if overwatered. Use your garden trowel to check the soil moisture around the clumps before watering. There's no need to fertilize chives, you want them to take their own "sweet" time to develop their distinctive flavor.

Regional Advice and Care
Chives don't require a lot of care, and there are few pests to bother them. You may have noticed this based on the healthy escapees in your lawn. The pale blooms attract butterflies. If you allow the chives to bloom, cut them back when the flowers have passed their prime and they will send up fresh blades. Remember, to improve your chives, divide them every few years. Share the extras with friends and neighbors! They can be hardy perennials in the southwest corner of the state where winters are often mild. In Ohio, you can snip chives long into winter.

Companion Planting and Design
Let chives be a star in the garden! They'll only be about 12 to 18 inches when they bloom, so plant them where you can see the pale purple blooms against the dark green blades.

Try These
I like the traditional chives, *Allium schoenoprasum*.

Common Sage

Salvia officinalis

Botanical Pronunciation
SAL-vee-uh oh-fiss-ih-NAH-liss

Bloom Period and Seasonal Color
Early summer; soft purple flowers

Mature Height x Spread
3 feet x 2 feet

Most people recognize the scent of sage and associate it with stuffing for the holiday turkey, but sage flowers are also edible and make fine additions to seasonal salads, imparting a hint of sage flavor. The soft, slightly fuzzy leaves are pale gray-green in color. These leaves are the most attractive feature of common sage. It is pretty enough to grow for its soft look alone. Being useful as well as good looking is always a plus! Its aromatic leaves have taken sage back up on the popularity list. Fresh sage is an ingredient in many new recipes. It is available fresh—for a price—at your local grocery store. But why pay for trimmings of this lovely herb when you can grow the whole plant in your own garden?

When, Where, and How to Plant

Starting sage from seed can be a little tricky, and it may take as much as two years before you can harvest. Get starts or divisions at your local plant swap instead, or just purchase good quality plants. Wait until the danger of frost has passed before planting. Select a sunny, well-drained spot with plenty of room for your sage. It seems that common sage prefers a more alkaline soil. Since alkaline soil is what we have the most of in southwest Ohio, then sage sounds like the perfect plant! Sage tends to do well even when soil conditions become dry, such as at the end of summer.

Growing Tips

Tiny sage plants require more frequent waterings; don't let them dry out completely. Check the soil near the plants before watering. Mature sage plants prefer drier conditions. Fertilizing sage causes artificially rapid growth and reduces the amount of essential oil in the leaves. What good are more leaves if they have no flavor?

Regional Advice and Care

Slugs seem to favor young sage leaves, so consider slug controls. A few varieties are more susceptible to wilt than others. Never pick *all* the leaves! Leaves are necessary for photosynthesis. No leaves means no fuel for the plant to stay alive. Allow good air circulation between plants to help thwart possible diseases. Trim plants after flowering, but before they set seed. Sage is a woody perennial that will produce for a few years. Encourage better growth by dividing the plants every other year. You may need to replace sage plants at the five-year mark as they can become scraggly and have reduced leaf production.

Companion Planting and Design

Common sage can be planted as a backdrop for dark green parsleys. Try planting it in front of the garden fence for an interesting and inviting border.

Try These

Do a little research to find a variety that pleases you. I still think the standard common sage (*Salvia officinalis*) is best.

Common Thyme

Thymus vulgaris

Botanical Pronunciation
TY-muss vul-GAIR-iss

Bloom Period and Seasonal Color
Midsummer; tiny blooms ranging from white to lilac

Mature Height x Spread
1 ½ feet x 2 ½ feet

Are you looking for the courage to become an herb gardener? You will have found it when you plant thyme. In ancient Greece, the word *thymus* meant courage. Thyme is an easy herb to grow. Select a shrubby thyme or a creeping variety to add to your garden. Their scent is heavenly, both in the garden and in the house. You can add fresh thyme to a variety of dishes, from soups and stews to fish. Thyme sachets are a welcome scent in stored clothes, and they help keep moths away. To get the best flavor from the dried herb, cut fresh twigs and hang them to dry in the house, away from direct sunlight. Store the dried herb in an airtight container or in the freezer.

When, Where, and How to Plant

Start with young plants rather than seeds. Herb gardeners often divide their plants routinely, so check with your local plant groups or purchase good quality plants at a garden center. Since it is the leaves you will be using, bushy plants producing lots of leaves is the goal. After the danger of frost has passed, select a sunny spot with any type of loose and fast-draining soil. A dose of fish emulsion in the planting hole before adding thyme may help your new plant get a "jump start." Mature thyme benefits from a light mulching of pine straw.

Growing Tips

Tender plants less than 6 inches tall like more frequent waterings; keep soil moist but not soaked. Do not let plants dry out completely. As thyme matures, it will do well unless we have drought. If drought conditions occur, water about 1 inch per week less any rainfall. Avoid fertilizers; fertilization promotes rapid growth, but reduces the amount of essential oil in the leaves. No oil means no flavor. Why grow more leaves if they have no taste?

Regional Advice and Care

Give established thyme a little "haircut" once or twice each growing season to stimulate new leaf production. You may only get a few years out of each plant before it appears more "woody" than "leafy." Well-drained soil is probably one of the most important issues; fungal diseases can occur if thyme is kept too moist. Many native bees as well as honey bees are attracted to thyme. At the end of the growing season, pull full stems, hang them upside down, and allow them to dry away from direct sunlight. Be sure they are completely dry before storing in an airtight container.

Companion Planting and Design

Plant common thyme as a border for a walkway, or plant any of the creeping varieties among walkway stones. Brushing past them releases their aromatic scent.

Try These

I am partial to the look of the woolly thyme, *Thymus pseudolanuginosus*.

Dill

Anethum graveolens

Botanical Pronunciation
uh-NAY-thum grav-ee-OH-lens

Bloom Period and Seasonal Color
Late summer; umbels of tiny yellow blooms

Mature Height x Spread
4 feet x 2 feet

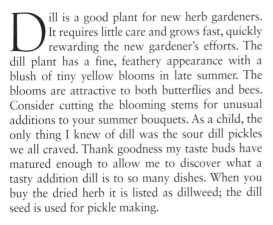

Dill is a good plant for new herb gardeners. It requires little care and grows fast, quickly rewarding the new gardener's efforts. The dill plant has a fine, feathery appearance with a blush of tiny yellow blooms in late summer. The blooms are attractive to both butterflies and bees. Consider cutting the blooming stems for unusual additions to your summer bouquets. As a child, the only thing I knew of dill was the sour dill pickles we all craved. Thank goodness my taste buds have matured enough to allow me to discover what a tasty addition dill is to so many dishes. When you buy the dried herb it is listed as dillweed; the dill seed is used for pickle making.

When, Where, and How to Plant

Look out! Dill is fast growing and can reach its mature height in just over 60 days. You can probably get a few "crops" during the growing season; plant a few seeds every three weeks to have fresh dill into early autumn. Start planting just after the danger of frost has passed. Select a sunny site with rich, well-drained soil. It should be protected from wind as dill becomes fragile once it gains heights beyond 2 feet. Space seeds 12 inches apart, covering them with no more than ¼ inch of soil. If seedlings look too crowded, simply thin them to 2 feet apart. Add garden markers to identify your herbs, as dill closely resembles fennel. Since it quickly flowers and goes to seed, be sure you plant it in a spot where you won't mind it self-seeding.

Growing Tips

Keep newly planted seeds moist. Taking into consideration any rainfall, they should receive 1 to 1½ inches of moisture per week. When plants are about 12 inches tall, I recommend giving them a compost tea to enrich them and encourage foliar growth.

Regional Advice and Care

Plant dill in a protected place rather than use unsightly stakes. Some light hand-weeding will be needed, especially when the plants are less than 8 inches tall. This may be the only care required. There are few pests or problems. Snip a few leaves every week to keep new leaves coming on. Take care not to have fennel growing near dill; these two plants can cross-pollinate and the result will be a useless hybrid. Wait to collect seeds until they start to ripen, then snip the whole flower head into a bucket so as not to lose them.

Companion Planting and Design

Because dill can be quite tall, consider using it as a backdrop for chives as long as the site offers wind protection.

Try These

I'm impressed by the tall varieties, such as 'Bouquet', blooming at nearly 4 feet tall!

Fennel

Foeniculum vulgare

Botanical Pronunciation
fen-IK-yoo-lum vul-GAIR-ee

Bloom Period and Seasonal Color
Late summer; umbels of tiny golden flowers

Mature Height x Spread
4 feet x 1 ½ feet

The herb fennel has been used to flavor foods and alcoholic beverages for centuries. Growing up, we used the other fennel, *Foeniculum vulgare dulce*, which is more like a vegetable. *F. vulgare dulce* looks just like the herb fennel on top, but it grows this wonderful celery-like bulb at the bottom. At my house, this was always identified by its Italian name *finnochio*. We would pull the bulb apart and eat it or use it as one uses celery. It imparts the same mild anise-like flavor as the leaves of the herb. The herb variety has a fine feathery appearance, is easy to grow, and is very pretty in the garden. Plant enough to use for culinary purposes as well as some to cut for unusual summer bouquets.

When, Where, and How to Plant
Sow seeds after the danger of frost has passed. Select a sunny spot with well-drained soil. To say that fennel is not fussy about soil would be an understatement. However, fennel does better with an enriched soil, especially if you live where there is clay. Amend with leaf compost and seasoned (composted) manure to give it a rich environment. Space seeds 12 to 18 inches apart. Lightly cover with no more than 1 inch of soil.

Growing Tips
As a seedling, fennel prefers soil to be moist, but take care not to overwater. After it reaches about 10 inches, it may do better under drier soil conditions than most herbs. So allow it to dry out between waterings. I do not recommend fertilizing fennel as you do not want rapid growth; it diminishes the essential oils in the plant.

Regional Advice and Care
Fennel doesn't require much care after the seedling stage. Use the leaves and the stem for flavoring, harvest the leaves before it goes to flower. Allow the leaves to dry and store them in an airtight container in the freezer to maintain flavor. Fennel is also enjoyed by caterpillars of the swallowtail butterfly family, and bees happily visit the flowers.

Companion Planting and Design
Fennel is best sited in its own corner of the garden. I recommend segregation because it can grow quite tall and unruly looking. As much as I value its culinary and medicinal contributions, fennel can be a bully in the garden. Be sure to label it to avoid confusing it with dill. Every once in a while you hear about dill and fennel combining into a strange hybrid with unfavorable results. Keep this in mind when siting these two herbs. Fennel is *allelopathic*, meaning it releases a chemical to inhibit the growth of other plants near it—so don't plant it near your vegetable garden!

Try These
Herb fennel (*F. vulgare*) is easier to grow than bulb fennel. You can use all parts of the herb—leaves, flowers, and seeds.

Garlic

Allium sativum

Botanical Pronunciation
AL-ee-um sa-TEE-vum

Bloom Period and Seasonal Color
Late spring and early summer; pale pink to white blooms

Mature Height x Spread
2 feet x 6 inches

Everybody is familiar with the papery-skinned, white garlic bulbs available at the grocery stores; these are known as soft-necked garlic. This is just one of nearly 600 varieties of garlic found around the world! Every country and every culture uses garlic, but few people recognize the plant in the garden. Being in the *Allium* family—along with onions—garlic has long, hollow, cylindrical leaves. They rise from the growing bulb in late spring and send up a single, leafless stalk. This stalk carries a beautiful bloom at its terminal end; pale pink to white flowers fill the globe-shaped head. If you're hoping for big cloves of garlic, you will need to cut the flower stalk off as it emerges so the plant uses its energy for bulb production rather than flower and seed production.

When, Where, and How to Plant
Select a sunny site with rich, but light soil. Garlic will grow in partial shade, but it prefers sun. Plant cloves—pointed end up!—no more than 2 inches deep and about 6 inches apart. A well-drained site is important as garlic will rot in too-wet soil. Garlic is somewhat cold hardy, and cloves can be planted as soon as the ground can be worked in spring or well into fall. Allow enough space around the bed so that you can easily use a forked garden tool when harvesting. You will have to decide about saving cloves for future planting or eating the whole crop! If you're in the cold zone in Ohio, with sustained winter temperatures of 5 degrees Fahrenheit or less, mulch any garlic that is left in the ground.

Growing Tips
Be attentive with the watering of garlic; while it needs regular moisture, it does not like to stay soaked. Fertilize in spring.

Regional Advice and Care
Researchers believe garlic may contain its own kind of fungicide and natural insect repellants. You may have noticed it seems to be nearly pest-free. By mid- to late summer, garlic leaves will be turning brown. Don't worry! Generally, this is a good thing. It means garlic is nearly ready for harvest. When you first notice the brown leaves, stop watering. You want the bulbs to dry somewhat before you dig them. At this point, you can gently lift out the bulbs using a garden fork. Allow them to dry in a covered but airy place for about a week. After this drying period, they can be stored in net or string bags (e.g., old potato or onion bags). Store them where they will have good air circulation to avoid mold.

Companion Planting and Design
Because you are likely to be digging around the garlic, make it easily accessible. It can be happy growing near the parsleys.

Try These
Soft-neck garlics, such as 'Early Red Italian' or 'Nootka Rose', are some of the easiest to grow.

Leek

Allium porrum

Botanical Pronunciation
AL-ee-um POH-rum

Bloom Period and Seasonal Color
Late spring; pale pink blooms (though not until their second season)

Mature Height x Spread
12 inches x 2½ inches

The leek is an odd cousin of the onion. It sends up wide, flattened leaves that overlap in a somewhat braided fashion. The bulb itself is more flat than round. As all members of the *Allium* family do, leeks send up one leafless stalk with a flower capsule on the end. When the capsule breaks open, flower buds spill out to form a beautiful globe. Allow a few leeks to go to bloom so as not to miss their rarely seen beauty. Otherwise, cut back the flower stalk as it begins to emerge, then dig and eat the leek bulb. Domestic leek has a mild onion flavor, unlike its wild cousin—ramps, *Allium tricoccum*. This wild leek, found in moist woodlands throughout the state, has a hot, harsh onion flavor.

When, Where, and How to Plant
Leeks are a "spring thing." They prefer soil temperatures lower than 77 degrees Fahrenheit, so plant as soon as the danger of frost is over. They are rather slow growers; I suggest heading off to a nursery for plants rather that waiting for seeds to germinate. Leeks prefer a site with all-day sun and rich, fertile, well-drained soil. Mix in leaf compost and seasoned manure if you need to enrich your soil. This will also lighten the heavy clay soil of southwest Ohio. Plant leeks about 6 inches down. They are generally grown in hilled soil, like celery or potatoes, to develop long white stalks. You can "hill" some soil around them once the plants reach about 1 inch in diameter.

Growing Tips
The soil used for hilling should be light and well drained; you don't want leeks to stay wet. Give them a little compost tea at about their 60-day mark to add extra nutrients.

Regional Advice and Care
As with most members of the *Allium* family, there just isn't much to bother leeks. However, should your plants turn up with rust, it is best to remove all infected plants in order to avoid spreading the disease to any remaining plants. Harvest leeks at 1 inch in diameter if you can't wait! Water about 1 inch weekly until about two weeks before harvest, then withhold water. This causes bulbs to form protective scales and "harden off." This important process will help leeks have a longer storage life. If you have to thin crowded plants, include them in your next salad or soup!

Companion Planting and Design
Because leeks do better in hilled soil, they should be grown off by themselves. You could choose to accent the back of a bed of leeks with a taller herb, such as sage.

Try These
Both 'Durabel' and 'American Flag' are considered cold hardy and should do well in all parts of Ohio.

Marjoram

Origanum majorana

Botanical Pronunciation
uh-RIG-uh-num ma-ju-AY-nuh

Other Name
Sweet marjoram

Bloom Period and Seasonal Color
Late summer; blooms in white

Mature Height x Spread
1 to 1½ feet x 1 foot

Marjoram, as its alternate common name suggests, is "sweet," especially when compared to another family member, oregano. Marjoram has a mild oregano flavor. Try substituting it in sauces and fresh salad dressings, but add the fresh leaves just before serving for the best flavor. Often overlooked by new herb gardeners, marjoram is easy to grow and care for. Allow a few stalks to go to flower. The flowers are also edible, but the small white clusters of blooms are pretty in their own right. For use in cooking, you want to grow full bushy plants (full of leaves instead of flowers). At the end of the season, pull the whole plant, hang it upside down, and allow it to dry away from direct sunlight. Keep only the leaves and discard the stems.

When, Where, and How to Plant

Marjoram seeds are slow to germinate. You can start seeds indoors in late winter and move the seedlings to garden beds after the danger of frost has passed. Or you can "jump start" this part of your garden by buying young plants to install. Select a sunny spot with well-drained soil. Marjoram likes the soil a little drier than most herbs, so consider turning a little sand into the soil before planting. Sweet marjoram is considered a tender perennial, but you will find most folks treat it as an annual. Marjoram is a mild-mannered member of the mint family. Unlike its minty cousins, peppermint and spearmint, it will not grow wild and invade other parts of the garden.

Growing Tips

While mature marjoram prefers a slightly drier soil, don't allow young plants to dry out. Check them every few days and water as necessary, up to 1 inch a week (this includes rainfall). I would not recommend any fertilization for sweet marjoram. The use of fertilizers will dilute the aromatic qualities of its essential oils.

Regional Advice and Care

Sweet marjoram is generally not bothered by pests or disease, making it nearly care-free in that respect. Hand-pull weeds as they pop up around young plants, as tools may damage these tender plants. If you decide to thin out crowded plants, pick off the tender aromatic leaves to use right away. You will keep marjoram producing new leaves by pinching off a few leaves weekly after the plant is nearly at its mature height, and also by pinching back the flower stems when they start to shoot up.

Companion Planting and Design

Since sweet marjoram will grow to a height of 12 to 18 inches, it will look nice clumped just behind your chives. Don't forget to feel for the square stem, as sweet marjoram is a member of the mint family!

Try These

I like the compact look of the old species, *Origanum majorana*.

Parsley

Petroselinum crispum

Botanical Pronunciation
pet-roh-sel-EE-num CRISP-um

Bloom Period and Seasonal Color
Early summer; blooms are insignificant

Mature Height x Spread
1½ feet x 1 foot

When you plant parsley, plant plenty! Besides all of the dishes you will be adding parsley to, you will be sharing it with the wonderful black swallowtail butterfly. Its colorful caterpillar will munch away at your parsley, so plant enough to share. If you can sacrifice a few plants for the caterpillars, you will be rewarded with up-close views of the black swallowtail butterfly. Parsley is versatile and lends delicate flavor to anything to which it is added. Rich in vitamin C, parsley can share this benefit with you only when it is eaten fresh. When you heat up parsley in cooking, you destroy the vitamin C. The flavor, however, remains intact! Nibble leaves to freshen your breath and to aid in digestion after a big meal.

When, Where, and How to Plant
Most varieties of parsley are easy to start from seed. Wait until after the danger of frost is over, then select a sunny to partially sunny spot. Parsley requires at least a half-day of sun for good growth. It also likes rich soil, so turn in some leaf compost and seasoned manure before planting. The area should be well drained, so that plants are not staying soaked. Parsley is actually a biennial, although it is usually raised as an annual. You may want to drape some cheesecloth on young plants so that the swallowtail caterpillars don't munch them right to the stem.

Growing Tips
Once established, parsley prefers to dry out a little between waterings. But take care not to let parsley growing in full sun go too long without water as you could find it wilted and limp. If that happens, you may be playing "Taps" for the parsley. If you mixed in some good compost just before planting, it is not necessary to fertilize parsley.

Regional Advice and Care
Parsley is nearly care-free. You will need to hand-pull weeds from around the tender emerging plants. Short of a few butterfly caterpillars dining on it, there is little else that bothers parsley. Once parsley goes to flower, it is on its way out. To harvest at the end of the season, cut the stems at the base of the plant. Bundle them into small bouquets of no more than about 1 inch (the collective stems), tie with cotton string, and hang them upside down to dry away from the direct sunlight. Once they are completely dry, break off the leaves to store and discard the stems.

Companion Planting and Design
Parsley is great as a border or in beds with showy annuals.

Try These
I like the way the curly varieties form tight bunches. 'Extra Triple Curled' or 'Krausa' are more tolerant of Ohio summers and less susceptible to disease.

Peppermint

Mentha piperita

Botanical Pronunciation
MEN-thuh pip-er-EE-tuh

Bloom Period and Seasonal Color
Early summer to early fall; blooms of tiny purplish flowers

Mature Height x Spread
3 feet x as wide as you will allow it

Members of the mint family are easy to discern from other plants as the majority of its members have square stems. Feel the stem of peppermint or spearmint, and compare it to a stalk of parsley or sage. With this simple lesson, you will quickly become a mint "expert" and be able to identify this plant family in the garden, at the nursery, or out in the wild. Peppermint is the strongest tasting mint; it only takes a few fresh leaves crushed in a dish to highlight its flavor. This flavor can overpower, so use it sparingly. The strength of the peppermint flavor diminishes with drying; this is true for any of the mints. Growing mint is so easy you will be showing off your mint bed in no time.

When, Where, and How to Plant
Peppermint, as with most mints, grows quickly if given half a chance. Check your local herb group's plant swap; there is always plenty of mint to be had. Or purchase plants at a garden store. You can begin planting after the danger of frost has passed. Select your site carefully because if it is too shady, peppermint will grow lanky and lean reaching for the sun. However, peppermint does not want full sun all the time. Mix a little leaf compost into the soil before planting. Give young plants plenty of room; space them no closer than 2 feet apart! Often mint does well in spots too moist for other herbs, just consider using a barrier (or container) to keep the mint contained—or you'll be hawking mint starts to everyone!

Growing Tips
Give the planting hole a drink of water, about 1 pint, before adding mint. Keep newly installed plants well watered, but not soaked. Do not fertilize! You want slow, steady leaf production, not artificially rapid growth. Rapid growth reduces the essential oils.

Regional Advice and Care
Easy-to-care-for peppermint does better when trimmed a few inches every few weeks, after it reaches 20 inches. If you want the small but pretty flowers, stop cutting. Mints are susceptible to wilts and rusts. If rust invades, consider clearing the whole bed or cutting it back to the ground. Clear away all clippings. Occasionally loopers, aphids, or grasshoppers visit, but not often enough to cause concern. Consider insecticide usage *carefully* since you are growing peppermint to consume. Insecticidal soap or horticulture oil may be the answer. Some folks cut perennial mint back to the ground every few years to rid the bed of unkempt plants and stimulate vigorous growth.

Companion Planting and Design
Mint can take over, so pluck it out of places you don't want it, or plant it with a barrier. Keep peppermint either at the back of a bed, because it can get quite tall, or better yet—give it its own bed!

Try These
I like the strong "original" peppermint, *Mentha piperita*.

Sweet Basil

Ocimum basilicum

Botanical Pronunciation
OSS-ih-mum bass-IL-ee-kum

Bloom Period and Seasonal Color
Midsummer; pale purple blooms

Mature Height x Spread
2 feet x 3 feet

Growing up in an Italian family meant lots of basil. Basil growing in the garden, basil growing in pots, and basil growing in my grandfather's hand-cast garden vessels set among the annuals! At the end of the growing season, fragrant basil bouquets were hung upside-down to dry in the house for winter use. This pleasant member of the mint family has the characteristic square stem and sends up a layered flower spike like other mints, but that's where the resemblance ends! Basil is sweet and savory at the same time. Add fresh basil leaves to salads, salad dressings, and most meat or fish dishes. From traditional tomato sauces to a zipped-up macaroni and cheese, there's always room for basil. With a variety of colors and leaf shapes, basil fits most gardens.

When, Where, and How to Plant

Wait until the danger of frost has passed and the soil temperature stays around 60 degrees Fahrenheit or warmer. Select a sunny, well-drained site. Turn in some leaf compost to enrich the soil before planting. Basils are easy to start from seed, or you can install young plants. When planting, consider the "finished product," each plant will grow to nearly 2 feet tall and spread as much as 3 feet. If you thin crowded plants, use the leaves in the kitchen. Young leaves are nice additions to salads.

Growing Tips

Lightly moisten seeds and young plants daily. They will fail if the soil's too dry. You don't want them "swimming" in moisture, but do keep them moist, at least until plants are 8 inches tall. Basil needs at least 1 inch of water per week. Use a light mulch, such as pine straw, to retain moisture. Do not fertilize basil, as this reduces the essential oils produced in the leaves.

Regional Advice and Care

Trimming basil will keep it producing tender leaves and cause it to grow full. Hand-pull weeds from around young basil plants. Pinch off the flower stem when it first starts to shoot up to direct energy into leaf production instead of flowers. Basil can get quite "leggy" if allowed to flower, though the tiny flowers are pretty. Occasionally aphids or slugs bother basil, though generally not enough to be concerned about. To harvest, pull off fresh leaves, rinse, and blot dry. These can be kept in the freezer. Otherwise, pull the whole plant, cut off the root section, and tie the bouquets together with cotton string. Hang them to dry in a spot away from direct sunlight and with good air circulation.

Companion Planting and Design

Basil varieties are so handsome! Group several different ones together to form a subtle mosaic. They are also attractive planted in amongst showy annuals!

Try These

Sweet basil is the "old" standard. My dad calls this "Italian Chanel No. 5"!

Wild Bergamot

Monarda fistulosa

Botanical Pronunciation
mo-NAR-da fist-yoo-LOW-suh

Bloom Period and Seasonal Color
July and August; blooms in delicate, pale purple

Mature Height x Spread
2 to 3 feet x 2 feet or more

This member of the mint family is well known as a native prairie species. (Yes, we have native prairie in Ohio!) Because of this, wild bergamot can tolerate drought conditions better than some shallow-rooted plants. Always get seed or young plants from reputable nurseries; never take bergamot from the wild. Digging it from the wild is illegal unless you have written permission from the property owner. This wonderful native will attract hummingbirds, butterflies, and bees. Pick the young tender leaves to use for an aromatic tea, or pluck individual flowers from the flower head to add to your summer salad. If you choose to dry wild bergamot, cut it when the bloom is full, but not past its prime. Dry completely before storing.

When, Where, and How to Plant
Install young wild bergamot after the danger of frost is over. It prefers a sunny spot, but also tolerates partial shade. It may lean toward the sun if planted in too much shade. If you are dividing a clump, take a big soilball with it; it tends to be deep rooted and will transition better with some of the original soil. When transplanting a big clump, be sure the new hole accommodates the soil clump you are installing. Give the hole a good soaking before transplanting. Gently but firmly heel in the transplant so there is no air space below the clump before backfilling with soil.

Growing Tips
Wild bergamot tolerates some extreme conditions and thrives at the height of our summer heat. It is drought resistant, but blooms are definitely better with regular waterings. It's not necessary to fertilize.

Regional Advice and Care
Wild bergamot is a low-maintenance plant. You may choose to thin out jam-packed clumps to allow for better air circulation and reduce the risk of leaf mildew. This long-lasting perennial will self-seed, if allowed. Begin harvesting the tender leaves once the plant is at least 24 inches tall. You can also collect the fresh flowers. These young leaves and flowers can be used fresh or dried to make a pleasant tea.

Companion Planting and Design
Wild bergamot will be nearly 3 feet tall when it blooms, so place it at the back of the bed. If your bed is a medley of tall bloomers, try any of the coneflowers as a companion plant. Wild bergamot looks good mixed in a tall summer bed or give it a spot to go "wild" in the yard. Plant bergamot in the yard where you have a hard spot to mow. You'll have a pretty oasis of flowers and one less place to mow.

Try These
I think the soft color of the native wild bergamot (*Monarda fistulosa*) adds a little "wild elegance" to the garden.

ORNAMENTAL GRASSES

FOR OHIO

O rnamental grasses come in all colors and sizes. There are grasses such as blue fescue that grow to only 6 inches high and other grasses that grow to 8 feet high, with numerous varieties growing to all heights in-between. There are ornamental grasses with green blades, with green-and-white blades, with green blades and yellow blotches, and with purple blades all season long. There are even some varieties with red blades. When you buy ornamental grasses in spring, take this book along to help you select the one you want. In spring, it won't make any difference if the final growing height is 6 inches or 6 feet, they'll all look the same height in the pot with their grass blades just starting to grow. They won't reach their mature height until mid-August. When they finally do reach their mature height, they will start to develop their seedheads, which add to their ornamental beauty and last until a wet snow breaks down the blades and the seedheads.

How to Plant, Transplant, and Divide

Ornamental grasses are easy to plant. Since they are only available as container plants, select your planting site, and slide the container off the root clump. As you remove the soil clump from the container, loosen any roots that are wrapped around it. When planting any ornamental grass, dig a hole twice as wide, and no deeper, than the soil clump. Use the existing soil to backfill, first breaking up all the backfill soil to pieces no larger than a golf ball. Backfill and water-in well to settle the soil. That's all there is to it.

After grasses have been planted several seasons, some varieties have a tendency to die out in the middle of the clump. Still other grasses might start to get too wide for the selected planting site. In any case, ornamental grasses are easy to transplant. The best time to divide and transplant is in spring as the new blades just start to grow. Decide how many divisions you wish to make. Be sure to first cut back all of the previous season's grass blades. With a sharp spade, start cutting the roots in a downward motion (much like cutting a pie), making clumps of at least 12 inches wide down the depth of your spade. If you're dividing because the center has died, discard the dead center and replant the "pie slices" close together to form a new, full plant. If you want to spread your wealth of grasses around and replant clumps in other areas, go for it. Just be sure to replant your divisions at the same depth that they were originally growing. Do not consider dividing until the original grass plant has been in the ground for at least three years.

Landscape Value

Ornamental grasses can solve many aesthetic landscaping problems, or they can simply be beautiful in their own right. Two of the biggest eyesores in an "outdoor living room" are those cable boxes and electrical transformers. Ornamental grasses do a beautiful job of camouflaging these unsightly necessities. And talk about a fast-growing, yearly screen to hide the side of a garage or to block the view of a neighbor's nasty yard! Ornamental grasses will fit that bill too. And picture your mailbox appearing to grow out of a clump of ornamental grass. The medium-height grasses also look great planted by themselves out in the lawn, looking like a green fountain softly gracing the lawn area. The most-often-asked questions by homeowners looking for ornamental grasses are, "Is this pampas grass?" or "Do you sell pampas grass?" I don't know how it started, but a lot of homeowners who are not familiar with ornamental grass varieties think that all ornamental grass is "pampas grass." Pampas grass is only one of many ornamental grass varieties, and it is not hardy in Ohio.

Ornamental Grass Maintenance

The only work to maintaining your ornamental grass is removing the old blades and seedheads in late winter. The easiest way to do this is by tying up your medium-to-tall grasses in three different places of height. Tie them up tight! Then cut off the bundle as close to the ground as possible, cutting the brown blades with a chainsaw or a trimmer. Old grass will tumble over in a bundle like an old tree, making cleanup a breeze! Always do this before next year's grass starts to grow.

Ornamental grasses have great aesthetic value as a landscape "problem-solver" and they are just beautiful!

Blue Fescue

Festuca ovina 'Glauca'

Botanical Pronunciation
fes-TEW-ka oh-VYE-na

Other Name
Garden fescue

Bloom Period and Seasonal Color
Icy blue foliage turning copper-tan in winter;
light green flowers in late June

Mature Height x Spread
8 to 12 inches x 8 to 12 inches

Blue fescue is a cute plant. I don't usually refer to plants that way, but this one is a very small tuft of grass with great silver-blue color. It stays in spiky mounds of about 12 inches high. The flowers form in late June to July and wave above the foliage. The foliage color is icy blue during the growing season, turning a copper-tan for winter. It works well as a low-growing border plant. You can even use it in a mass planting as you would another groundcover. Blue fescue is relatively fast growing, but needs good drainage to thrive. Many plants are sold as "blue fescue," but for the best results in your garden, look for the named selections. You'll find slightly different sizes and foliage colors—all cute!

When, Where, and How to Plant

Plant blue fescue anytime the ground is not frozen. Remember, if you buy blue fescue in the early spring, it won't look as pretty as it does when it has new blades—but soon it will! Blue fescue prefers nice, loamy soil. It will tolerate some clay, though it needs good drainage. Avoid poorly drained soils and heavy clay. Blue fescue grows best where it is shaded from hot afternoon sun in summer, especially in Zone 6. To plant, follow the directions listed in this chapter's introduction. Space plants 2 feet apart or less, depending on the cultivar.

Growing Tips

Water new plants until established; after that, fescue is drought tolerant. Fertilizers are unnecessary.

Regional Advice and Care

Blue fescue is a cool-season grass, which means it grows primarily in the spring and fall. In the heat of midsummer, your plants will appear somewhat dormant. Watch for more growth in the fall. Coming out of winter, blue fescue will be brown, not blue. In early spring, cut back the old brown blades to within 2 to 3 inches of the ground. Shear off the flowers whenever you feel they become unattractive. If your fescue starts to die out in the center, your plants are giving you a signal—they need to be divided. Divide fescue in spring or in early fall. Consult this chapter's introduction for more on dividing grasses. As far as bugs and diseases go, blue fescue is trouble-free.

Companion Planting and Design

Blue fescue makes a neat specimen plant. It can be used as an edging or mixed with other perennials that need good drainage, such as Stokes' aster, 'Vera Jameson' sedum, and lavender. Try it as a ground-cover on hard-to-mow slopes. Plant on 2-foot centers, and it will be solid in three to four years.

Try These

One of the best and most durable blue fescues is 'Elijah Blue' (8 to 12 inches tall). It has beautiful icy blue foliage, grows fast, and endures our summers better than other fescues.

Feather Reed Grass

Calamagrostis x acutiflora

Botanical Pronunciation
ka-la-mo-GROSS-tis ak-yoo-tih-FLOR-uh

Other Name
Reed grass

Bloom Period and Seasonal Color
Mid-May through winter; variegated foliage;
blooms in greenish purple changing to tan

Mature Height x Spread
1½ to 3 feet (3 to 5 feet in bloom) x 1 foot

Although it starts the season as a foliage clump, feather reed grass blooms early, forming graceful flower spikes that move in the slightest breeze. Its upright growth habit makes it desirable to plant several together in the same bed—then watch the wind work those beautiful flower heads all summer long. The feathery flowers that emerge are pink maturing to tan in the fall. The blades are narrow and solid green during the growing season. Some ornamental grasses are huge and hard to fit into a modest-sized garden—not this one. It forms a clump of foliage about 3 feet high; its flowers shoot up several feet more. The cultivar named 'Overdam' is slender, allowing it to be used in many unique landscape situations. 'Overdam' has green blades with white edges and soft pink flower plumes.

When, Where, and How to Plant
Plant container-grown feather reed grass anytime the ground is not frozen. This grass is adaptable and tolerates a wide range of soil types, including clay as long as it is well drained. It prefers full sun, but will tolerate a half-day of shade (plants in shade will flower less and be less upright). Plant feather reed grass in the garden about 18 inches apart, following the directions in this chapter's introduction.

Growing Tips
You won't need to fertilize these care free grasses. Clumps are drought-tolerant once established, but provide water to new plantings during dry spells. Check the surrounding soil, and water if it's dry.

Regional Advice and Care
It has no important pest or disease problems to worry about. Sometimes foliar rust appears, but it doesn't seem to bother the plants. Feather reed grass starts growing early, so cut it back to about 6 inches in late winter. Follow the method listed in this chapter's introduction to make cleanup easier. After all, you don't want to be outside raking in late winter! Feather reed grass doesn't need division as frequently as some other grasses, but if your clumps start to die out in the middle, divide them in spring following the instructions in this chapter's introduction. Keep new divisions moist.

Companion Planting and Design
If you are skeptical about ornamental grasses, give this one a try. Feather reed grass is a cinch to use in the garden where its vertical habit makes a great accent. Combine it with perennials, or use it in a shrub border. Mass it in a group planting or as a narrow, low screen. Plant a grouping to camouflage a cable box or electric transformer in your yard—use your imagination! These plants add interest to the garden almost all year long.

Try These
I highly recommend 'Overdam'. If you have more room, grow the non-variegated form usually sold as 'Karl Foerster' (5 to 6 feet tall by 2 to 2½ feet wide). It is bigger, but not unwieldy, and complements other perennials effortlessly.

Fountain Grass

Pennisetum alopecuroides

Botanical Pronunciation
pen-ih-SEE-tum al-oh-pek-yur-OH-id-eez

Bloom Period and Seasonal Color
August through fall; creamy tan flower plumes

Mature Height x Spread
3 feet x 2 to 3 feet

I would have to say that fountain grass is probably the most popular ornamental grass to date. It is easy to use in the landscape—many landscape professionals love it and include it in their designs. Why? Its glossy, narrow foliage forms a shimmering clump topped by lovely foxtail flowers. The species forms a dramatic clump almost 4 feet high and wide. One cultivar I especially recommend, 'Hameln', is a smaller selection (reaching 2 to 3 feet). It is a bit easier to use in the garden and is equally as attractive. Each plant resembles a little round, fuzzy pillow highlighted by fluffy tan-colored plumes that grow just a few inches above the foliage. Even heavy winter snow does not disfigure this plant, just cut it back in the spring.

When, Where, and How to Plant
Fountain grass transplants easily (as do all ornamental grasses). Plant anytime the ground is not frozen. Fountain grass will grow and flower in full sun to a half-day of shade. It grows in all types of soil, but grows best where the drainage is average to good. Fountain grass is available in containers of various sizes. Plant whatever size fits your budget, knowing that it will grow. Plant 2½ to 3 feet apart, following the directions listed in this chapter's introduction.

Growing Tips
As with all ornamental grasses, keep new plantings moist until the roots are established; after that, grasses seldom need watering. Ornamental grasses rarely need fertilizer.

Regional Advice and Care
Fountain grass is care-free—no bugs or diseases will bother it. Cut back all old foliage in late winter or early spring before new foliage starts growing. A hedge trimmer is great for this. If your clumps start to die out in the middle, it's time to divide. Do this in spring just as new growth appears. Digging a mature clump requires effort. Read this chapter's introduction for details on dividing grasses.

Companion Planting and Design
Fountain grass is a great-looking plant for any landscape situation. Combine it with perennials, use it as an accent with bedding plants, mass it like a groundcover, or treat it as a shrub. Its special winter appearance makes it a valuable year-round ornamental. Add bulbs such as daffodils, and you'll have early spring color too.

Try These
'Hameln' grows to only 2 to 3 feet; each plant looks like a little round, fuzzy pillow. 'Little Bunny' is the smallest of all fountain grasses, growing only 10 to 12 inches high. A cultivar of Oriental fountain grass (*Pennisetum orientale*) called 'Karley Rose' is a real winner. It has delicate, smoky pink, bottlebrush flowers from June through fall. If you see it, try it. 'Red Head' grows to only 2 to 3 feet with blooms of reddish maroon (purple-brown) in midsummer. 'Piglet' only grows to a height of 12 to 18 inches with a creamy tan bloom in late summer to early fall.

Japanese Blood Grass

Imperata cylindrica

Botanical Pronunciation
im-per-AH-tuh sil-IN-dree-kuh

Other Name Blood grass

Bloom Period and Seasonal Color
Red foliage throughout the growing season

Mature Height x Spread
1 to 2 feet x 2 feet

Plant this ornamental grass in full sun, and red foliage you shall have. Most of the red foliage growth will be on the tips, greening out towards the ground. Plant blood grass in mass plantings and you will have a beautiful sight in spring, summer, fall, and even into winter when the foliage turns a brownish copper. Japanese blood grass is low growing at only 1 to 2 feet tall. It spreads itself by means of underground stems, but it is certainly not aggressive in its growth habit. Blood grass does not flower, so don't expect those flower heads that other ornamental grasses display. Even though blood grass gives you no flowers, it more than makes up for it with its beautiful red foliage.

When, Where, and How to Plant
Plant Japanese blood grass anytime the ground is not frozen. In early to mid-spring, you'll swear you're buying a pot full of soil and nothing else. If you want to see it growing, view it at your garden center in May. For the best foliage color, plant in full sun. But I have it planted in my yard in an area that gets only four hours of afternoon sun, and it still looks great. Any type of soil will do. Blood grass likes a little soil moisture. To plant, dig a hole as deep as the soil clump and twice as wide. Remove the plant from the pot and loosen any wrapped roots. Use the existing soil to backfill, breaking up the soil particles to the size of golf balls. Water-in well.

Growing Tips
Once established, your blood grass won't need much care or fertilizer. It prefers moist soil though, so a good soaking during dry spells (once weekly) would be nice.

Regional Advice and Care
Japanese blood grass is low maintenance—no bugs or disease. The most you'll do is cut it back to within 3 inches of the ground in late winter. To trim it back, mow off the foliage at 3 inches with a rotary power mower. If you want to spread the wealth, divide and transplant blood grass in spring before the new blades grow taller than 8 inches. If any part of your planting reverts back to a green form, dig and remove those sections.

Companion Planting and Design
Plant Japanese blood grass in areas where you can view it from both outside and inside the house. Plant large sweeps in open areas to make a dramatic landscape statement. Use blood grass in rock gardens, around water ponds, or anywhere in the landscape that needs great foliage color.

Try These
You may also see plants sold as 'Red Baron' or 'Rubra'. This is the same plant, so don't hesitate to obtain some for your home.

Maiden Grass

Miscanthus sinensis 'Gracillimus'

Botanical Pronunciation
miss-KANTH-us sy-NEN-sis

Other Name
Japanese silver grass

Bloom Period and Seasonal Color
July through fall blooms in purplish bronze
turning silvery-white

Mature Height x Spread
5 to 7 feet x 3 to 5 feet

Here is a tough and beautiful grass for your garden. This one has a striking form, it doesn't mind heat and humidity, and it grows in most soils—even clay. Maiden grass is sometimes referred to as "silver grass" because its thin, fine-textured blades are silver-and-green and it has silvery white, plume-type flowers in late summer and fall. The silver-green blades often have wonderful fall color turning golden brown after a killing frost and the plant provides great winter interest as well. Maiden grass isn't small; plants can reach 5 to 7 feet tall and 3 to 5 feet wide, but it is perfect as a dramatic accent. There are many selections of maiden grass for Ohio; see more listed in this entry.

When, Where, and How to Plant

Plant container-grown maiden grass anytime the ground is not frozen. It grows best in full sun to half-day shade. Maiden grass grows well in all types of soil and will tolerate conditions from somewhat wet to somewhat dry. Follow the directions for planting in this chapter's introduction, spacing plants at least 3 to 4 feet apart. Give maiden grass plenty of room to grow and develop its beautiful form.

Growing Tips

Miscanthus species prefer moist soils and therefore appreciates water during dry spells. Did you know that grasses will tell you when they need water? The leaf blades will roll in, indicating drought stress. You won't need to fertilize maiden grass.

Regional Advice and Care

In Ohio, maiden grass is free of pests and disease. Prune it back to 3 inches from the ground in early spring, before the new growth appears. Follow my suggestion listed in this chapter's introduction to make it easier. Wear gloves with this one; the leaf blades are sharp. If your plants start to die in the middle, divide them in the spring. For more specifics, see this chapter's introduction. Discard the dead center and divide the remainder into 12- to 16-inch clumps that can be replanted as one new plant or separated into individual clumps in their own areas.

Companion Planting and Design

Maiden grass really makes a statement in any home landscape. It makes a good screen, a grassy hedge, a background plant for other lower-growing grasses or ornamental plants, or a fantastic lawn specimen. It's gorgeous by a pond or water feature.

Try These

Besides 'Gracillimus', there are lots of other selections to consider. One of the best, 'Morning Light' (5 feet tall), has variegated green-and-white blades that appear almost silvery in the garden. Porcupine grass, or 'Strictus', (5 to 6 feet) has green blades highlighted with golden horizontal bands. For small gardens, forms of dwarf maiden grass are sold under the name 'Yaku Jima'. They grow to only 3 to 4 feet.

Northern Sea Oats

Chasmanthium latifolium

Botanical Pronunciation
chas-MAN-thee-um lat-ee-FOH-lee-um

Other Name
Spangle grass

Bloom Period and Seasonal Color
July through fall; blooms in green turning to coppery brown

Mature Height x Spread
3 feet x 2 feet

Northern sea oats has attractive bamboo-like foliage and produces flat flowers that look as though they belong on a box of oat cereal. This is one ornamental grass that will tolerate a lot of rough conditions, including shade. The beautiful green spikelets—a favorite of flower arrangers for both fresh and dried arrangements—turn a copper color in fall and provide interest all winter. Sea oats has a vase-shaped form, and you can use it where other grasses wouldn't dare to go—in shady perennial beds, woodland gardens, and by a water feature. You can put it in sun as well. It is important to know that northern sea oats is a self-sower, sometimes producing lots of seedlings. See the Regional Advice and Care section for hints on controlling all those babies.

When, Where, and How to Plant

Plant northern sea oats anytime the ground is not frozen. You might have a hard time locating this plant because some nurseries are not familiar with it. It will grow in average soil that has good drainage. Northern sea oats grow well in shade or sun (with adequate moisture) and tolerate difficult conditions, including dry shade. In sun, the blades will be a lighter green than those grown in shade, which will be a much bluer green. To plant, dig a hole as deep as the soil clump and twice as wide. Take the plant out of the container and loosen any wrapped roots. Place the plant in the hole and backfill with the existing soil. Water-in well to settle the soil.

Growing Tips

Plants in full sun will need regular watering to keep the soil moist. In average or better soil, no fertilizer is needed. A layer of organic mulch will help to conserve moisture as well as reduce self-sowing.

Regional Advice and Care

This plant is resistant to bugs and disease. Cut it back to 3 inches from the ground in late winter to early spring, before new growth starts. Sea oats reseed themselves, but are not considered invasive. In happy conditions though, you'll get a lot of seedlings. To control the number of new plants that develop from the seed, apply a weed seed preventer, to the bed area in mid-March and again in mid-May. Or just knock them out with a hoe in the spring. Clumps can be divided in the spring, consult this chapter's introduction for specifics. Keep new divisions moist.

Companion Planting and Design

Plant several of the plants in a bed, or use them around a water feature. They combine well with hostas, astilbe, and 'Palace Purple' alumroot. Don't forget to cut the flower heads for indoor arrangements. A full bunch is spectacular in a vase and lasts all year.

Try These

'River Mist' grows to 2 to 3 feet with variegated foliage and blooms midsummer and late summer to early fall.

Purple Fountain Grass

Pennisetum setaceum 'Rubrum'

Botanical Pronunciation
pen-ih-SEE-tum se-TAY-see-um

Bloom Period and Seasonal Colors
Purple-maroon foliage; midsummer through fall blooms in rose-red

Mature Height x Spread
4 feet x 2 feet

Here is an ornamental grass that *cannot* be "planted anytime the ground is not frozen." Purple fountain grass is not winter hardy in Ohio, but I'm making room for this extremely colorful ornamental grass. It probably provides the most seasonal color of any grass with its rose-red spikes of flowers in mid- to late summer. Purple fountain grass blades grow 2 feet high, 3 to 4 feet high in bloom, and have a purple-maroon color. Yes, purple fountain grass *is* an annual, just like geraniums and impatiens, but get ready to enjoy this grass. Best of all, unlike perennial varieties, this grass is available in 3-inch pots for very little cost per pot.

When, Where, and How to Plant
Plant purple fountain grass after the danger of heavy frost is over in your area. You will most likely find this plant in the area of the garden center where they display their annuals. It is usually found growing in 3-, 4-, and 6-inch pots. That means you have a nice price range from which to select. Just remember, purple fountain grass is an annual in Ohio. See this chapter's introduction for planting tips.

Growing Tips
When planting in mixed patio pots with other flowering annuals, choose companion plants that don't require frequent watering. Purple fountain grass does not like wet feet. Purple fountain grass does like a feeding of a timed-release fertilizer.

Regional Advice and Care
Though purple fountain grass is an annual, it is a low-maintenance, bug- and disease-resistant ornamental grass. Although the roots freeze and die during the winter, the tops still give you a nice winter look—much like a dried arrangement. Discard the plants in early spring and wait until mid-May to plant new ones.

Companion Planting and Design
You can plant purple fountain grass in mixed patio pots or in flower beds with other annuals and perennials. Purple fountain grass looks great in patio pots mixed with 'Wave' petunias, coleus, cobbitty daisies, and Million Bells®, or any other summer-blooming annuals that love it hot and somewhat dry. Purple fountain grass also makes a beautiful statement when planted in mass in its own bed or underplanted in a group around ornamental trees. As long as the planting site gets a half a day of sun or more, let your creative juices flow.

Try These
Burgundy giant fountain grass (*Pennisetum* 'Burgundy Fountain') is another annual grass with 1-inch-wide leaves in solid burgundy red. Red foxtails develop on a rapidly growing plant that grows 5 feet high and 3 feet wide in one season. Wow! Now that's fast!

Ribbon Grass

Phalaris arundinacea 'Picta'

Botanical Pronunciation
FAL-ah-ris a-run-din-uh-KEE-uh

Other Name Gardener's garters

Bloom Period and Seasonal Color
Striped foliage in cream and green

Mature Height x Spread
1 feet x 2 feet (and spreading)

It seems that ornamental grasses are all the rage nowadays, but here is one that has been around since long before Grandma. Ribbon grass, with its green-and-white striped foliage, makes a quick statement in the garden. You can almost watch it grow. It is quite aggressive, which could be an asset when you plant it on hillsides to control erosion or in a difficult spot by a driveway. But when you use ribbon grass in the garden, be prepared to control its growth. Use it in shadier areas where its beautiful creamy white-and-green blades will brighten up the site, and plant it around deck and patio areas where you relax at night. Moonlight will illuminate the ribbon grass, giving a beautiful glow to the garden.

When, Where, and How to Plant
Plant ribbon grass anytime the ground is not frozen. To make sure you like its appearance, wait until around the middle of May, when the new blades are growing in a pot, before you buy it. Ribbon grass does well in hot, sunny locations and in shaded areas of the landscape. It does well in all types of soil. It appreciates good drainage but will tolerate—in fact prefers—some soil moisture. For "how tos" on planting, see this chapter's introduction.

Growing Tips
When planted in hot, sunny, sloped areas, an occasional drink of water during dry spells will be appreciated. No fertilizer is needed for ribbon grass.

Regional Advice and Care
Ribbon grass, like all ornamental grasses, is low-maintenance and resistant to bugs and disease. Use your lawn mower to mow down the brown blades of last year's growth; do this in late winter or early spring, before new growth begins in April. Ribbon grass can be aggressive. Be prepared to prune away all unwanted growth with a spade. It transplants easily, so if you have a large area to fill, start with a few plants and continue to divide and fill in the other areas with your own transplants. Do this anytime during the growing season.

Companion Planting and Design
Ribbon grass provides a *great* solution for an erosion problem on a hillside or other hard-to-mow areas. It is fast-growing and will tolerate shade. It could be the perfect groundcover in an area where little else will grow. Just keep it away from your well-prepared garden beds where it will become a thug.

Try These
There is a great form of ribbon grass that has stronger cream-and-white variegation flushed with pink in the spring. It is sold both under the name 'Feesey' and the more poetic 'Strawberries and Cream'. This form is reported to be less invasive.

PERENNIALS

FOR OHIO

The term *perennial* is most often used to describe flowering plants that typically survive more than two years. We should call them herbaceous perennials, because they are soft-stemmed plants. They die to the ground after a killing frost or two, but their roots live over winter, giving you new leaf growth and flowers each year. Perennials keep coming back every year if they have a happy growing space. (Extremely cold temperatures following a dry fall can make the roots of many perennials vulnerable to freezing, thus causing them to die; if we have a dry fall, water in late fall to reduce the risk of root failure).

Finding a Happy Home

The great majority of perennials require good soil drainage. Some varieties tolerate all kinds of Ohio *soil*, but they still need good *drainage*. If they're constantly exposed to wet soil, roots will rot and plants will die. This can happen during the growing season, or over winter in areas where large snow coverings thaw and puddle water around the sleeping perennial roots.

Many garden books describe a lot of plants that do best in full sun. But the only exposure we have for full sun is south. If you insisted on full sun for all the sun-loving plants, that would mean that 75 percent of your plants would be located on the south side of your house, away from any shade or ornamental trees. In a perfect world, we could do this, but it's not a perfect world. Pay attention to the *minimum* amounts of sun that these sun lovers will tolerate so you will be happy with the outcome. I grow many sun lovers that get less than six hours of sun. They do great and so will yours.

Planting Potted Perennials

The best and only way to purchase new perennials is to buy ones already growing in a pot. Even when buying in early spring when there is very little, if any, new growth showing, the roots are established in the soil in the pots. You will find new perennials growing in 3- and 4-inch pots, and in 1- and 2-gallon pots. First, make sure the location you are choosing is where the perennial wants to grow. If your new perennials are not listed in this chapter, get as much information as you can get from the place you're buying them. Dig a hole twice as wide, but no deeper than the soil clump. Break up the backfill soil so no pieces are bigger than a golf ball. With heavy clay soil, add up to 30 percent organic matter (peat humus or compost) to the backfill soil. Remove the plant from its pot, and loosen any roots that are wrapped around the soil clump. Place the plant in the hole and backfill. Water-in well. Fertilize with a water-soluble plant food, following the directions on the container.

Beebalm planted with black-eyed Susans makes for a beautiful late summer show.

When buying perennials in early spring, select plants that have not been in heated greenhouses that cause them to develop more quickly than they would otherwise. This tender, early growth could be very vulnerable to late season frosts and freezes. Buy potted plants that are not any further developed than those that have been in the garden over winter.

Dividing Perennials

Perennials, by variety, need to be divided about every three to five years. A telltale sign is a dramatic drop in bloom. Another sign is when the center of a plant dies and the good parts are to the outside of the clump. The best times to divide are fall (September to mid-October) or early spring as new leaves grow. Make a circular soil cut with a garden spade around the clump. Dig down the depth of the spade. Then take the spade or a large knife and half or quarter the clump. Leave half to a quarter in place, and transplant the balance to another part of your landscape. Fill in the cavity left in the original planting site with additional garden soil.

What Perennials Are Best?

There are many perennials to choose from. I picked my favorites because . . . well, heck, it's my book! They may not be your favorites. Do not be afraid to try other perennials that you'll find at your favorite garden centers. There are too many to limit yourself to my favorites alone.

Aster

Aster spp.

Botanical Pronunciation
AS-ter

Other Name
Fall aster

Bloom Period and Seasonal Color
August through October; blooms in purple shades of blue, magenta, pink, white

Mature Height x Spread
1 ½ to 4 feet x 2 to 3 feet

Fall is a season of mixed emotions. Summer annuals are coming to an end, leaves are starting to fall ... but wait, what's that gorgeous color in the garden? Well, it could be mums. But if the colors are purple, lavender-blue, magenta, pink, and white, all looking like starry daisies, then those plants—ladies and gentlemen—are fall asters. They start blooming in late August and bloom into October and many are native to the United States. These two, *Aster novi-belgii* and *A. novae-angliae*, do well in Ohio. For ease of culture, look for the cultivars noted here. Save a spot in your landscape for a few of these scene-stealers to perk up your fall garden.

When, Where, and How to Plant
Plant container-grown asters whenever they're available. If planting in fall, do it early to allow roots time to establish. Asters do best in full sun, but light shade still produces lots of color. They will grow in all types of well-drained soil as long as you keep the soil moist. Asters need good air circulation, so space plants adequately—don't crowd them. Follow the general directions for planting in this chapter's introduction.

Growing Tips
Keep soil moist, but not wet, in hot, dry weather. To prevent problems with foliar disease, avoid overhead watering. Fertilization is generally unnecessary with asters. If you fertilize, follow the directions on the label of your favorite plant food.

Regional Advice and Care
Insects aren't a concern, but some asters are prone to foliar disease. To avoid mildew, improve air circulation by giving plants plenty of room, follow these watering suggestions, and select disease-resistant cultivars. Some asters need pinching to prevent the stems from flopping. Look for self-supporting compact selections. If you decide to pinch, which will double your blooms and shorten your plants, cut back stems to the height you want them to bloom as spring turns to summer. Stop pinching by mid-July. Asters need occasional division to keep plants vigorous. Transplant and divide asters in spring, making each division at least 6 inches in diameter.

Companion Planting and Design
Combine asters with 'Autumn Joy' sedum and ornamental grasses for a nice combination.

Try These
For New England asters, bright magenta-pink 'Alma Potschke' is my favorite. It grows to about 3 feet high and wide and needs no pinching to maintain loads of flowers. Another New England aster is 'Purple Dome' (mounds of royal purple color). For New York asters, 'Professor Kippenburg' has stood the test of time. It has lavender-blue, semidouble flowers topping out at 1 to 1½ feet tall. 'The Wood's of New York' asters are excellent dwarfs, making them great for borders or small gardens. They have dainty, yellow-centered daisylike flowers over fine-textured foliage and bloom in summer continuing well into fall. Wood's asters come in Blue (bluish purple), Pink (bright pink), and Purple (rich purple).

Astilbe

Astilbe x arendsii

Botanical Pronunciation
a-STIL-bee ar-END-see-eye

Other Name
False spirea

Bloom Period and Seasonal Color
Late June to early August (by variety); red, pink, peach, white blooms

Mature Height x Spread
1 to 3 feet x 1½ to 2 feet

Need more ideas for the shade garden? Consider astilbe. Astilbe has attractive, glossy fernlike foliage. That in itself makes it a great plant, but add to that beautiful flowers alive with color, and you've got a terrific summer-blooming plant that comes back year after year. Considered a woodland plant, astilbe grows best where it is protected from direct sun but gets good natural light. Some forms have bronzy foliage or garnet-red new growth. The feathery plume-type flowers come in vibrant reds and magentas, as well as soft pinks, peach, and sparkling white. If you can spare them, astilbe plumes make an excellent cut flower; be sure to cut the flower stems when the flowers are no more than half open.

When, Where, and How to Plant

Plant nursery-grown astilbe—available in 3- and 4-inch pots—in spring. Plant larger 1- and 2-gallon potted astilbe anytime the ground is not frozen. Astilbe prefers moist, but not wet, soil that's loose and loamy. It prefers shady areas that have good sky light or morning sun. The key to success is the soil. If you have average soil, add organic amendments. To plant, consult the general instructions in this chapter's introduction. Space plants 1½ to 2 feet apart.

Growing Tips

Astilbe wants to be kept moist during hot, dry weather. To conserve moisture, apply a 1- to 2-inch layer of bark mulch around their roots but not on their stems. Fertilize in spring with a timed-release fertilizer.

Regional Advice and Care

Pests and disease rarely trouble astilbe. Remove spent flowers. Divide clumps every four to five years in spring to keep astilbes blooming well. Make each transplanted clump at least 6 inches in diameter. Replant at the same depth they were growing in their old home.

Companion Planting and Design

Astilbe makes a great mass planting if they're all the same color, or use in mixed borders. It look great when in bloom *and* makes a nice glossy, green plant that defines any bed line well. Plant hostas nearby for a great combo.

Try These

Here are my favorite pink, white, red, and peach varieties. 'Erica' (28 to 36 inches) has large pink flowers. 'Bridal Veil' (1½ to 2 feet) has glossy foliage producing cream-colored flower spikes. 'Fanal' (2 feet) has deep red flowers and blooms earlier than others. 'Peach Blossom' (2 feet) offers beautiful salmon-pink flowers. I also like *Astilbe simplicifolia* 'Sprite' (1 foot), a Perennial Plant of the Year. It has shell pink flowers that last up to six weeks. Vision series has tall feathery blooms (three colors) foliage (14 inches tall). Vision White (white flowers with deep bronze-green foliage), Pink (light pink flower plumes against coarsely textured, blue-green foliage) and Red (reddish purple with deep bronze-green foliage). Montgomery astilbe (12 inches) has dark red plumes and green foliage that emerges bronze in fall.

'Autumn Joy' Sedum

Sedum 'Autumn Joy'

Botanical Pronunciation
SEE-dum

Other Name Showy stonecrop

Bloom Period and Seasonal Color
August to frost; blooms in pink turning to russet

Mature Height x Spread
1½ to 2 feet x 2 feet

Talk about an easy perennial to grow! One of the common names of sedum is "live forever," and it does that. 'Autumn Joy' grows all by itself in the hot, dry soils that southern Ohio is famous for; indeed, it grows in all types of well-draining soil. The leaves are thick and fleshy, resembling a succulent. The flower heads first start to form in mid- to late August, then the color changes begin. At first they appear to be white, but as September arrives the flower heads change color and become a warm pink. In two weeks they deepen to a pinkish red. By October they turn to a rust color, and finally to brown after several hard freezes. These dried-looking flowers add winter interest to the garden.

When, Where, and How to Plant
Install new plants anytime they are available. 'Autumn Joy' grows in just about any type of garden soil; it actually prefers clay soil that is well drained and never stays wet after a rain. This sedum grows best in full sun but will grow very well in only four to five hours of sun. Follow the directions for planting in this chapter's introduction. Space about 2 feet apart.

Growing Tips
Water new plants; once established 'Autumn Joy' is heat and drought tolerant. Do not overfertilize; follow the instructions on the container. In average to fertile soil, fertilizer is probably unnecessary.

Regional Advice and Care
There are no bugs or diseases to worry about. During winter, sedums have bare stems with dried flowers on top. Some call this winter interest; others think it looks yucky. If you think it's yucky, prune off bare stems in late fall to within 3 inches of the ground.

Companion Planting and Design
'Autumn Joy', like fall mums and fall asters, adds lots of great color to September landscapes. Locate fall bloomers where they can be enjoyed from outside and inside your home. Mix 'Autumn Joy' with dwarf fountain grass, hydrangeas, and other plants that provide winter interest.

Try These
I love 'Autumn Joy', but there are lots of other sedums. 'Ruby Glow' (12 to 14 inches) has deep, pinkish red flowers beginning in late summer. 'Vera Jameson', another low-grower, has dusky plum foliage and pink flowers. Dazzleberry series (6 to 8 inches) blooms earlier than most. The huge, brilliant raspberry flower clusters are up to 9 inches in diameter. Disease-resistant foliage retains its fantastic smoky blue-gray color from spring through fall. 'Angelina Stonecrop' has brilliant chartreuse-yellow, needlelike foliage that forms a quick groundcover. 'Lime Zinger' is a very hardy ground-cover with fantastic lime green leaves edged in bright cherry red. 'Mr. Goodbud' has very large, dense heads of light purple buds contrasting with dark purple flowers on a more compact plant. 'Chocolate Drop' (12 inches) has rose pink flowers on lightly scalloped, dark chocolate brown leaves that are glossy with a rubbery texture.

Balloon Flower

Platycodon grandiflorus

Botanical Pronunciation
plat-ee-KO-don gran-dih-FLOR-us

Other Name Chinese bell flower

Bloom Period and Seasonal Color June until
September; violet-blue, pink, white blooms

Mature Height x Spread
8 to 24 inches x 18 to 24 inches

Balloon flower is near the top of my list of my favorite, low-maintenance perennials. It's absolutely care-free. Balloon flower blooms for several months, has no pest or disease problems, and plants survive for years. The stems grow straight up, producing dark green leaves that are silvery underneath. The first buds appear at the top of the stems in early June. Each flower then opens with five broad, pointed petals to form a fat blue star (or pink or white). Balloon flower continues to produce flowers into September. This perennial emerges from the soil a little later than most perennials. Be patient. Plant balloon flower where you can view its fluorescent blue flowers in the moonlight. Why is it called balloon flower? Just look at the inflated buds.

When, Where, and How to Plant
Plant new nursery-grown balloon flowers in 3- to 4-inch pots in spring to summer. One-gallon containers can be planted anytime the ground is not frozen. Balloon flower will grow and prosper in almost any soil, just be sure there is good drainage. Plant in locations with full sun to a half-day of sun. For new installations, loosen the existing soil to a depth of 6 to 8 inches. Dig a hole as deep and twice as wide as the soil clump. Loosen any roots that are wrapped around the soil clump. Backfill, and water-in well to settle the soil.

Growing Tips
Fertilize in spring as plants start to grow, using the balanced plant food of your choice and following its package instructions. Give balloon flower an occasional drink during hot, dry weather.

Regional Advice and Care
Remove the old blooms as they fade. This will keep your plants looking healthier and blooming more. Balloon flower rarely needs division; the fleshy taproots can be tricky to divide. Remember, balloon flower is one of the last perennials to emerge in spring. Mark your plants in the fall to avoid damaging the tender shoot during your spring cleanup. When cutting balloon flower stems, use a match to singe the cut end of the flower stem. This stops the flow of milky sap out of the stem, giving your cut balloon flowers a much longer bloom time in the vase. Pests are not troublesome, but watch out for slugs.

Companion Planting and Design
Great perennial companions for balloon flower are lady's mantle, yarrow, daylily, white baby's breath, 'Powis Castle' artemisia, and any of the tall summer phlox.

Try These
'Apoyama' is a dwarf, growing only 8 inches tall, and has purple-blue flowers. 'Mariesii' has purple-blue flowers on compact 12- to 16-inch stems. 'Mother of Pearl' and 'Shell Pink' both have light pink flowers. 'Fuji' is available with pink, white, or blue flowers, grows to 24 inches tall, and is great as a cut flower.

Beebalm

Monarda didyma

Botanical Pronunciation
mo-NAR-da DID-ee-muh

Other Name Oswego tea

Bloom Period and Seasonal Color
July to September; red, pink, wine-red, purple, white flowers

Mature Height x Spread
1 to 4 feet (by variety) x 3 feet

This is truly a story about the birds and the bees. Beebalm gets its common name from its flowers' ability to attract honey bees. But don't tell that to the hummingbirds! Plant beebalm in an area near a porch or window where you can enjoy the entertainment provided by the hummingbirds it attracts. Though traditionally red, there are now forms with pink, white, purple, and garnet flowers. In the garden, beebalm often succumbs to a foliar disease called powdery mildew. Plant mildew-resistant cultivars for the best performance. Overall, beebalm is trouble-free and easy to grow. It spreads through underground roots that push up new stems. It's not considered invasive, but you will need to thin out new shoots to keep it contained.

When, Where, and How to Plant

Transplant existing beebalm in spring. Install new plants anytime they are available during the growing season. Plant in full sun to morning sun. It grows in all types of soil as long as the drainage is good. For new plants, follow the directions in this chapter's introduction. Space at least 1 to 1½ feet apart to allow air circulation.

Growing Tips

Beebalm is considered drought tolerant, but timely watering during dry weather prevents water stress, which means it's less susceptible to mildew. Consider mulching to conserve moisture—just keep it away from the stems. There is very little need to fertilize beebalm, as that could cause plant stems to get too long and require staking. A little bit every couple of years will be sufficient.

Regional Advice and Care

Deadhead any spent flowers. This will keep beebalm looking neater and will also encourage later, additional bloom. To avoid mildew (its only weakness), plant resistant cultivars and follow the watering advice given here. If plants become diseased, cut them down and remove affected stems and foliage from the garden. Thin and replant beebalm every three to four years. Take divisions that are at least 4 to 6 inches in diameter. Discard the old centers, and space plants on 12-inch centers.

Companion Planting and Design

Plant in groups of three or more in an area large enough for plants to spread. Beebalm makes a great planting along fence rows and in areas set aside for that wildflower look.

Try These

Some of the best mildew-resistant selections include 'Jacob Cline' (3 to 4 feet), a great choice in the traditional deep red. 'Raspberry Wine' (3 to 4 feet) has wonderful wine-red flowers. If you like pink, try 'Marshall's Delight' (2 to 3 feet), which is a disease-resistant, clear pink form, as well as 'Petite Delight' (12 to 15 inches), which is surprisingly dwarf. 'Coral Reef' (36 to 42 inches) has flowers in shades of pink that are easy to grow and multiplies quickly. 'Pink Lace' is a dwarf that produces heads of pink flowers with purple centers in mid- to late summer.

Black-Eyed Susan

Rudbeckia fulgida var. *sullivantii* 'Goldsturm'

Botanical Pronunciation
rud-BEK-ee-a FUL-jih-duh sul-lih-VANT-ee-eye

Other Name Gloriosa daisy

Bloom Period and Seasonal Color
July through September; orange-yellow blooms

Mature Height x Spread
14 inches to 3 feet x 2 to 3 feet

Even the blackest thumb can look like a horticultural genius when planting black-eyed Susans. Just give them average soil, lots of sun, and good drainage. Schedule your lawn party for early August and your Susans will make you look good. Without a doubt, this is the most impressive perennial in my home landscape. It simply needs no help from me. 'Goldsturm' black-eyed Susans are *sensational*. The black-centered, orange-yellow flowers start in mid-July, continue through August, and, with deadheading, you'll have flowers until frost. Regardless of the weather, black-eyed Susans will flower and flower and flower. This plant multiplies rapidly, making it a great perennial plant that, if given enough bed space, will double its flower production every year.

When, Where, and How to Plant

Plant nursery-grown black-eyed Susan anytime in spring, summer, or fall. You will find several pot sizes available. 'Goldsturm' grows in just about any garden soil as long as there is moisture and good drainage. Full sun is best, although I grow mine in just-morning sun, and I get lots of blooms. For specifics on planting, consult this chapter's introduction. Space 2 feet apart.

Growing Tips

Fertilize when *Rudbeckia* first starts growing in spring. Use a timed-release fertilizer that you only have to use once. Although reportedly drought tolerant, black-eyed Susans appreciate moisture. A little water—say, 1 inch of water every two weeks, less any rainfall—during dry spells will lead to healthier, more lush plants.

Regional Advice and Care

Deadhead flowers as they finish blooming. When all the flowers have finished, around the middle of August, prune the entire plant back to 10 inches from the ground. Wait a couple of weeks, and your Susans will bloom again. There are no bugs or diseases that bother this plant. You can divide existing black-eyed Susans as the plants start growing in early spring. Transplant clumps at least 6 inches in diameter and replant at the same depth. Keep new divisions moist until established.

Companion Planting and Design

Black-eyed Susan's beautiful orange-yellow flowers blend in well with other flowers in the same bed. Add a little blue salvia, some nicotiana, and a border of wax begonias, and you have an annual and perennial bed that needs little care and even less water. Other perennials mix well to give you that wildflower look; check out purple coneflower for starters.

Try These

'Goldsturm' is incredible and hard to top. If you have a small garden, try 'Viette's Little Suzy', a selection of *R. fulgida* var. *speciosa*. It behaves much like 'Goldsturm', but it's smaller; clumps reach about 12 to 14 inches. 'Little Goldstar' is compact, standing just knee-high, covered with a dome of closely spaced, starburst-shaped, 2- to 2½-inch, golden yellow blossoms. 'Goldquelle' has large, daisylike, double lemon yellow flowers with contrasting green centers that turn yellow with age.

Blanket Flower

Gaillardia x *grandiflora*

Botanical Pronunciation
gay-LAR-dee-uh gran-dih-FLOR-uh

Other Name
Gaillardia

Bloom Period and Seasonal Color
June into August; deep red edged-with-yellow flowers

Mature Height x Spread
1 foot x 1 to 1½ feet

Blanket flower is another of my favorite summer-blooming perennials. For a plant that only grows to 12 inches, it provides *tons* of color. The large showy flowers, which are maroon in the center with rays of red petals tipped with golden yellow, begin blooming in June and keep going into August. The vibrant colors reminded someone of a Native American blanket, and that is how it got its name. Blanket flower is tough too; it can survive in hot, dry, poor soil. If it has a flaw, it's that it tends to be short-lived. The selection 'Goblin' can live for many years in happy planting locations or as little as two years in so-so situations. Every yard has room for some of these colorful perennials.

When, Where, and How to Plant
Plant container-grown blanket flower in spring or early summer. Plants are available in 3-, 4-, and 6-inch pots and 1-gallon containers. Blanket flower will grow in all types of soil as long as it has very good drainage. You can even choose a planting site that's hot and dry, where other perennials will not grow. A full day to a half-day of sun is fine. For new plantings, loosen the existing soil to a depth of 6 to 8 inches. Dig a hole as deep and twice as wide as the soil clump. Loosen any wrapped roots, backfill, and water-in well to settle the soil.

Growing Tips
In spring, as your plants start to grow, give them some balanced fertilizer according to the package instructions. Blanket flower is drought tolerant, so you won't need to drag out your hose.

Regional Advice and Care
There are no bugs or diseases to bother blanket flower. When planted in rich garden soil, it may flop a little, though it will still be colorful. Plants stay more compact in average to poor soil (just make sure there's good drainage). Cut off spent flowers weekly to keep new blooms coming. Divide and transplant in spring as soon as new growth appears. Plant divisions at the same depth they were growing previously. Space on 12-inch centers.

Companion Planting and Design
Blanket flower looks great as a border for taller-growing annuals and perennials. The beautiful colors of the flowers make 'Goblin' a showpiece for any landscape. *Gaillardia* also works well mixed with other perennials, such as lavender, coreopsis, coneflower, and black-eyed Susans.

Try These
Try 'Baby Cole', a dwarf, growing only 6 to 8 inches with red daisylike flowers with yellow tips on the petals. If you prefer a solid-colored flower, 'Burgundy' has wine-red flowers and reaches a height of 2 to 3 feet. 'Mesa Peach' (peach-colored flowers dipped in golden yellow) and 'Yellow' (soft yellow flowers) have large, 3-inch daisylike flowers that bloom early and don't fade all season. 'Arizona Sun' has large, fiery red flowers edged with a ring of vivid yellow over a long bloom season.

Bleeding Heart

Dicentra spp. and hybrids

Botanical Pronunciation
dy-SEN-truh

Other Name
Valentine flower

Bloom Period and Seasonal Color
Spring through summer; pink, red, or white blooms

Mature Height x Spread
15 to 18 inches x 15 to 18 inches

The traditional bleeding heart, *Dicentra spectabilis*, is graceful and beautiful in bloom. The problem is its short bloom period—only a month in spring. *D.* 'Luxuriant', a well-known cultivar, is not quite as graceful, but it will bloom with arching 15-inch sprays of reddish pink, heart-shaped flowers from June until October. Now *that's* a long time! Its attractive foliage is deeply serrated, bluish green, and more finely textured than that of *D. spectabilis*. And it doesn't do a disappearing act. All varieties of bleeding hearts prefer a lightly shaded woodland atmosphere with rich, moist, well-drained soil. Have a heart, and plant one or many if you have the right location.

When, Where, and How to Plant
Plant new, nursery-grown bleeding hearts from 3- to 4-inch or 1-gallon containers from mid-March until fall. Smaller potted sizes will be most plentiful in April and May. Plant bleeding hearts in humus-rich soil that has good drainage, and in shade with good natural light. They tolerate morning sun, but *no afternoon sun*. Plant nursery-grown bleeding heart in a hole as deep as it was growing in the pots. Dig the hole twice as wide as the container, backfill, and water-in well to settle the soil. Mulch to conserve moisture.

Growing Tips
Fertilize with a timed-release fertilizer in spring, following the package instructions. Keep bleeding hearts watered during hot, dry days of summer, especially if they're planted among competing tree roots. Water about 1 to 2 inches once a week if there is no rain.

Regional Advice and Care
There are no bugs or diseases that bother bleeding hearts. They reseed themselves for additional plants the following spring. Transplant and divide existing bleeding hearts in early spring as new growth appears. When transplanting existing clumps of bleeding hearts, dig a clump at least 6 inches in diameter, and replant at the same depth it was growing originally.

Companion Planting and Design
'Luxuriant' is a great addition to any shady bed or woodland garden. It's a perfect complement to hostas. Common bleeding heart works best when planted in groups among evergreens and flowering shrubs. This plant will go dormant and "disappear" until next spring. That's why it's a good idea to plant bleeding heart with hostas, ferns, and other shade lovers to fill the void.

Try These
Who can resist the old-fashioned valentine flower? *D. spectabilis* is the common bleeding heart that has pink, heart-shaped flowers in midspring. This one grows 2 to 2½ feet tall by 1½ to 2 feet wide; its foliage dies back to the ground after blooming. *D. spectabilis* 'Alba' is the same, except it has white, heart-shaped flowers. 'King of Hearts' has clusters of cherry pink, heart-shaped flowers. 'Valentine', an old-fashioned favorite with a vibrant look, displays clusters of heart-shaped, deep red flowers from arching red stems over a long bloom season.

Cardinal Flower

Lobelia cardinalis

Botanical Pronunciation
low-BEE-lee-a kar-dih-NAL-iss

Bloom Period and Seasonal Color
July to September; brilliant red, purple blooms

Mature Height x Spread
36 to 40 inches x 24 inches

Cardinal flower can be seen from a quarter of a mile away. The brilliant red flowers are borne on single, tall, sturdy stems reaching up 3 feet or more. Unfortunately, cardinal flower is not suited for every home landscape. To see if yours qualifies, keep in mind that cardinal flower prefers partial shade, but will tolerate full sun if it's planted in great soil or if it's growing in the cooler summers of northern Ohio. The red color and size of its flowers may tempt you into trying some soon. One last tease—cardinal flower is a real attraction for hummingbirds. Even if you don't have the right spot for cardinal flower to live over winter, treat it like an annual and enjoy it for a single growing season.

When, Where, and How to Plant
Plant nursery-bought plants in spring. You will find cardinal flower available in 3-, 4-, and 6-inch pots. For most of Ohio, plant in a semi-shaded area; morning sun will do just fine. If you live in northern Ohio, full sun should be okay. Remember, cardinal flower spreads when happy, and it will need some room to spread. Find the most fertile soil site you have; most of us don't have the loamy soil that this plant wants, but you can add organic amendments to make a happier home for cardinal flower. Follow the instructions for planting perennials in this chapter's introduction.

Growing Tips
Cardinal flower prefers moist soil. Water when Mother Nature gets skimpy with her rainfall. ("Skimpy" would be a week without any rain.) A layer of mulch will help conserve moisture. Fertilize once with a balanced plant food as the plants start to grow in the spring. Read the instructions on the container to determine how much to use.

Regional Advice and Care
There are no bugs or diseases that bother cardinal flower. Divide established plants in early spring or early fall. Discard the old centers. Replant your transplants at the same depth they were growing originally. This plant readily reseeds itself, especially in moist areas of the garden.

Companion Planting and Design
Don't be afraid to try different cardinal flowers. The beautiful blooms are worth the effort. You could also plant these in containers, making sure the soil is good and the exposure works. Place the container in an unheated garage for winter. Be sure to water the container monthly over the winter. Go ahead, try it!

Try These
'Compliment Scarlet' (40 inches) is the beautiful red of the native cardinal flower. It resembles the wildflower, but it's a hybrid and therefore bigger and bolder. 'Vedrariensis' is another hybrid. This one has beautiful purple spikes that bloom from July into late September. The Fan series is a little more compact than most lobelias; its flower spikes are in 3 colors: 'Fan Deep Rose' (scarlet red), 'Fan Blue' (blue-violet) and 'Fan Burgundy' (red).

Catmint

Nepeta x faassenii

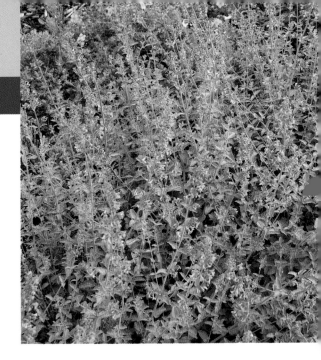

Botanical Pronunciation
NEP-eh-tah fah-SEEN-ee-eye

Bloom Period and Seasonal Color
May through early October; lavender-blue flowers

Mature Height x Spread
18 to 28 inches x 10 to 24 inches

This is a clump-forming perennial originally from Asia. This plant has very aromatic, lance-shaped leaves that are smooth and dark green. Flowers are in upright, whorled cymes and bloom from June through August. This plant is a great substitute for lavender as it's a lot better grower in some of Ohio's heavy clay soil. Older varieties of yesteryear were known to attract kitty cats but newer cultivars don't seem to have the same attraction. However some homeowners today might argue the point. Either way, it's a great plant. The lavender-to-blue trumpet-shaped flowers form a flower spike on the top of each stem. It blooms in late spring to early summer and will bloom again if you cut the plant halfway back after its initial bloom.

When, Where, and How to Plant
Potted or container plants can be planted anytime the ground isn't frozen. This plant does best when grown in full sun and well-drained soil. Space your plants on 18-inch centers for a full bed. Follow the planting instructions that are explained in the beginning of this chapter.

Growing Tips
Water this plant when the rain has been sparse. Take a garden trowel and dig down 3 inches around the plants roots to check for moisture. Take a sample of soil, place it in your hand, and squeeze. If the soil holds together, wait another day or so to add water. Catmint does not like wet feet. Fertilize in spring with a granular all-purpose plant food.

Regional Advice and Care
Select sterile and less aggressive varieties. They will offer all the beauty without you consistently trying to keep the plant within its allotted boundaries. There is no need to deadhead the spent flowers for a tidier appearance. If plants get tall, cut the plant back two-thirds after the first bloom. There are no pests that seem to bother this plant.

Companion Planting and Design
Plant taller-growing varieties towards the back of the bed. Mix in with other perennials that grow a little shorter in height that are listed in this chapter. Daylillies of different colors and bloom times go well with 'Walker's Low'.

Try These
'Walker's Low' grows 24 to 36 inches. The popular 'Six Hills Giant' grows to 30 inches and produces sterile seeds (that can be a good thing). 'Blue Cloud' and 'White Cloud' grow 15 inches tall and bloom as their names imply. Try 'Blue Wonder', with dark blue flowers, and 'Snowflake' with creamy white flowers.

Columbine

Aquilegia cultivars

Botanical Pronunciation
a-kwi-LEE-jee-a

Other Name
Granny's bonnet

Bloom Period and Seasonal Color
May into early June; red, white, yellow, blue, violet, and many bicolors blooms

Mature Height x Spread
1 to 3 feet x 1 to 2 feet

The graceful, spurred flowers of columbine hybrids add beautiful colors to any perennial bed. These hybrids grow best in well-drained, ordinary garden soil. The best color will come from growing in lots of sun, but columbine will disappear if that sunny location gets too hot. Columbine plants growing in part shade will stay around into late summer, though with fewer flowers. It's up to you. All columbine plants live for only two to three years, but don't despair—they reseed themselves, giving you more flowers, often with different color combinations. It's exciting to see what new color combinations you will get in May to early June. All are great attractions to hummingbirds. Check out the picture for a glimpse of this perennial.

When, Where, and How to Plant
Plant columbine hybrids in spring. Large, 1-gallon, container-grown plants will be available in late May, many of which will be in bloom. Columbines like full sun and well-drained soil. However, the bloom period will be longer—although with fewer flowers—if the hybrids get a little shade. The soil does not have to be extremely good. Columbine has a taproot, so loosen your garden soil fairly deep, about 8 to 10 inches. Dig a hole as deep and twice as wide as the soil clump. Loosen any wrapped roots, backfill the soil, and water-in well.

Growing Tips
Fertilize in spring, following the instructions on the container. Lightly mulch around the roots of columbine to help keep them cool during the summer. In an unusually dry spring, water your plants weekly as the soil dries.

Regional Advice and Care
If leafminers appear (you'll notice the winding trails on the leaves), remove the infected foliage and discard it. Columbine will produce more foliage. Hybrid columbines do not like to be divided or transplanted. Don't fret; you'll get lots of new ones from their self-sown seeds. These new plants will also give you bloom colors that, in some cases, you've never had before. If you enjoy these volunteer plants, do not use weed seed preventive in early spring in your beds that have columbine; it will kill the seed from last year's plants.

Companion Planting and Design
Plant columbine in groups of five, or plant it close to other perennials whose leaves will shade its roots. Columbine hybrids look great when mixed in a bed of other spring- and summer-blooming perennials.

Try These
'McKana Giant' hybrids (3 feet tall) are known for their large blooms of pastel, mixed-color flowers that last five to six weeks. The 'Music' hybrids (2 feet tall) have bicolor blooms of lavender, red, yellow, and white. The flowers last five to six weeks if given a little shade. They grow extremely well in average soil. A couple of newer varieties are the Songbird series and the Cameo series.

Coral Bells

Heuchera 'Palace Purple'

Botanical Pronunciation
HEW-ker-a

Other Name
Alumroot

Bloom Period and Seasonal Color
May to July; reddish purple foliage; creamy white blooms

Mature Height x Spread
1 to 1½ feet x 1½ feet

The perennial coral bells has been around for many years. *Heuchera sanguinea* is an old-time species, well known for its neat clumps of green leaves and for producing small, bell-shaped flowers on wiry stems from May into June. Then came 'Palace Purple' coral bells. Perennial growers and experts thought so much of it that 'Palace Purple' was pronounced a Plant of the Year by the Perennial Plant Association. This gorgeous plant has wonderful foliage; the leaves are metallic and dark reddish purple, making coral bells a highly desirable plant for the landscape all season long. The flowers it produces from May into July aren't showstoppers, but they are airy and delicate and make a nice addition to the foliage, which is what this plant is all about.

When, Where, and How to Plant
Plant container-grown coral bells in spring and summer. All coral bells want to be planted in average to good, well-drained soil. Coral bells tolerate full sun, but you will find 'Palace Purple' keeping its best summer leaf color where it gets relief from the hot afternoon summer sun. Turn to this chapter's introduction for planting specifics.

Growing Tips
Prevent new plants from drying out. Supply additional moisture to the roots during hot, dry weather, but do not keep them wet. When planting coral bells in hot sun, apply a 2-inch layer of shredded bark mulch around their roots, keeping the mulch off the plant stems. Fertilize with a slow-release garden fertilizer in spring.

Regional Advice and Care
There are no pests or diseases to bother 'Palace Purple'. Coral bells tends to grow upward on a woody plant center above the soil every few years. Dig up elevated clumps and remove the old growth. Replant the young plants that are growing with their own roots. Some gardeners remove the flowering stems to focus attention on the foliage. Transplant coral bells in early spring as the new growth starts to appear. Take divisions of at least 3 to 4 inches in diameter. Replant divisions at the same depth they enjoyed in their previous home.

Companion Planting and Design
Two great companions for 'Palace Purple' in partly shady areas are astilbe and hosta. 'Palace Purple' also makes a great landscape appearance when planted in clusters among foundation-type shrubs and evergreens. Remember, the leaves will grow a lot larger after planting than they appear in the garden store.

Try These
If you like 'Palace Purple', you'll like 'Chocolate Ruffles'. Its textured leaves are bronzy brown on top and burgundy underneath. Colorful foliage is great but don't forget that coral bells' blooms can also bring a lot of color to the garden. 'Bressingham' hybrids have shiny leaves and red, pink, coral, or white flowers on spikes that bloom in early summer. There are several new varieties: 'Apple Crisp', 'Caramel', 'Fire Chief', 'Georgia Peach', 'Lime Marmalade', 'Miracle', 'Mocha', 'Peach Flambe', and 'Southern Comfort'.

Coreopsis

Coreopsis verticillata 'Moonbeam'

Botanical Pronunciation
kor-ee-OP-sis ver-ti-si-LAH-tuh

Other Name Tickseed

Bloom Period and Seasonal Color
June to frost; yellow blooms

Mature Height x Spread
1½ to 2 feet x 1½ feet

Now here is a perennial that knows how to bloom during the summer. Starting in June, 'Moonbeam' coreopsis is covered with thousands of soft yellow, daisylike flowers—and they just keep on coming! It is no surprise that the Perennial Plant Association (founded by Dr. Steven Still of Columbus) named 'Moonbeam' as one of the first winners of the Perennial Plant of the Year designation. Of course, to win the award a plant has to offer more than just flowers and 'Moonbeam' certainly does that. This plant has fine, ferny, almost threadlike foliage and a very neat mounding habit. It doesn't succumb to disease or attract pests, it requires very little watering, it's easy to divide—hey, it even has winter interest. This plant deserves more awards.

When, Where, and How to Plant

Plant container-grown coreopsis in spring or summer. 'Moonbeam' will grow in any kind of soil that drains well. Hot, dry, sunny locations produce many flowers. 'Moonbeam' will also perform well in a half-day of shade. Follow the general instructions for planting in this chapter's introduction.

Growing Tips

Once established, 'Moonbeam' coreopsis needs little care. It is very drought tolerant—don't worry about watering unless we hit a period of drought, then water. It needs no special fertilizing regime.

Regional Advice and Care

'Moonbeam' is not susceptible to any bugs or diseases. You can maintain its height by trimming it back to 8 inches after each bloom period finishes. Trim back, and more blooms will cover the plant again in three to four weeks. Use a hedge shear to prune. Most threadleaf coreopsis should be divided and replanted every three to four years. 'Moonbeam' needs less frequent division. If you notice that more of the blooms are coming from the outside of the clump, discard the center and replant the outside portions toward the inside of the clump. Divide in spring when the ferny growth starts to appear. Make each clump at least 6 inches in diameter. Replant your transplant clumps at the same depth they were growing originally.

Companion Planting and Design

Plant 'Moonbeam' in any bed or border that needs yellow blooms, whether it fills the bed or is used as the front. Good companion plants are purple coneflower, Stokes' aster, and gayfeather. Use it around low-growing, spring-flowering perennials—such as creeping phlox—that tend to disappear when the weather turns hot.

Try These

'Zagreb' is similar to 'Moonbeam', except it grows lower and has golden yellow flowers. It is less of a clump-former and more of a spreader. There are other types of coreopsis that provide lots of color. I like 'Sunray', a selection of *Coreopsis grandiflora* that grows 2 to 3 feet tall and has 2-inch golden yellow flowers. It blooms forever and is nice with annuals or perennials. There are several newer varieties: 'Route 66', 'Crème Brulee', 'Mercury Rising', 'Jethro Tull', and 'Sienna Sunset'.

Cranesbill Geranium

Geranium sanguineum

Botanical Pronunciation
jer-AY-nee-um san-GWIN-ee-um

Other Name Perennial geranium

Bloom Period and Seasonal Color
Mid-spring through summer; blue or lavender

Mature Height x Spread
8 to 12 iches x 18 inches wide

This geranium family member of perennials is very underused because homeowners don't know of it and its value to a landscape. It has a long-lasting bloom period, from April through June, and is available in several bloom color choices. This plant has very attractive foliage. Between the foliage and bloom color, this plant makes an excellent showing as a border plant or a row lining the top of a garden wall. The seedheads of the finished flowers resemble a crane's bill, hence this plant's common name. Cranesbill geranium also has beautiful red fall leaf color that can last well into winter. Some of the newer varieties will tolerate summer's heat and bloom into late summer. This plant can be considered a groundcover in partial shade to full sun.

When, Where, and How to Plant
Cranesbill is available in early spring in 4- to 6-inch pots and 1-gallon containers. These are available all spring and can be planted anytime the ground is not frozen. Perennial geraniums grow best in full sun to partial shade in locations with well-drained soil. Once your plants are established they become very drought tolerant. Refer to planting know-how at the introduction to this chapter.

Growing Tips
When checking for soil dryness, use a garden trowel and dig down 3 inches around the soil clump. If it's moist, wait a day or two. Overwatering on any plant is a lot worse than underwatering. Feed with a "start and grow" (a timed-release) fertilizer that will slowly feed your plants for the rest of the season.

Regional Advice and Care
Spent flowers self-clean, no pinching off of old blooms. These geraniums are considered very low maintenance. After a few weeks of bloom, your geraniums might start to look a little garden weary, showing some yellow leaves and sparse bloom. At this point take some garden or hedge shears and cut all your plants back to a few inches from the ground. This is an easy plant to grow; it does not attract pests or have any problems.

Companion Planting and Design
Mix with other low-growing perennials in a rock garden or in a mixed, low-growing perennial bed. You could also interplant with some low-growing annuals for lots of color the remainder of the growing season. Cranesbill geraniums make great border plants that will really accent a perennial bed.

Try These
'Max Frei' has a longer blooming season on a plant that grows 8 inches high. 'Rozanne' has large cup-shaped, deep blue flowers that will tolerate our summer heat and bloom all summer. 'Dark Reiter' has dark purple dissected foliage with lavender flowers.

Daylily

Hemerocallis hybrids

Botanical Pronunciation
hem-er-oh-KAL-iss

Other Name
Hybrid daylily

Bloom Period and Seasonal Color
June until October; the color choices are huge

Mature Height x Spread
1 to 3 feet (by variety) x 2 to 3 feet

Did you know that daylilies are not true lilies at all? Although they are in the lily family of Liliaceae, they get their common name because the flowers resemble true lilies and each individual flower blooms for a day. Rumor has it that there are over 40,000 named varieties of daylilies (now tell me if you can't find one to please you). There are countless flower colors and forms—some are double, some are ruffled, and some are fragrant. There are short, tall, and medium-height daylilies. Talk about low maintenance; these plants grow completely on their own. New dwarf selections have come along over the last dozen years. Some of the best of these are also repeat bloomers. Such cultivated varieties as 'Stella d'Oro' and 'Happy Returns' will spot-bloom from June to October. More varieties are on their way.

When, Where, and How to Plant
Plant container-grown daylilies anytime during the growing season. Daylilies grow in any type of well-draining soil. Plant in lots of sun, although my own daylilies get only four hours of sun and bloom very well. Loosen the existing soil to a depth of 6 to 8 inches. With new plantings, dig a hole as deep and twice as wide as the soil clump. Loosen any wrapped roots. Backfill, and water-in well. Space about 2 feet apart.

Growing Tips
Daylilies are very drought tolerant, but if you have time, water plants during extended dry spells. Fertilize in the spring with a balanced plant food, following the package instructions. Feed repeat bloomers again in early summer.

Regional Advice and Care
There isn't any bug that bothers daylilies. Remove spent flower stems on your repeat blooming daylilies as soon as they finish to keep them flowering several more times each season. With all the rest of the one-time blooming daylilies, cut off the spent flowers and all the leaves back to the ground. This will cause all the one timers to bloom again this fall. Try it—it works! Divide all daylilies as the new growth emerges in early spring. Make sure the new divisions are at least 6 inches in diameter.

Companion Planting and Design
Daylilies create a beautiful transition between the lawn and woodsy, natural areas. They also look great in mass groups in and among groups of evergreens. Daylilies will grow in shade; don't expect as many flowers, but the foliage will act as a tall groundcover.

Try These
There are many daylily varieties for you to choose from. Here are some good repeat bloomers: The popular choice is 'Stella d'Oro' with gold flowers on 1-foot stems. 'Happy Returns' has lemon yellow flowers on 1½-foot stems; the flowers are small and ruffled. 'Little Business' has raspberry-red flowers on 1-foot stems. 'Pardon Me' is a newer variety to try.

English Lavender

Lavandula angustifolia

Botanical Pronunciation
lav-AN-dew-lah an-gus-tee-FOH-lee-uh

Other Name
Lavender

Bloom Period and Seasonal Color
June to August; lavender, blue, pink blooms

Mature Height x Spread
1 ½ to 2 feet x 1 ½ to 2 feet

Lavender has been a perennial that, in the past, was known more widely as an herb. Its biggest contribution was for its special fragrance used in sachets and potpourris. But then came 'Hidcote', and now this herb is a hard-working and beautiful garden perennial. 'Hidcote' is a compact grower (12 to 15 inches tall) with gray-green foliage and slender, deep purple-blue flower spikes. It blooms for about eight weeks. All lavender prefers a sunny location and average soil that drains very well, both in the growing season and in winter. Lavender grows well in alkaline soil, which is good news for most of us in Ohio. English lavender can withstand the heat of summer too. Just don't water it too much during the hot, dry summer. The roots prefer to remain on the dry side.

When, Where, and How to Plant
Plant lavender anytime the plants are available in spring, summer, or early fall. Lavender is a tough plant that does well in dry soil. Too much moisture, either from rain or from irrigation, can be its enemy. If you have lots of winter snow, make sure the soil in which you plant your lavender has good drainage. Plant in areas of full sun for best growth and bloom—but it will perform well with only five hours of sun. Space plants 2 feet apart. Follow the general guidelines for planting in this chapter's introduction.

Growing Tips
Lavender is very drought tolerant and will need very little watering. Do not fertilize this plant; it grows very well in average soil.

Regional Advice and Care
Pests aren't a problem, and good drainage should eliminate any disease concerns. In poorly drained sites, lavender may succumb to root rot. Lavender will appear almost as an evergreen, suffering very little dieback in the winter, unlike other perennials. Prune all the stems back to about 6 to 8 inches in early spring every year or two to promote more compact growth. Shear back the old flowering stalks whenever you find them unattractive. Lavender is essentially a small woody shrub, so division isn't recommended. If you need to transplant a clump, do it in spring.

Companion Planting and Design
Lavender is a wonderful plant to place near a patio, and it makes a great edger plant. Try it along a sunny brick or stone walk or as a border for a rose bed. If you have raised beds installed to improve drainage, it will prosper there.

Try These
'Hidcote' is probably the best and the hardiest, but if you love lavender, try one of these others. 'Munstead' is dwarf, growing to 15 inches tall and wide. 'Jean Davis' has light pink flowers and bluish leaves. It grows to 18 inches tall and wide, blooming in summer and again in late fall. 'Rosea' has soft pink flowers on 15-inch stems. Some newer varieties to try are 'Blue Cushion', 'Dilly Dilly', and 'Provence'.

Forget-Me-Not

Myosotis scorpioides cultivars

Botanical Pronunciation
my-oh-SO-tis skor-pee-OY-dees

Bloom Period and Seasonal Color
Late May until fall; blue flowers

Mature Height x Spread
6 to 10 inches x 18 to 24 inches

Don't forget about forget-me-nots. Forget-me-nots could be the perfect plant for that damp-to-wet area in which other perennials fail to grow. As you read about the many cultivars of perennials in this chapter, you will notice one common denominator: almost all the other perennials mentioned want good soil drainage regardless of soil type. Well, forget-me-nots are the exception to that rule. They want to grow in soil that is well moistened and never dries out, along a stream, pond, or low area that tends to have gravel mixed in with the soil. Most landscapes don't have this kind of situation, but if you have an area that stays wet and other types of plants have not fared well in it, try forget-me-nots.

When, Where, and How to Plant
Plant forget-me-nots in spring from plants growing in 3-, 4-, or 6-inch pots. Moist, sunny or shady areas of the landscape are best. Loosen the existing soil to a depth of 6 to 8 inches. Dig a hole as deep and twice as wide as the soilball. Loosen any roots wrapped around the soilball, backfill, and water-in well to settle the soil. Remember, forget-me-nots grow very low to the ground, bloom for a long period of time, and quickly cover the ground like a blanket with beautiful blue flowers.

Growing Tips
Forget-me-nots grow best in a woodland garden near a water source—this could be moisture that you provide through a sprinkler. Water plants when rain is inadequate to keep the soil moist. Apply

fertilizer to the plants as they start to grow in spring. Follow the instructions on the container to determine how much to use.

Regional Advice and Care
If allowed to stress because of insufficient water, mildew and mites could pose a problem. Transplant existing forget-me-nots in spring as the new leaves start to appear. Transplant divisions of existing forget-me-nots that are at least 6 inches in diameter. Replant existing transplants at the same depth and planting conditions from which they came.

Companion Planting and Design
A woodland garden is the ideal spot, especially if you have a stream, pond, or other water feature. Forget-me-nots mix well with hardy ferns, hostas, and primrose. When planted in a happy spot, they will grow and prosper for many years. Planting forget-me-nots on the edge of a woodland, or in other shady areas with good sky light, will give you a beautiful carpet of blue flowers.

Try These
'Semperflorens' is a great variety to plant; it begins flowering in May and its blooms last into August. It's very compact-growing too. *Myosotis sylvatica*, commonly called woodland forget-me-not, is more tolerant of dry soil conditions; the parent plant may not winter over, but don't worry—it reseeds itself quite readily.

Garden Mum

Chrysanthemum x *morifolium*

Botanical Pronunciation
kris-AN-theh-mum mor-ih-FOE-lee-um

Other Name
Hardy mum

Bloom Period and Seasonal Color
August to late October; yellow, bronze, purple, white, red, pink, lavender, orange blooms

Mature Height x Spread
1 to 3 feet x 2 feet

True garden mums bloom in the fall, not summer. The common denominator of the whole group is the fact that all chrysanthemums like full sun, good drainage, and having their spent flowers removed, thus prolonging the bloom period. Fall mums start blooming in August and their blooms can continue until November. Fall mums are frost proof—don't worry about covering those beautiful flowers when temps dip into the freeze zone. Garden mums look like green veggies in the spring and summer. I recommend growing your mums in a sunny, out-of-the-way location—then transplanting them in the fall into a sunny, in-your-face location so they can show off all that color. Leave in the new location until spring. Then transplant them back to their out-of-the-way growing spot until next fall.

When, Where, and How to Plant

Plant garden mums in spring or in late summer to fall. Choose locations in average garden soil that drain well. Garden mums should at least get morning sun; full sun is best. To plant, loosen the existing soil to a depth of 6 to 8 inches. Remove the mum from its container, loosen any wrapped roots, and plant in a hole as deep and twice as wide as the soil clump. Backfill and water-in well.

Growing Tips

If soaking rains are scarce, provide water for your mums to keep moisture in the soil. Fertilize with a general or slow-release garden fertilizer, following the package directions.

Regional Advice and Care

There are no bugs or diseases that will attack your garden mums. Keep mums pinched—by that I mean keep them short—until the middle of July. If you want your mums to bloom at 18 inches tall, keep them pinched back to 12 inches until mid-July. You can count on another 6 inches of growth until they form bloom buds. If you want your mums taller, follow the same math. Remove spent flowers to allow secondary buds to bloom. Divide mums in spring as they start to grow. Plant transplants as deep as they were growing in their previous location; dig transplant clumps that are at least 6 inches in diameter.

Companion Planting and Design

Great summer companion plants for fall mums are cosmos, black-eyed Susans, and Shasta daisies. These summer bloomers will give a mixed bed lots of color until the mums kick in.

My Personal Favorite

There are *hundreds* of mums; it's virtually impossible to pick one favorite. Make sure you buy plants that are hardy. Mums from florists, usually called pot mums, have very large blooms and are usually not hardy in Ohio. These mums, if received in bloom in spring, can be planted outside and will bloom again in fall. They are not winter hardy, however, and usually don't winter over.

Gaura

Gaura lindheimeri

Botanical Pronunciation
GOW-ra lind-HY-mer-ee

Other Name
Whirling butterflies

Bloom Period and Seasonal Color
July into August; white fading to pink blooms

Mature Height x Spread
3 to 4 feet x 2 feet

I was introduced to this perennial several years ago. I had heard of it, but didn't connect one of its common names—whirling butterflies—to its appearance. Then I saw it and said, "Wow, it does look like small butterflies on top of that plant." It is a heat- and humidity-tolerant plant, and it grows well without needing the water hose. Gaura is a great plant to use on sunny hillsides that are difficult to water; it will turn such a planting situation into a picture worth taking. In the wind, it's a joy for kids of all ages to watch as it spins. Keep gaura blooming longer by cutting off the spent flowers. It's no big deal . . . just do it every couple of weeks.

When, Where, and How to Plant
Plant gaura in spring and summer. If you are not sure about this one, wait and buy it in 1-gallon containers in July when it's in bloom. If you like its looks, as I do, plant it and enjoy. Plant these whirligigs in full sun. This perennial grows in all types of well-drained Ohio soil. Dig a hole as deep and twice as wide as the soil clump. Loosen any wrapped roots and plant. Backfill with the existing soil, and water-in well. Use mulch to cover the soil to 2 inches, but don't let the mulch come in contact with the plant stems.

Growing Tips
Whirling butterflies is easy to grow and is also drought tolerant, though it wouldn't hurt to give it a little water during drought. Fertilize when the plant first starts growing in spring. Read the instructions and fertilize according to the directions on the container.

Regional Advice and Care
Whirling butterflies is largely free of disease and insects. Remove the flowering stalks as they are spent to increase bloom. Gaura grows from a taproot so it is difficult to move or transplant.

Companion Planting and Design
The blooms of whirling butterflies really do dance in the wind like butterflies. Plant in groups of three to five plants to get the full effect of this summer-blooming perennial. Plant where you can observe it from both outside and inside the house, in a solid bed, or mixed with other perennials. Try whirling butterflies with 'Autumn Joy' sedum and fountain grass.

Try These
Many gaura cultivars are hitting the garden market-place, most offering pink flowers. The first was 'Siskiyou Pink' (3 to 4 feet). 'Crimson Butterflies' is only 15 inches high and has pink flowers and crimson foliage. All of the new guys are heat- and drought-tolerant plants, but not all are perfectly hardy. Gardeners in Zone 5 areas of Ohio may have trouble overwintering these plants.

Gayfeather

Liatris spicata

Botanical Pronunciation
ly-AT-riss spi-KAH-tuh

Other Name
Blazing star

Bloom Period and Seasonal Color
July to September; rosy purple, purple, white flowers

Mature Height x Spread
1 to 3 feet x 2 feet

An Ohio native, gayfeather, also called blazing star, is a perennial accustomed to the harsh temperature swings of the Midwest. It can take very cold winters and very hot summers; it will also give you loads of rosy purple vertical spires from July into September. It starts to grow with grassy-looking leaves that form short clumps of growth. Then, in July, a leafy flower spike pushes upwards from the center of the plant. When the spike reaches its top height, green buds form and start to open from the top of the flower bud down, producing rosy purple, fuzzy flowers. In full bloom, the flower spikes resemble a bottlebrush. Blazing star is care-free even in so-so soil. It also attracts butterflies and makes an excellent cut flower.

When, Where, and How to Plant
Plant gayfeather anytime the plants are available. For the best results, choose locations with moist, well-drained soil. It prefers fertile to average soil, but will tolerate average to poor soil. It grows best in full sun, although you can have nice plants and good bloom with five to six hours of morning sun. To plant, refer to the directions in this chapter's introduction.

Growing Tips
Fertilize early each spring with an all-purpose fertilizer as new growth appears, following the instructions on the container. In fertile soils, fertilization is unnecessary. Water during dry spells, enough to keep the soil moist, not wet. Mulch will help keep the soil moist.

Regional Advice and Care
There is no major pest problem with gayfeather. Mildew can attack during hot, humid weather. When this type of weather exists, water the soil when it's dry to eliminate moisture stress. Prune off spent flower spikes to encourage more flowering spikes. Tall plants may need staking. Divide existing gayfeather in early fall. Lift and separate the corms and replant on 12- to 15-inch centers. Replant your divisions in their new home at the same depth at which they were growing originally.

Companion Planting and Design
Gayfeather has quite a vertical impact when planted in groups of nine to twelve plants. It also blends in well with other perennials in a mixed bed. Combine it with plants such as 'Moonbeam' coreopsis, yarrow, *Artemisia* 'Silver Mound', and white-blooming summer phlox.

Try These
The species can get too tall and require staking, so the best choice for the garden is 'Kobold'. This selection has rosy lavender-purple spikes of bloom growing 1½ to 2 feet tall and wide. It blooms July through August and does best in full sun. If you have an informal meadow garden and you like butterflies, try the meadow blazing star, *Liatris ligulistylis* (3 to 5 feet). A favorite of monarchs and goldfinches, it has long-lasting, rosy lavender flowers that bloom from August into September.

Hellebore

Helleborus orientalis

Botanical Pronunciation
hel-eh-BORE-us or-ee-en-TAY-liss

Other Name Lenten rose

Bloom Period and Seasonal Color
Late winter to early spring; pink, white, purple, yellow, red, green blooms

Mature Height x Spread
15 to 18 inches x 15 inches

A plant I truly love and one that is finally growing on the hearts of homeowners is a plant known as hellebore. It has evergreen foliage and an extended bloom period. Add low maintenance to its list of positives and you too will see why this is a great addition to any landscape. As delicate as the plant seems, hellebores can survive severe heat and drought. The colorful parts of the flower are actually sepals, the outer covering of any flower. With traditional hellebore, the sepals are facing downward. Newer cultivars and hybrids are being introduced with upright and outward-facing "flowers" in a variety of colors. This plant is a must for any landscape. It will be easy to find the perfect spot in the garden.

When, Where, and How to Plant
Always buy your hellebores in pots of any size whose plants are already root established. Plant these anytime during the year, when the ground is not frozen. Pick a spot for your hellebores in full to partial shade in moist, well-amended soil. Space plants 12 to 15 inches apart. These plants are available in a variety of colors. Young starter plants may not bloom the first year after planting. **Note:** Plant hellebores in areas not convenient to children as the plant can be considered poisonous.

Growing Tips
Water plants when the soil is dry to keep the roots moist. Established plants that have been installed for one or more years will be drought tolerant, as will larger transplants; not only will they provide bloom but will be drought tolerant as well. Fertilize in the spring with a slow-release fertilizer such as a start and grow type.

Regional Advice and Care
Hellebores' evergreen foliage is tender and may tatter or scorch during severe cold winters. If air circulation is poor plants could develop blackspot. The same holds true with crown rot if the plants are growing in extreme wet weather and poorly drained soils. Divide established plants in early spring taking clumps at least 8 to 10 inches in diameter.

Companion Planting and Design
Plant these plants around the base of shrubs growing in shady areas. Combine with other shade-loving perennials for extended flower color to the shady bed.

Try These
Helleborus niger (Christmas rose) is white with pink-tinged flowers appearing earlier than the Lenten rose. Grow it in a protected spot away from prevailing west winds so you can enjoy the early blooms. 'Pink Frost' has upward-facing flowers in shades of pink, white, or rose. Winter Jewels™ series are vigorous growing plants with lots of color choices.

Hibiscus

Hibiscus moscheutos hybrids and cultivars

Botanical Pronunciation
hi-BIS-kus mos-KEW-tos

Other Name
Rose mallow

Bloom Period and Seasonal Color
July to October; red, pink, white blooms

Mature Height x Spread
3 to 6 feet x 4 to 5 feet

When we hear the name hibiscus, most of us think of Hawaii—not Ohio—and those tropical plants with showy flowers and glossy leaves that have to be kept indoors during the winter. But there is another kind of hibiscus. And believe it or not, these hibiscus hybrids are even showier than the tropicals. This hardy perennial reaches shrublike proportions growing 3 to 6 feet tall depending on the selection. The exotic flowers are huge—the size of a dinner plate—and come in shades of crimson, pink, or white. You may read in other books that hibiscus likes consistently moist soil, but don't worry. I know from experience that hibiscus is fairly drought tolerant and will do just fine in ordinary Ohio garden soil.

When, Where, and How to Plant
Plant container-grown hibiscus in mid- to late spring. Choose locations with good to average soil. Rose mallow is native to marshy situations and prefers consistently moist soil, but once established in the garden it tolerates some drought. It does well in full sun, as well as areas receiving only three to four hours of sun. Plant in areas away from the wind, which can damage the large flowers. Loosen the existing soil to a depth of 8 to 10 inches. Space plants 3 to 4 feet apart. Turn to this chapter's introduction for more specifics on planting.

Growing Tips
Fertilize your hibiscus with any all-purpose fertilizer in spring as new growth appears. Water new plantings the first year; after that, your plants should be able to go it alone. Mulch during the summer heat to help retain soil moisture around the plants.

Regional Advice and Care
Don't worry about any pests or diseases on this guy. You may wish to groom your plants by removing flowers as they pass. To improve the winter look in your landscape, cut back hibiscus to the ground. Mark the spot where it is, so you don't accidentally plant something else there next spring. Don't laugh! As far as I know, hibiscus is the last perennial to start to grow, and you may not see signs of new growth until mid-May. Hibiscus can be divided in spring, but on a mature clump this is a major undertaking.

Companion Planting and Design
Use this plant's shrublike appearance to make a real color statement in your landscape. Plant several hibiscus in a cluster, and plant variegated maiden grass to the rear. This combination is rich and colorful.

Try These
'Southern Belle' (3 to 5 feet tall) blooms in white, rose, red, or pink, with most having a red eye in the center of each flower. The blooms of 'Lord Baltimore' (4 to 5 feet) are a pinkish red and average 7 to 10 inches in diameter.

Hosta

Hosta spp. and hybrids

Botanical Pronunciation
HOSS-tuh

Other Name
Plantain lily

Bloom Period and Seasonal Color
July into September; grown primarily for
attractive foliage; white or lavender blooms

Mature Height x Spread
6 to 48 inches x 1 to 4 feet

Hostas! They are, in my estimation, the most popular perennial around. This is amazing, considering they are not known for any flower. It's the leaf that is appealing to so many. Hostas come in many shades of green and many combinations of variegation. Hostas also come in all growing sizes, with some as small as 6 inches and others growing to 48 inches tall and wide. Perhaps the real reason hostas are so popular is fact that they are so easy to grow. You would have to try hard to kill a hosta. All hostas do well in shade, with the variegated types tolerating morning sun and green-leafed varieties growing in full sun. Hostas do have lavender or white flowers that appear in late summer.

When, Where, and How to Plant
Plant new hostas anytime plants are available; the best selections will be in spring and summer. All hostas perform well in medium shade to morning sun. Some varieties, especially those having yellow in their leaves, need some morning sun for good leaf color; varieties that have blue leaves prefer less sun. Moist, well-drained, fertile soil is ideal, but hostas adapt; good drainage is important. Planting tips can be found in this chapter's introduction.

Growing Tips
Keep soil moist during hot weather. Mulch hostas 2 inches deep with a high-quality shredded bark mulch. Fertilize with a timed-release plant food, following the instructions on the container. To discourage deer, apply an application of Milorganite around your hostas in October and again in March.

The deer don't like the odor but you won't mind; the aroma is non-offensive to us and it feeds your plants too!

Regional Advice and Care
Slugs and snails *love* hosta leaves, especially during wet weather. Use organic diotomaceous earth or slug bait to combat them. Deer also find hostas very tasty. Spray your hosta leaves monthly with a bitter-tasting substance found in some deer repellent products. Divide and transplant hostas in early spring, as the leaves just start to grow. Take clumps that are at least 6 inches in diameter. When transplanting, replant the clumps no deeper than they were growing in their previous home.

Companion Planting and Design
If you've got shade, you've got a 101 ways to use hostas. They perform well as edgers, groundcovers, in foundation beds, and in drifts with other perennials. Large hostas make dramatic accents and work well in containers.

Try These
Wow, I have a lot of favorites. 'Aphrodite' has deep green, large leaves with extremely fragrant flowers that are wonderful as cut flowers; this double-flowering hosta is one of my all-time favorites. 'Krossa Regal' has blue-green leaves with lavender flowers on a plant that grows 3 feet tall and wide. 'Gold Standard' has gold leaves with green edges.

Ligularia

Ligularia spp.

Botanical Pronunciation
lig-yoo-LAR-ee-uh

Other Name
Ragwort

Bloom Period and Seasonal Color
June through August; blooms in deep orange-yellow to yellow (by variety)

Mature Height x Spread
3 to 5 feet x 2 to 4 feet

Now here is a summer-blooming perennial that is great for areas where you have found it difficult to add perennial color and foliage interest. Ligularia is a shade-loving plant that comes in several varieties, offering a choice of leaf size and color as well as bloom color choices from yellow to bright orange. Leaf size varies with the variety, but all ligularia leaves are considered large, bold, and beautiful. Ligularia varieties grow between 3 and 5 feet tall and can spread to 4 feet. Plant under shade trees, around garden pools, or in other shady to morning sun areas where they have some room to spread. A great perennial for all of Ohio and one that will have your neighbors asking, "Hey, what's that neat-looking plant?"

When, Where, and How to Plant
Plant container-grown ligularia in spring or summer. It prefers moist, but not wet, locations that get all day shade or morning sun, but no hot afternoon sun. Strong sun causes the foliage to wilt and look terrible. Prepare the planting site by loosening the existing soil to a depth of 8 to 10 inches. Space plants 3 to 4 feet apart—even though that may appear too far apart at first. Turn to this chapter's introduction for more details on planting.

Growing Tips
Because ligularia has large broad leaves, they lose a lot of water through those leaves. If it's particularly hot during the summer, the leaves will wilt and then perk up in the evening. Cool and moist are the key words—no other care is required, not even fertilizer or dividing unless you want more plants.

Regional Advice and Care
Slugs can make a few holes in the leaves in the spring, but there are plenty of slug baits to take care of them. Ligularia doesn't grow particularly fast, but its clumps do get larger. Divide in spring, as it starts to grow, about every three years or when it expands beyond its location. Occasionally remove old leaves to keep it looking neat.

Companion Planting and Design
Any shade-loving annual or perennial mixes well with ligularia, including astilbe, large-leafed hosta, coral bells, and bleeding heart. Just be sure your companion plants grow large enough to not get buried by the ligularia.

Try These
Ligularia stenocephala 'The Rocket' grows dramatic 5-foot spires of bright golden yellow flowers from June through July; foliage grows 4 to 5 feet high and 2 to 4 feet wide. *L. dentata* 'Othello' offers purple leaves with golden daisylike flowers from midsummer to fall; it grows 3 to 4 feet high and 2 to 4 feet wide. *L. dentata* 'Britt Marie Crawford' has deep orange-yellow flowers in midsummer and dark, glossy, chocolate-maroon leaf tops with dark purple on the undersides; it grows 3½ feet high and 2½ feet wide. A couple of others to try are 'Little Rocket' and 'Midnight Lady'.

Peony

Paeonia hybrids

Botanical Pronunciation
pay-OHN-ee-uh

Other Name
Garden peony

Bloom Period and Seasonal Color
Late May into June; white, pink, crimson-red, or bicolor blooms

Mature Height x Spread
2 to 3 feet x 2 to 3 feet

A peony plant is capable of living 100 years or more. How's that for a hardy perennial! To maximize the life and happiness of your peonies, you must dig a ten-dollar hole for a three-dollar plant—peonies want to be planted in a large, oversized hole located in full sun. Get them off to the right start, and you'll be enjoying the sumptuous blooms for decades. Many cultivars (there are over 900) have large double flowers that bloom in white, pink, red, or bicolor. Peonies bloom sometime during early midsummer. Ants in your pants can be bothersome, but ants on your peony buds are nothing to worry about. They like the sweet sap that bleeds from the tight flower buds, but they cause no harm.

When, Where, and How to Plant

Plant container-grown peonies in spring or early summer. Try to plant peonies in full sun. They will bloom in partial shade, but too much shade can mean no flowers. Peonies grow in average, well-drained soil, but they reach their maximum height when placed in an oversized hole and backfilled with soil that's been improved by adding rotted manure, organic peat, compost, and bonemeal. For new plants, dig a hole 18 inches wide and deep. Amend existing soil as mentioned Be sure to plant the points, or eyes, no more than 1 inch deep. The most common reason peonies never bloom is that they're planted too deep. Backfill with the amended soil and water-in well.

Growing Tips

Fertilize in spring with a balanced fertilizer following label directions. Peonies appreciate a drink of water during dry spells. Place a peony metal ring or the top half of a tomato cage around your peony as it starts to grow. This will keep peonies from flopping over when those large blooms get wet.

Regional Advice and Care

In general peonies are tough and pest- and disease-free. They are susceptible to a disease called *botrytis*. To avoid problems, cut back foliage in fall and remove it. Divide and replant existing peonies in early fall or in early spring. Be sure each new division has at least three growing points, or eyes. When relocating transplants, plant the clumps no deeper than they were growing in their old home.

Companion Planting and Design

Plant in mixed beds with other perennials or shrubs, or plant them by themselves out in the open lawn.

Try These

If I had to pick one . . . can I pick two? 'Bowl of Beauty' (32 inches tall) *is* a thing of beauty. The sumptuous flowers have fuchsia-pink outer petals filled with a ruff of creamy white petals often flecked with pink. Another favorite is 'Rubra Plena' (18 to 24 inches), an heirloom variety sometimes called the Memorial Day peony. It always attracts attention for its early blooming time and its double, dark red flowers.

Phlox

Phlox paniculata

Botanical Pronunciation
FLOKS pan-ick-yoo-LAY-tuh

Other Name
Garden phlox

Bloom Period and Seasonal Color
July to September; red, pink, white, rose, lilac, orange flowers, some with colored eye zones

Mature Height x Spread
3 to 4 feet x 2 to 3 feet

Summer-blooming garden phlox comes into flower in white, rose, pink, blue, purple, lavender, orange, red, and combinations of these colors with dark-colored eyes. You won't get a better choice even when buying ice cream. *Phlox paniculata* is sometimes referred to as summer phlox because no perennial brings so much color to the summer border. Each flower head is made up of small florets that form a huge rounded cluster measuring up to 6 inches tall and wide—now that's large and showy! An unsightly foliar disease called powdery mildew can be a problem, but hybridizers have really done a great job with summer phlox, making them not only more colorful, but also more disease resistant. When given good air circulation, cultivars such as 'David' will be mildew-free.

When, Where, and How to Plant
Plant container-grown phlox anytime during the growing season. Phlox likes full sun. If such a site is not available, choose morning sun over afternoon sun. Phlox will grow in all types of soil as long as there's good drainage. With new plants, loosen the existing soil to a depth of 6 to 8 inches. Add a little organic material if your soil is on the clay side. To plant, follow the directions in this chapter's introduction. Plant new or transplanted phlox on 2-foot centers.

Growing Tips
Phlox is fairly drought tolerant, but do water once a week during the hot, dry periods of summer. Maintaining even soil moisture and exposing your phlox plants to good air movement will reduce the risk of mildew on the leaves. Feed your phlox with a timed-release fertilizer in spring.

Regional Advice and Care
Mildew does not cause serious health problems for the phlox, but it certainly makes the plant look bad. Planting resistant selections and following the watering advice given here will minimize the risk. There are no other problems or bugs to . . . bug it. Deadhead plants to avoid self-sowing. Phlox needs to be divided every three to four years. Dig clumps in spring and make new divisions at least 4 inches in diameter. Replant transplants at the same depth they were growing previously. Enrich the soil with organic matter before planting divisions.

Companion Planting and Design
Tall phlox makes quite a colorful statement in the landscape. Use it in a mixed perennial bed with other summer-flowering perennials, such as gay-feather, Stokes' asters, and veronica.

Try These
'David' is mildew-resistant and has fragrant pure white flowers growing to 3 feet tall. The Perennial Plant Association named it a Plant of the Year. The Chicago Botanic Garden found 'Katherine'—a beautiful lavender-blue phlox with a white eye—to be the most disease resistant of the garden phlox. There are many varieties: 'Bubblegum Pink', 'Coral Crewe Drop', 'Coral Flame', 'Cotton Candy' and 'Grape Lollipop'. If you see a beautiful phlox in a garden or at a nursery find out which one it is!

Purple Coneflower

Echinacea purpurea

Botanical Pronunciation
ek-in-AY-shee-uh pur-PUR-ee-uh

Other Name Coneflower

Bloom Period and Seasonal Color
Mid-June to early September; blooms in pink, red-violet, white

Mature Height x Spread
2 to 3 feet x 2 to 3 feet

Wow! The large, showy flowers of purple coneflower really have summer impact. The original plant was native to the prairie and had pinkish, shuttlecock-shaped flowers with petals that drooped down. The new selections are bigger, brighter, and have a flower shape that more closely resembles a daisy. The white forms are stunning too. Purple coneflower is a magnet for butterflies—they land right on the orangey center cone. And, if you like birds, leave some of the dried seedheads and you'll attract goldfinches. All coneflowers are easy to grow. They make perfect cut flowers that will last a couple of weeks in a vase. These dark centers remain showy after the petals fall, and they make a great addition to any dried arrangement.

When, Where, and How to Plant

Plant nursery-grown container plants from mid-March until the garden store runs out. The best selection of 3- and 4-inch potted plants will be from mid-March until mid-May. One-gallon containers should be available all spring and summer. Plant coneflower in full sun to part shade; it will do well in average, well-drained soil. Container-grown plants should be planted at the same depth they were growing in their pots, but dig the hole twice as wide. Backfill and water-in well—and don't forget to loosen the roots. Space at least 2 to 2½ feet apart.

Growing Tips

Coneflower is a low-maintenance and heat- and drought-tolerant plant. Keep new plantings moist. Purple coneflower doesn't need heavy fertilization.

In poor soils, fertilize in spring with a balanced fertilizer according to the container's instructions.

Regional Advice and Care

Deadhead to encourage more blooms later in the season. It will also prevent self-sowing; volunteer seedlings are rarely as nice as the parent plant. Birds love the seed though, so in naturalistic parts of your garden, put your clippers away. Purple coneflower doesn't need frequent division. If you notice the clump is getting too large or bloom count is down, divide and transplant in spring as new growth appears. When dividing existing coneflower, take clumps of at least 6 inches in diameter. Replant the clumps no deeper than they were originally growing.

Companion Planting and Design

Originally a prairie flower, this perennial can be planted in masses for that wildflower look. Mix with black-eyed Susans and low-growing ornamental grasses. It is a great addition to any perennial bed or border.

Try These

'Magnus' has large (4-inch diameter), pinkish purple flowers on a plant that grows to 3 feet tall. 'White Swan' offers white flowers with copper-orange centers on a plant growing to 3 feet tall. For mass planting, plant on 2- to 3-foot centers. 'Kim's Knee High' has a nice compact form reaching about 2 feet high; this one is great for shade. Also try Big Sky series, 'Butterfly Kisses', 'Cheyenne Spirit', 'Hot Papaya', 'Now Cheesier', 'The King', 'Red Knee High', and the PowWow series.

Russian Sage

Perovskia atriplicifolia

Botanical Pronunciation
per-OFF-skee-uh at-ry-pliss-ih-FOH-lee-uh

Other Name
Azure sage

Bloom Period and Seasonal Color
July through fall; blue and violet blooms

Mature Height x Spread
3 to 5 feet x 3 to 4 feet

Just a few years ago, Russian sage was pronounced the Perennial Plant of the Year by the professional group, the Perennial Grower's Association. This plant certainly has all the qualities that make a particular plant a winner. The foliage has a nice sagelike fragrance, it has airy blue flowers that appear in midsummer and last the balance of the growing season, it's drought tolerant, and finally it's deer resistant too. Prune the tall stems back in early spring to one foot from the ground. This will give you more new growth and thicker stems. You will also enjoy this plant's fragrance as you cut back your plants during spring pruning.

When, Where, and How to Plant

Russian sage, because of its popularity, is readily available in 4- to 6-inch pots and 1-gallon containers at your neighborhood garden centers all during the planting season. But don't wait—plant early and enjoy a long season. Russian sage, like so many other perennials needs to be planted in full sun, in soil that offers good drainage. Plant more than one on 30- to 36-inch centers. Follow the planting instructions as written in this chapter's introduction.

Growing Tips

Russian sage is very drought tolerant but it does appreciate an occasional drink during hot dry periods. Water from below with a hand-held hose to prevent overhead watering, which will weigh down the tall stems. Fertilize as it starts to grow in the spring with an all-purpose plant food.

Regional Advice and Care

Russian sage is a low-maintenance plant with no problems to speak of. Leave your Russian sage unpruned during the winter for interest and (your) increased happiness. Some of the old leaves and silver stems will give you a beautiful dried arrangement appearance. There are smaller-growing varieties if you want some to use in dried arrangements. This plant is not subject to any serious pest problem.

Companion Planting and Design

Because of its potential growing height per variety, plant the taller-growing varieties to the back of planting bed. Makes an excellent blooming, fragrant hedge of various sizes per variety. Plant several around base of a flag pole out in the yard, add some red and white to that circular bed and get ready to salute.

Try These

'Peek-a-Blue' is just like a miniature example of its taller growing cousin. Grow 'Filigran' for a more compact 30-inch-tall, finer-textured plant. Others are 'Blue Haze', pale blue flowers; 'Blue Spire', finely dissected leaves and deep violet flowers; and 'Longin'. This variety is more narrow leaf and it's more upright; leaves are not as dissected as other varieties.

Salvia

Salvia spp.

Botanical Pronunciation
SAL-vee-ah

Other Name
Perennial sage

Bloom Period and Seasonal Color
Summer; blue, rose, pink or violet flowers

Mature Height x Spread
2 to 3 feet x 3 to 4 feet

Salvia has been a mainstay in perennial gardens for years. These long bloomers add charm to the garden and its color adds a lot of class to a flower arrangement. Plant salvia in areas viewable from inside the home as well as the outside so you can enjoy the butterflies and hummingbirds that come to pay a visit. This plant also has a history outside its garden charm. It has been used medicinally to heal problems with the liver, stomach, and heart as well as controlling fevers. Perennial salvia will provide years of color from one plant. It makes quite a statement if you need to include blue in your landscape. **Note:** *Salvia officinalis* is sage, which is usually planted in the herb garden and used for cooking.

When, Where, and How to Plant
Plant potted salvia of all sizes in the growing season. The best selections will be found in the spring from your favorite garden centers or nursery stores. Grow salvia of all varieties in lots of sun and well-drained soil that's kept moist (which you can supplement through the hose). Plant on 18-inch centers. If they get a little too much shade, the stems will flop and will need staking. See the chapter introduction for more planting tips.

Growing Tips
Perennial salvia performs best when it has moist soil. Avoid the use of any water-soluble plant foods; they make the stems grow fast and encourage floppy and poor flowering as well. Feed once a season with a "start and grow" timed-release fertilizer in the spring.

Regional Advice and Care
To extend the bloom time, cut off spent flower spikes as they occur. Just remove the faded flower stems back to the side (buds and stems). Leave stems standing in late fall to help its winter hardiness. Do your heavy stem pruning in the spring. You can divide salvia by digging up clumps after they've been planted 3 years. Do this in early spring as it wakes up from winter. Just note that re-establishing is slow because of its long, stringy root system.

Companion Planting and Design
Salvias make a beautiful low hedge planted on 15-inch centers along sidewalks or the front of any planting bed. In a perennial bed, it mixes well with any yellow or orange perennial.

Try These
There are many varieties of perennial salvia. *Salvia* 'Caradonna' has violet-blue spikes and dark purple spikes on stems blooming 2 feet. 'Eveline' grows to 2 feet on stems of two-toned pink and purple.

Shasta Daisy

Leucanthemum x superbum

Botanical Pronunciation
lew-KANTH-ih-mum soo-PER-bum

Bloom Period and Seasonal Color
Mid-June through September; yellow-centered white flowers

Mature Height x Spread
10 to 36 inches x 12 to 24 inches

Next time you are in the greeting card department, check out the number of friendship cards that have daisies on them. They even decide if she (or he!) loves you or loves you not. Shasta daisy looks just like the ordinary meadow daisy, only much bigger and better. These perennials will bloom and bloom all summer if you deadhead the spent flowers. In the right location—sun and good drainage—Shasta daisies are very easy to grow. There are many cultivated varieties from which to choose. The taller-growing Shasta daisies make for great cut flowers. All bloom from mid-June through September. Shasta daisies are fun and fresh and look great in the garden combined with other perennials. Plant some—and I'll bet she (or he) *does* love you!

When, Where, and How to Plant
Plant small pots of daisies in spring or early summer. One-gallon plants can be put in anytime the ground is not frozen. Plant Shasta daisy in good to average garden soil. Make sure your planting location has good drainage. Shastas prefer full sun, but you will get almost as much bloom from plants getting a half-day of sun. Read the planting tips in this chapter's introduction for specifics. Space plants about 1½ to 2 feet apart.

Growing Tips
Water Shasta daisies during hot, dry weather. Don't keep them wet—let them dry out between waterings. The soil moisture dictates the amount of bloom you will enjoy. Fertilize Shasta daisies in spring with a balanced plant food, following the directions and schedule on the container.

Regional Advice and Care
Shastas have no disease problems. If aphids appear, use a strong water spray from your hose to wash them off. Deadhead to promote rebloom. For larger-growing varieties, cut back all the stems halfway after initial bloom. This will make for fuller plants that bloom again. Divide every three years to keep them free-flowering. They couldn't be easier to divide. Dig up the clump when the foliage first comes out of the ground in spring. Discard the center and replant the younger, outer shoots. Replant at the same depth they were growing originally.

Companion Planting and Design
Shasta daisies are a cheerful addition to any bed or border. Combine them with irises, lilies, daylilies, and yarrow. 'Snow Lady' is grown like an annual and can be used in bedding displays.

Try These
One pick is 'Snow Lady'. This Shasta has the traditional flowers along with a compact size (10 to 12 inches tall) and a long, almost three-month, blooming period. If you want a taller Shasta, you'll love 'Becky', the Perennial Plant Association's pick for a Plant of the Year. This one is tall (30 to 36 inches), but sturdy and produces large daisies from July through September. A few more to add to the list: 'Snowcap', 'Banana Cream', 'Sunny Side Up', and 'Real Neat'.

Turtlehead

Chelone species

Botanical Pronunciation
kee-LO-nay

Other Name Shellflower

Bloom Period and Seasonal Color
August and September; pink and purple flowers

Mature Height x Spread
3 feet x 12 to 30 inches

This is a very interesting plant. When it blooms in late summer the blooms closely resemble a turtle's head with its mouth open. It's a great perennial for spots in the landscape that could be difficult if not impossible for other perennials to grow, as it will live in wet or damp spots in the garden either in sun or shade. Turtleheads will give many areas of your landscape a quick splash of beautiful color that lasts into mid-September when other perennials are starting to wrap up their bloom colors.

When, Where, and How to Plant
Buy turtleheads in their own pots of various sizes and plant anytime during the growing season. See this chapter's introduction for complete planting instructions. Grow in full sun to half-day sun in well-drained soil.

Growing Tips
Water new plantings thoroughly but check the soil for moisture before assuming they're dry or you'll wind up overwatering your new plants. Remember to always check for moisture in the soil with a hand-held garden trowel. To fertilize these perennials and many others, use a timed-release fertilizer that will feed your plants all season with one spring application.

Regional Advice and Care
You do not have to deadhead or remove any spent turtlehead flowers. This plant will grow very bushy if you pinch back some of the new early spring growth. If your turtlehead plants become overgrown, take a spade and divide them in early spring as they start to grow. Turtleheads are slow to re-emerge the following spring so leave of few older stems intact so you can locate their presence in early spring. Turtlehead has no serious disease or insect problems.

Companion Planting and Design
Combine with mums, asters, and other fall-blooming flowers to increase your perennial color when most other perennials are getting ready for a good winter's nap. With children plant at least one for the kids to enjoy, especially in the fall.

Try These
The native 'White Turtlehead', *Chelone glabra*, will readily reseed itself and can be found growing in the wild in many locations. Also check out 'Hot Lips' with its bronzy green leaves turning to all bright green in a few weeks, with hot pink blooms.

Variegated Solomon's Seal

Polygonatum biflorum

Botanical Pronunciation
po-lig-oh-NAY-tum BI-floor-um

Bloom Period and Seasonal Color
Late March to mid-April; white flowers

Mature Height x Spread
24 to 36 inches x 24 to 36 inches

Solomon's seal adds a unique form to any shade garden. The 2- to 4-foot upright, arching, burgundy stems and white variegation on its leaf edges brighten the shade garden all summer long. But it's not done there. The leaves then turn a golden yellow in the fall. Its foliage can also be used in floral arrangements. This plant is another that was chosen as a Perennial Plant of the Year, partly because of its multi-season interest. Pairs of white bell-shaped flowers arranged on each stem enhance the look. Just let them grow and you'll enjoy them. This is a very easy plant to grow and can be extremely trouble-free.

When, Where, and How to Plant
Plant container-grown plants anytime during the growing season. The best selection of various-sized plants will be in the spring. Refer to the chapter's introduction for complete planting instructions. Plant in part to full shade and in moist, well-drained soils for best growing results. Space plants 18 to 24 inches apart.

Growing Tips
Give plants a good soaking their first growing season in your garden. Mulch with a 2-inch layer of bark or shredded bark chips. Fertilize with slow-release fertilizer in the spring. Feed once for the entire season.

Regional Advice and Care
Solomon's seal is one of the most low-maintenance plants that exist. If your have trouble growing these, try plastic plants the next time. There are no insect problems, including slugs. These plants will spread quite a bit, so get ready to share the wealth with neighbors and friends. Divide any established plants in early spring as they start to wake up. Take 8- to 10-inch clumps and plant to the same depth.

Companion Planting and Design
It looks great growing among hardy ferns, ginger, hostas, and daylilies. Plant a few in mixed containers with annuals. In the late fall as the annual flowers are fading, place the container with the Solomon's seals in an unheated garage, water once a month, and set it back outside in March.

Try These
Polygonatum commutatum is the great solomon's seal. This is the giant of the *Polygonatum* genus. It is normally 3 to 5 feet tall. Flowers are greenish white that form large groupings and are not ideal for the small garden. *P. odoratum variegatum* has green-and-white leaves.

Virginia Bluebells

Mertensia virginica

Botanical Pronunciation
mer-TEN-see-uh vir-JIN-ih-kuh

Bloom Period and Seasonal Color
April to May; blue blooms

Mature Height x Spread
1 to 1½ feet x 1 to 1½ feet

When we think of flowering plants that welcome us to spring, we usually think of spring-flowering bulbs, such as crocus, hyacinths, and daffodils. Well, Virginia bluebells, an Ohio native wildflower, also do a colorful job of saying "Welcome to spring." They begin to appear in April with attractive gray-blue leaves. Soon after, pinkish lavender bloom buds appear that then open up to a true-blue flower color. Bluebells prefer moist, loamy soil to clay. They do not like to be exposed to hot, late-spring sun; in fact, the entire plant disappears, going dormant in mid- to late-June. These woodland beauties reseed themselves, slowly filling in an entire shady area in a controlled and very attractive way. Plant these native bluebells and you'll enjoy them every spring.

When, Where, and How to Plant

Plant Virginia bluebells in spring and early summer before the foliage goes dormant. Choose locations in natural or tree shade—they can tolerate morning sun, but absolutely no hot afternoon sun. Plant them in good, loose soil that stays relatively moist but not wet. Bluebells want to be planted in soil with good drainage. When planting in average soil, add organic amendments to the existing soil to improve the overall soil condition; do this as you pre-loosen the soil. For new plantings, loosen the existing soil to a depth of 6 to 8 inches. Dig a hole as deep and twice as wide as the soil clump. Loosen any wrapped roots, backfill, and water-in well to settle the soil. Space plants about 1½ feet apart.

Growing Tips

Use a plant food for acid-loving plants, following the instructions on the container. If you have rich woodland conditions, fertilization will be unnecessary. During dry springs, add water occasionally to keep the soil moist.

Regional Advice and Care

There are no pests or diseases to bother your Virginia bluebells. Virginia bluebells rarely need division and, in fact, division can be a bit tricky. In happy conditions, they will self-sow and that's the best way to get new plants. You can move plants in spring or attempt division as the foliage starts to yellow.

Companion Planting and Design

Always surround bluebells with other shade-loving plants that will fill in for them when they disappear in summer. Use bluebells to underplant small, shade-loving plants such as 'P.J.M.' rhododendron, bayberry, and abelia. Plant Virginia bluebells with spring-flowering companion perennials, such as columbine, bleeding heart, hosta, and hardy ferns.

Try These

If you can grow Virginia bluebells, you can grow other Ohio woodland natives such as creeping phlox, wild ginger, crested dwarf iris, and wild columbine. For more information on native plants, consult Ohio State University's Bulletin 865 *The Native Plants of Ohio*. Go to their website address http://bygl.osu.edu/.

Yarrow

Achillea spp. and hybrids

Botanical Pronunciation
ak-ih-LEE-a

Other Name
Hybrid yarrow

Bloom Period and Seasonal Color
June till August; blooms in yellow, pink, white, red, lavender, copper

Mature Height x Spread
1½ to 3 feet (by variety) x 2 to 3 feet

This garden book is full of low-maintenance, easy-to-grow plants. Yarrow would certainly qualify for a spot in the top twenty-five. Yarrow has large flat-headed flowers that come in many colors with green or grayish green aromatic foliage that is attractive even when yarrow is in between bloom. By deadheading spent flowers, you can keep your yarrow blooming from June until September. Because it does best during hot, dry periods, plant it in the same bed with your spring-flowering bulbs. Yarrow's foliage will hide the tulip leaves as they mature. Yarrow also complements other summer-blooming perennials. It will grow in garden soil where many other perennials fear to tread. Most yarrow plants spread 2 to 3 feet. A little yarrow goes a long way and stays a long time.

When, Where, and How to Plant
Plant yarrow in 3- and 4-inch pots in April and May. One-gallon potted yarrow can be planted anytime the ground is not frozen. Plant yarrow in full sun for the best growth, though some shade is okay. It will tolerate any type of soil—average to poor preferred—as long as there's good drainage. Don't use bad soil as an excuse not to plant this one. Loosen the existing soil to a depth of 6 to 8 inches. With nursery-bought plants, dig a hole as deep and twice as wide as the soil clump. Loosen any wrapped roots. Backfill, and water-in well to settle the soil.

Growing Tips
Water new yarrow plants until they are established. Now, put the hose away, because yarrow is a heat- and drought-tolerant plant. Fertilize sparingly.

Yarrow can grow tall and sprawling in rich soils, requiring staking.

Regional Advice and Care
There are no bugs or diseases that give this plant any trouble. Remove spent flowers to keep your yarrow blooming all summer. Cut the stems back halfway when removing old flowers. Divide yarrow every four to five years in spring. Over time, you can create your own meadow of yarrow just from the divisions. Make each division a minimum of 6 inches in diameter. Replant no deeper than the yarrow was growing originally.

Companion Planting and Design
Plant yarrow in beds and borders and meadow-style gardens. Yarrow is beautiful with other summer-blooming perennials—daylilies, balloon flowers, Shasta daisies, and gayfeather. Ornamental grasses and silvery artemisia also make great companions.

Try These
Early-blooming 'Coronation Gold' (3 feet tall) has silvery foliage and golden yellow flowers. It is one of the best yarrows for general garden use. 'Anthea' (2 feet) is a softer yellow and promises to be a great garden performer. Newer yarrows called the Galaxy Hybrids are on the market in a range of soft and bright colors. One I like is 'Appleblossom' (2 to 3 feet). It has rosy pink flowers and performs well in Ohio. A few others to try are Seduction series, 'Moonshine', and 'Pomegranate'.

ROSES

FOR OHIO

The rose is our national flower, and it deserves to be—but in the past, the rose family has been a very challenging group of plants to grow successfully in Ohio. Fortunately, it's getting a lot easier. Many new varieties have been produced over the last twenty to thirty years, particularly in the last twenty or so, which have greatly improved our chances for success. Hybrid teas, floribundas, grandifloras, miniatures, groundcover roses, and climbing roses have been available for many years. Add to this original list the Meidiland® landscape roses, now climbing repeat-bloomers, and shrub roses of all colors and growing habits. Wow!

A Little Bit of T.L.C.

Roses perform best in a full day of sun. If you don't have this type of exposure, morning sun is the better half to have. Morning sun dries the dew off the plants, and that's important for reducing the risk of diseases, such as blackspot and mildew.

Bush and climbing roses with perennials

Roses like to be planted in an open area where they can get good air movement among the individual plants. Plant roses 5 feet apart to give each plant good growing space and air space. Many of the newer rose varieties are more disease and insect resistant, but certain groups—especially hybrid teas (and that's one reason I'm not including hybrid teas; they need more attention) and grandifloras—still need a little assistance. There are spray products that can be used to protect these roses from disease and insect attack. In general, roses love good, loamy soil. They will tolerate clay soil as long as the soil drains well.

How to Select a Rose

Roses are available three different ways: (1) bare-root plants whose roots are packed in moist packing material and wrapped in a plastic or foil-type bag; (2) "boxed" potted roses that are available

Container-grown roses is the best choice. To remove the rose from the container, lay it on its side and squeeze gently, then tease out its roots.

in early spring; and (3) roses that are already growing in their own soil medium in 2- or 5-gallon pots. The latter is the absolute best way to buy rose plants. These roses are usually potted during the winter and are well-established by the time they're available for you to buy. They'll cost more, but their value is much greater.

Be wary of the "boxed" roses. These are basically bare-root plants that have had their canes and roots pruned back (which is good), but the roots are placed in the cardboard box with moist sphagnum peat. The canes have been coated with wax to keep moisture from escaping the rose while it is being stored and offered for sale. Here's the real problem: You can't water the roots because that would ruin the box. These plants then have a very short shelf-life; they just don't stay viable for long. And too often, these roses remain for sale for several months, daily increasing the desiccation of these roses. I hope our retail nurseries will quit handling these. My advice when you select this type is "buyer beware." Remember, as is true of any living plant that you want to purchase, it won't get any better looking during the ride home. Always buy healthy, vigorously-growing plants, including roses.

Planting Bare-Root and Potted Roses

Bare-root roses come from the nursery with their roots in a plastic-coated paper bag or a cardboard box. Take the wrapping off the roots. Prune the roots back to 8 inches in length. If they are already at 8 inches, put a fresh ¼-inch cut in the root ends. Prune off any broken roots just above the break. Soak the roots in a bucket of water for 6 hours; then you're ready to plant. Dig a hole 16 inches wide and as deep as the roots are long. Break up all the soil particles so that none are bigger than a golf ball. Now, in the center of the hole build a pyramid of soil that ends at the top of the hole. Spread

If you plant a bare-root rose, drape the roots over a "cone" of soil in the planting hole.

the roots over the pyramid and backfill the balance of the soil. This process ensures complete soil coverage around the roots. Water-in very well to settle the backfilled soil. If no new buds or shoots are growing on the canes, cover the canes with additional soil to help push out new growth. Remove this excess soil as new growth starts to appear.

Potted roses are roses already growing in their own soil. To plant, dig a hole as deep as the distance from the bud union (that swollen area that all the rose canes are attached to) and the bottom of the soil clump. Dig your hole twice the width of the pot. Slide the pot off and backfill with your soil that you've broken up so no clumps are bigger than a golf ball. Water-in well to settle the backfilled soil.

Pruning Tips

There's lots of misinformation out there about how far to cut your roses back to encourage more repeat bloom. I'll try to make it simple. For long-stem cutting roses (hybrid teas and grandifloras), when the flowers have finished blooming on a particular stem, cut back the stem 20 to 80 percent of the way, making the cut just above a set of leaflets growing away from the center of the plant.

For cluster-blooming roses (all the rest), wait until each cluster has finished blooming then cut the stem halfway back, cutting just above a set of leaflets growing away from the center of the plant. Stop pruning back all rose stems in September and allow the seedheads (rose hips) to form and signal to the roots that it's time to get ready for winter. Let the roses continue to put on new blooms on their own. Just don't remove the spent flowers. Don't be surprised to see KNOCK OUT® roses blooming into November, maybe even December. Do not fertilize roses after September 1.

Do your heavy pruning of rose canes in early spring as the new buds start to swell. On all roses but climbers, prune all canes back to 8 inches or more, depending on whether or not any winter dieback has blackened your canes closer to the ground than

8 inches. In this case, prune back to good green cane color. Cut them back so no cane is longer than 8 inches.

Climbers will have the majority of their bloom the current year on canes that grew the prior year. Do not prune except for removing winter-damaged canes, or you will cut off the canes that are carrying this year's flowers; it's the same if canes have grown out of allocated space. *You* own the pruning shears.

How Will My Rose Stay Warm for the Winter?

Many roses need to be protected from cold Ohio winters. The base of each plant, known as the bud union, is the most vulnerable part. Leave the rose canes long, at least 3 feet tall. Do not prune climbers at all. Buy or make rose collars that are 8 inches high to encircle the base of each plant; you can use any material that will hold together for the winter. Fill the collar with any well-draining material, such as pine bark chips or oak leaves.

How Many Rose Varieties Are There?

There are literally thousands of rose varieties . . . more than we could count. Most garden centers and nursery stores try to sell roses that come from some of the best growers, nurseries such as Conard-Pyle's Star® Roses, Weeks, and Jackson and Perkins®. Buying roses grown at these great nurseries gives you greater assurance that you are buying high-quality plants, representing high-quality varieties.

Go ahead and try a rose—and enjoy! Each rose category in this chapter will describe all of the benefits of that particular type of rose. This family has really expanded to add lots of color with ease of growing and enjoying.

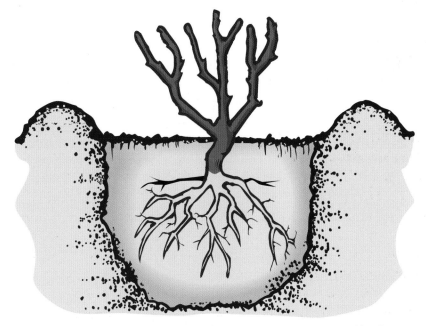

The bud union of grafted roses is the most vulnerable part and must be protected in winter.

Climbing Repeat-Blooming Rose

Rosa hybrids

Botanical Pronunciation RO-zuh

Other Name Cold-hardy rose

Bloom Period and Seasonal Color
Mid-May to a hard freeze in mid- to late fall; light pink, red, pink with yellow center, reddish pink

Mature Height x Spread
Up to 10 feet x 4 feet

Climbing roses are a romantic addition to the garden. Provide them with some space to climb and a fixture to climb on, and they will provide walls of color. But until these repeat-blooming roses were bred by Bill Radler, the developer of the KNOCK OUT® rose family, most climbers put on their bloom show around Memorial Day and that was *it* (not much of a memory was required of gardeners). Now though, through Mr. Radler's hybridizing, we have a class of climbing roses known as climbing repeat-blooming roses. Now the rose market is offering you very cold-hardy climber varieties that are produced on their own root and repeat their bloom periods with large flowers and strong colors.

When, Where, and How to Plant
You can plant container-grown climbing roses anytime during the growing season. Best selections would be to buy in the spring. Climbers of all types are sun lovers. Just make sure yours gets at least morning sun. Choose a location with good soil drainage. They will still thrive in good old Ohio clay. Your climbing roses will need a climbing support whether it's a trellis or a fence that you can attach the canes to. For details on planting procedures refer to this chapter's introduction.

Growing Tips
Fertilize climbers, new or old, with a granular rose food as the new leaves start to appear. Repeat again after the first flush of many blooms appear. Use the amount of fertilizer recommended on the fertilizer container. Water when the soil is very dry.

Regional Advice and Care
Climbing roses require a lot less care than the cousins hybrid teas and grandifloras. Your climbers will be fairly clear of any insects and disease. Climbing roses also produce more flowers on canes that are growing horizontally (on a fence support) or downward (on a trellis or arbor). Don't be in a rush to cut canes off. They will bloom next year on the canes that grow this year.

Companion Planting and Design
Make the taller-growing climbers as the background in a perennial garden or shrub bed with the smaller plants to the front for a great picture, especially if you're standing in the center of that colorful picture.

Try These
All of these are great repeat climbing roses. 'Morning Magic'™ comes in light pink, 'Winner's Choice'™ has red flowers, 'Bright Eyes'™ has pink flowers with yellow centers, and 'Cancun'™ has reddish pink blooms. 'Golden Showers' is an older variety making a comeback. It produces large, yellow double-flowering blossoms with honey-scented aroma. It is quite resistant to insects and disease and blooms from spring until fall. Other great varieties are 'Joseph's Coat (yellow-red), 'New Dawn' (pink), and 'Iceberg' (white).

Floribunda Rose

Rosa hybrids

Botanical Pronunciation
RO-zuh

Bloom Period and Seasonal Color
May through fall; blooms in red, coral, pink, white, yellow, bicolor

Mature Height x Spread
2½ to 4 feet x 2 to 3 feet

Floribundas make excellent landscape plants, producing almost constant blooms from Memorial Day until fall. Though descended from hybrid teas, in general they are shorter and produce flowers borne in clusters rather than one bloom per stem. The flowers are smaller than the hybrid teas, but you won't notice as floribundas produce so many more blooms—expect *loads* of color. Their growth habit and bloom qualifies them for use as a low-blooming hedge or border plant—or plant them in their own bed for fantastic yard color. As a rule, floribunda roses are easier to care for than hybrid teas, although they are susceptible to the usual rose problems and need winter protection in Ohio. These were the original shrub/landscape rose more than 90 years ago.

When, Where, and How to Plant
Plant bare-root roses in spring. Container-grown roses can be planted anytime during the growing season. Choose locations in full sun, if possible, or at least morning sun. Floribundas will grow in all types of well-drained soil. Space 4 to 5 feet apart to allow good air circulation. Refer to this chapter's introduction for a blow-by-blow description of how to plant and *please* follow those directions.

Growing Tips
Mulch with a 2-inch layer of organic mulch. If rainfall is scarce, provide your plants with about 1 inch of water weekly. Roses are heavy feeders. Feed with a rose fertilizer in spring about two weeks after spring pruning, and continue feeding as often as recommended on the fertilizer container. Don't feed after early August.

Regional Advice and Care
Floribundas need a maintenance schedule to avoid diseases such as blackspot, although some floribundas are more disease resistant. There are several products that combine systemic insecticide with rose food. Just follow the instructions. Handpick and discard any yellow infected or fallen leaves to avoid additional blackspot. For disease control, spray any product that contains the fungicide called propiconazole that's a systemic and lasts in the rose leaves for four weeks. In early spring, prune floribundas back hard to live wood, creating a strong open framework. Deadhead throughout the growing season until mid-September. After that, let the flowers go to seed (called rose hips), which signals the roots to shut down. Most winter damage to roses happens because the plants are still actively growing when the real cold weather hits. For winter protection tips, see this chapter's introduction.

Companion Planting and Design
Cheerful floribunda roses can be used as edgers, in rose beds, and in mixed borders. They look great in masses or in groups of at least three.

Try These
'Showbiz' produces showy clusters of lightly scented, scarlet-red blooms on vigorously growing, but compact plants. It is not as prone to blackspot disease as are some other varieties. Other great varieties are 'Angel Face' (lavender), 'Europeana' (dark red), 'Iceberg' (white), and 'Rainbow Sorbet' (yellow/orange/pink).

Grandiflora Rose

Rosa hybrids

Botanical Pronunciation
RO-zuh

Bloom Period and Seasonal Color
Mid May through October blooms in pink, red, white, yellow, bicolor

Mature Height x Spread
5 to 6 feet x 3 to 4 feet

As a group, grandiflora roses have large, perfect blooms much like the hybrid teas. But they differ from hybrid teas in a few significant ways. Grandifloras produce clusters of flowers, like a floribunda rose, although the flowers are like a hybrid tea in shape and size. Grandifloras are vigorous plants and grow taller than a hybrid tea, often reaching 5 to 6 feet. When it comes to hardiness, grandifloras are similar to hybrid teas; they will need protection to survive an Ohio winter. Because of their size, grandiflora roses are often used in the background of a rose bed or mixed border. With their long stems and floriferous nature, these are great roses for cut flower use.

When, Where, and How to Plant
Plant container-grown roses anytime the ground is not frozen, although spring is preferred. Choose a spot in full sun with average to fertile soil. Grandifloras should be spaced 5 feet apart for good air circulation; don't cheat. Follow planting instructions in this chapter's introduction. Full sun is best for planting locations and roses want to be planted in well-draining soil.

Growing Tips
If rainfall is scarce, water deeply (about 1 inch of water per week). Avoid wetting foliage, which can promote disease. Mulch with 2 inches of organic mulch. Roses are *heavy* feeders. Feed with a rose fertilizer a few weeks after spring pruning and repeat as directed on the container. In Ohio, stop feeding in early August. Be ready to prepare your roses for winter cold protection.

Regional Advice and Care
All grandifloras need a maintenance schedule. Blackspot can be a problem. Fungicides are available to spray on the rose leaves; remove any yellow infected leaves from the plant and discard. Several products combine systemic insecticide with rose food. Just follow the instructions and pour it on the soil around each bush. To avoid overwintering disease spores, always remove any prunings or fallen leaves. Turn to this chapter's introduction for winter protection tips. In spring, prune back hard to live wood at an outward-facing bud, leaving an open framework of strong canes. When dead-heading, cut back old flower stems 75 to 80 percent, making the cut just above an outward growing set of leaves. See this chapter's introduction for more pruning details.

Companion Planting and Design
The tall grandifloras can be used as a screen or hedge. Because of the extra height, they should always be planted to the back of a rose bed in which you're mixing grandifloras with hybrid teas and floribundas.

Try These
Try 'Lasting Peace' (coral-orange), 'Love's Promise' (bright red), 'Pink Flamingo' (pink), and 'Dream Come True' (yellow/pink blend). The hybridizer of 'Dream Come True', Dr. Pottschmidt, is from Cincinnati. He's a doctor who, after many years of bringing new babies into this world, retired and now delivers new roses for all to enjoy.

Landscape Rose

Rosa hybrids

Botanical Pronunciation
RO-zuh

Other Name
Hedge rose

Bloom Period and Seasonal Color
Mid-May until hard freeze in the fall; blooms in red, yellow, copper, lavender, white, bicolors

Mature Height x Spread
4 to 6 feet x 3 feet (depending on variety)

When thinking of hedge plants, are roses your first thought? Probably not, but it's time to think again. Roses make fantastic, informal hedges—serving as a great barrier and providing beautiful flowers and ornamental fruit as well. This group of roses is not only gorgeous and easy to grow but you can find unlimited uses for this rose family. If you're looking for disease resistance and reblooming shrubs that come in a range of color, then try landscape roses. Grow this group alongside the KNOCK OUT® family of roses to add an easy, top-performing line of shrubs to your landscape.

When, Where, and How to Plant
Potted roses in general can be planted anytime during the growing season. Choose a sunny to partly sunny location with well-drained soil. Shrub roses are tough and can handle many planting situations, including areas with only four hours of sun. Follow the general rose planting directions in this chapter's introduction. Water-in well to settle the backfilled soil.

Growing Tips
Landscape roses have excellent resistance to insects and disease. For the few bugs that like your roses for lunch, apply a systemic soil drench per label instructions. Pour the mixture around the base of your roses and you won't have bugs for a year. These roses are very cold hardy, so no winter protection is required. Prune back in early spring.

Regional Advice and Care
Deadheading (cutting off spent blooms) is not necessary. In spring, remove any weak-looking or broken canes. If you are growing your landscape roses in patio pots, place them in an unheated garage in December and leave them there until the end of March. Remember to water the pots once a month while they are in the garage.

Companion Planting and Design
Roses are not only great hedge roses, they are also great to plant on a hillside that may be hard to mow and besides, lawn grass sure doesn't bloom like this group of blooming shrubs. They are a good background anchors for a bed of perennials or annuals for seasonal color

Try These
Try any of these: 'Phloxy Baby'™ (medium pink finishing light pink), 'Thrive'™ (dark red), 'Bonica'™ (pastel pink), 'Bubble Double'™ (light pink), 'Milwaukee's Calatrava'™ (white), 'White Out'™ (white), or 'Tequila'™ (orange-copper).

Miniature Groundcover Rose

Rosa hybrids

Botanical Pronunciation RO-zuh

Other Name Drift series

Bloom Period and Seasonal Color
Mid-May through fall; blooms in apricot, peach, pink, yellow-blend, red

Mature Height x Spread
18 to 18 inches x 2 to 3 feet (per variety)

Drift roses are a cross between full-sized groundcover roses and true miniatures. From the groundcover roses they kept toughness, disease resistance, and winter hardiness. From the miniatures they inherited a well-managed size and the ability to repeat bloom often. The low, spreading habit of drift roses is perfect for small gardens and combination planters. They truly complement any garden. They brighten up borders, fill in empty spaces, and spread colorfully around other established plants. They are available in seven varieties in the Drift seres and continue to bloom from spring to a hard frost in the fall. They are naturally dwarf with very pretty, with dark glossy leaves until frost. These roses stay in constant bloom all summer into fall.

When, Where, and How to Plant
Drift roses are a wonderful example of miniature groundcover roses. Mini-groundcover roses are available in 1-, 2- and 3-gallon sizes. Plant these anytime of the year when these beautiful roses are offered for sale. Plant in areas with soil that drains well. Full sun is terrific but they will please you with just morning or just afternoon sun. Refer to this chapter's introduction for planting instructions. These roses also do extremely well in patio or other type planters. Water pots well once a month.

Growing Tips
Fertilize mini-groundcover roses with granular rose food or an all-purpose plant food in early spring and again after their first flush of blooms. Once established they become very drought resistant.

Regional Advice and Care
Apply a systemic soil drench per label instructions to keep all insects off your roses for an entire growing season. Deadheading (removing old flowers) is not necessary. Early spring, prune back your roses to contain them in their allotted space. No extra winter protection is needed as this family of roses is very cold hardy. To overwinter roses in containers, just place in an unheated garage from December through May.

Companion Planting and Design
It's hard to describe just how much pleasure you'll derive enjoying all the color you will get viewing these low-growing, weeping plants. Plant a variety of colors or plant a low rose hedge of all the same color. For this hedge effect plant them on 4- to 5-foot centers.

Try These
Use your "horticultural paintbrush" and let your imagination do the rest. The colors in your paint cans are Red Drift, Coral Drift, Popcorn Drift (a creamy yellow), Peach Drift, Apricot Drift, Pink Drift, and the Sweet Drift (a lovely clear pink). Plant a bed of a solid color or mix your colors, if possible. Plant in areas of your yard that's viewable to your neighbors. Share the beauty; that's what great neighbors would do.

Shrub Rose

Rosa hybrids

Botanical Pronunciation RO-zuh

Other Name Hedge rose

Bloom Period and Seasonal Color
Mid-spring through late fall; blooms in yellow,
red, pink, white, pink blend

Mature Height x Spread
3 to 6 feet x 3 to 6 feet (as permitted)

The category "shrub rose" is a catchall term, defined by use, that includes a range of new and old roses, such as polyantha roses, hybrid rugosa roses, modern shrub roses, landscape roses, and old garden roses. In general, they need lots of sun to prosper—at least a half-day of morning sun. In exchange, you will get flowers that never stop. Plant shrub roses as a hedge, as a border for a rose bed, or mix them in with other perennials and shrubs for extended summer color; none will out-bloom a shrub rose. Many have ornamental fruits called rose hips, as well. Beauty aside, shrub roses are rugged, care-free, and winter hardy. You won't have to look far to find a place for one in your landscape.

When, Where, and How to Plant
Plant container-grown shrub roses anytime the ground is not frozen. Bare-root roses should be planted in spring. Choose a location with lots of sun and good soil drainage. Follow the general planting directions listed in this chapter's introduction. If you're creating a hedge, space adequately to provide the air circulation all roses need. Consult the label or nursery staff to determine the right spacing for the plant you purchase.

Growing Tips
Don't let your newly planted shrub roses dry out. Although some shrub roses are quite drought tolerant, find out the watering needs for your variety. A 2-inch layer of organic mulch will help conserve moisture. Other than rose food in spring, they don't require much maintenance.

Regional Advice and Care
Shrub roses are low maintenance. They can have a few bugs or a little blackspot during the rainy seasons or as a result of poor planting sites. Pruning is minimal, although you may want to remove some branches to improve their shape and open up the center to air. As with any rose, remove any dead or damaged canes in spring. You can prune them back hard in spring to reduce their height if desired. Deadheading won't be necessary. These roses are winter hardy and won't need any protection.

Companion Planting and Design
Shrub roses are versatile. Mass them as screens or hedges, or enjoy one as a specimen plant. They can be planted in shrub borders, used as foundation plants, and combined with perennials.

Try These
My absolute favorite variety is any member of the KNOCK OUT® family. There are seven different varieties (including KNOCK OUT®, Double KNOCK OUT®, Pink KNOCK OUT®, Double Pink KNOCK OUT®, Blushing KNOCK OUT®, Sunny KNOCK OUT®, and Rainbow KNOCK OUT®). Most are award-winners that will give you great color with little to no maintenance. This rose variety will bloom in as little as four hours of daily sun, a great help to many gardeners.

SHRUBS
FOR OHIO

Shrubs, or bushes, are woody perennials. They make up the group of plants most often purchased and installed by homeowners. They can be needled evergreens, broadleaf evergreens, or deciduous plants that drop their leaves in fall. Even builders who consider landscaping a nuisance will take the trouble to install ten or twelve shrubs in front of a newly built home, a message for prospective buyers that says, "Hey, this house is ready for you to move into."

Think Globally, Buy Locally

In January and February in Ohio, we're eager for any sign of spring. The mail-order catalogs begin to arrive, and our minds shift into planting gear. Be careful, though. Don't be taken in by prices that seem too good to be true, descriptions of unfamiliar plant varieties, and pictures of plants that are artist's illustrations instead of actual photos. Many of these plants may be small enough to fit through a slide-in mailbox!

Well-placed shrubs add incredible beauty to beds and foundations. Go ahead! Include deciduous shrubs as foundation plantings.

It's always best to buy locally, so you can see what you're getting before opening your wallet.

Planting Your New Shrubs

Most of Ohio does not enjoy good garden soil. We usually have clay soil of varying degrees of thickness, but that's not all bad. Clay soil retains moisture, which reduces plants' additional watering needs during those periods of hot, rainless weather. We'll have more on watering new trees and shrubs a little later. First, let's dig the planting hole.

All shrubs are available as balled-and-burlapped (B & B) or container-grown (in pots) plants. The planting procedure for both types is the same. Dig your hole as deep as the soil clump

The *Ilex* genus can have berries other than red, such as *Ilex opaca* 'Canary'.

or rootball and at least twice as wide. Take a spade and break up the backfill soil particles so that no pieces are bigger than a golf ball. A few shrubs, as mentioned in the individual listings of this chapter, appreciate some soil amendments. This means adding organic peat or compost to the existing backfill, replacing no more than one-third of the existing soil. Mix amendments with the existing soil and then backfill. Water-in very well, taking a spade to mix the backfill with the water in the filled hole to eliminate any air pockets. Make sure the plant is level with the planting bed when finished. Mulch your newly installed shrubs to a depth of 2 inches—no deeper—and keep the mulch off the trunks or stems of your plants, even if it's just an inch away. No plant wants its trunk or stems covered with mulch. There is more information about the use of mulch in this book's introduction. Use mulch wisely.

The Best Time to Plant Shrubs

For many years, too many people have been under the impression that the best time to plant trees and shrubs is spring. I often got calls around Memorial Day from homeowners asking if it was too late to plant. Add to this the fact that garden centers close out their inventory around June 1, and there wasn't anything left to buy even if a homeowner wanted to.

Well, guess what? The best time to plant trees and shrubs is the *fall*. The roots of plants installed in the spring basically sit until the soil cools down in the fall. Even plants that need to get root-established for their first winter will establish quicker when planted in September to October. The roots of all plants develop the majority of their year's growth in the fall, even as late as December. You see, the top stops growing

Dig the planting hole as deep as the rootball and twice as wide; put the container in the hole to confirm it's large enough.

After planting, backfill and water-in well.

in early fall and all the plant's energy then goes into new root development. You'll notice that Mother Nature does all her planting in the fall. But unfortunately, we homeowners are inspired by spring fever; there's no such phenomenon as "fall fever." So while it is safe to plant any tree or shrub anytime the ground is not frozen, planting in the spring takes a lot more maintenance on your part, especially if we have a very hot and dry summer. Nevertheless, spring is still when most people plant shrubs.

Watering—The Most Difficult Task

The most difficult thing to teach a homeowner is how and when to water. Wind, temperature, type of soil, and rainfall all play a major role in how often to water. Timely watering during hot, dry weather helps any plant, but do check the soil down to 5 inches first. The only way you can tell when the soil around your plantings is dry is by checking all the soil in your planting beds with a garden trowel, digging down 4 to 5 inches to see if there's moisture. If there is moisture, wait until there's not. More newly installed plants have died within the first planting season by overwatering than under-watering. Always check the soil before grabbing the hose. Just because one bed area is dry doesn't mean the whole yard is dry.

A general rule to go by is that plants need 1 inch of water per week, including rainfall, throughout the growing season—that means in November and December too. It is better to err on the dry side than the wet side. Underwatered plants droop and wilt; they respond positively when watered. Overwatered plants droop and wilt like a dry plant, but because their roots are kept wet and can't breathe air like you and me, they start rotting and—oops, there goes the plumbing!

Fertilizer Can Be Too Much of a Good Thing

Most trees and shrubs don't need to be fertilized when planted. In fact, many a plant has burned up because we want the shrubs to grow so fast that we easily overfeed and burn the new roots. The fertilizer recommendations given with each shrub variety are for after the shrub has been installed for one year.

How Much Sun Is Sunny?

You will note that in this chapter, many varieties of shrubs are listed as needing a light exposure of sun to part-shade. Shrubs that thrive in full sun will also thrive in planting locations that receive a half-day of sun and a half-day of shade. On the other hand, if you find a variety that's shade-loving, chances are very good that it will also tolerate a half-day of morning sun; however, never make that half-day of sun the hot, afternoon sun.

How Big Will My Shrub Get?

Throughout this chapter, the mature height and width of each individual shrub is listed. These various sizes listed are the average size that you can keep your shrub by pruning. Remember, no tree or shrub ever stops growing until the day it dies. When you shop your garden center or nursery store, many of the plant signs and plant labels will list the mature size of the plants you're selecting. Again, these are average sizes that tell you the size at which that plant looks its best. You will have to prune to keep the plant at that size.

Mix and Match

For years, the front of every home was framed with evergreen, needle-type shrubs. There were junipers and yews, and yews and junipers—with an occasional arborvitae thrown in. Within the last twenty years, landscape designers as well as homeowners have realized, "Hey, I don't look at my shrubs in the winter, does anyone else?" The answer of course is, "No, I'm too cold to worry about whether the shrubs in front of my house are evergreen." This discovery has opened up an all-new type of landscape design that allows front plantings to be a mixture of evergreen and deciduous shrubs.

Deciduous shrubs offer much more seasonal color during the growing season than do simple mixes of evergreen needles and leaves. Deciduous shrubs also have many different leaf colors, and many have blooms to boot. A mixture of deciduous and evergreen shrubs makes for a very colorful attractive landscape. Deciduous shrubs even make interesting, leafless winter attraction, as well. So go ahead, mix them.

Abelia

Abelia x *grandiflora*

Botanical Pronunciation
uh-BEEL-yuh gran-dih-FLORE-uh

Other Name Glossy abelia

Bloom Period and Seasonal Color
Early spring to fall; leaves change colors
throughout the seasons; stark white blooms

Mature Height x Spread
2 to 4 feet x 3 to 5 feet

Glossy abelia is a semi-evergreen (though it's evergreen in the South) shrub with arching branches and a rounded shape. It has glossy, dark green, opposite leaves. The fragrant, funnel-shaped flowers produced in clusters are white, tinged with pink, and about an inch long. Glossy abelia begins flowering in midsummer and continues until the first frost. There are several named cultivars in the trade, including some with darker pink flowers, some with yellow or variegated leaves, some with a creeping habit, and some that stay small. I feel this plant is underused in the landscape and this is your invitation to plant one of these showstopping plants in your yard today. If you only have room for one abelia, choose 'Twist of Orange'; it is a beautiful plant in bloom and leaf color.

When, Where, and How to Plant
Plant container-grown abelia anytime the ground is not frozen, but the best selections will be in spring. Read the planting tips in this chapter's introduction for guidance.

Growing Tips
Follow a regular watering schedule during the first growing season to establish a deep, extensive root system. Feed with a general-purpose fertilizer before new growth begins in spring.

Regional Advice and Care
There are no serious insect or disease problems. This moderate grower is considered deer-resistant and easy to care for. For a tidy, neat appearance, shear annually to shape. Pruning time is in spring as new leaves emerge.

Companion Planting and Design
Glossy abelia is a cherished performer in the mixed shrub border because of its long season of blooms, from June to October. Use it for hedging, to separate garden areas, as a screen, or along a foundation. This plant is pretty in front of large, dark evergreens. This semi-evergreen is sure to add some zest to your landscape and would be a great addition to any yard.

Try These
'Twist of Orange' has beautiful variegated foliage with green, gold, orange, and red variegated foliage. A moderate grower, 'Twist of Orange' will reach about 4 feet tall and wide. 'Kaleidoscope' puts on a show with its ever-changing leaf color throughout the growing season. Leaves emerge in early spring with lime-green centers and bright yellow edges on bright red stems. In summer, the yellow matures to golden and in the fall the foliage deepens to shades of orange and fiery red.

Azalea

Rhododendron spp. and cultivars

Botanical Pronunciation
roh-do-DEN-dron

Bloom Period and Seasonal Color
Early April to May; purple, pink, red, orange, yellow, white blooms

Mature Height x Spread
3 to 15 feet x 3 to 15 feet (by variety)

Did you know that azaleas are all rhododendrons (that is, they are all members of the genus *Rhododendron*)? The large-leaf rhodos have a difficult time in much of Ohio because of our heavy, alkaline soils. Azaleas, on the other hand, adjust much better to our Ohio soils. Although there are hundreds of varieties, some grow here much better than others. Many gardeners yearn for those gorgeous drifts of azaleas, and even in Ohio you can have an impressive display, but you must choose the right plants and the right site. Azaleas are often classified as evergreen or deciduous; however, the evergreen varieties will still mostly turn color in fall and lose their foliage in the spring. If you long for azaleas, read on.

When, Where, and How to Plant

All azaleas do best when they are planted from spring to early fall. In Ohio, what azaleas need is protection from the northwest winter wind. Choose locations in good natural light or sun where they are blocked from the wind. My azaleas do best on the southeast side of my house. Azaleas have fine-textured root systems. They prefer well-drained, moist, rich, acidic soil. Good drainage is a *must*. If your soil consists of heavy clay, seriously consider mound planting. Follow the general planting directions listed in this chapters introduction.

Growing Tips

Azaleas are fussy in that they want moist soil *and* good drainage. Keep your plants moist; mulch is important to help conserve moisture. There are many soil acidifiers that can be added to alkaline planting beds. Feed azaleas in spring as new growth appears. Be careful not to overfeed, which can "burn" the roots. If you want more information, consult *Growing Rhododendrons and Azaleas in Ohio* distributed by Ohio State University. It is available through their website, http://ohioline.osu.edu/hyg-fact/1000/1078.html.

Regional Advice and Care

Few insect problems threaten this group, but root rot caused by poor drainage can be a serious problem. If you need to prune, always do so within 45 days after they finish blooming to avoid affecting the following year's blooms.

Companion Planting and Design

Azaleas are beautiful in mixed shrub borders and lightly shaded yards, or along woodland edges.

Try These

There are two groups of hybrid azaleas that are beautiful, tough, and well-suited to Ohio. 'Great Lakes' evergreen azalea was bred in northern Ohio. Look for the ones with the first name of "Girard's" in the series name, such as 'Girard's Rose'. The 'Northern Lights' azaleas are hardy, deciduous shrubs bred in Minnesota. Their fragrant flowers come in a wide range of colors. Look for "Lights" as the second part of the name, such as 'White Lights'. If you have the right conditions for the large-leaf rhodos, my favorite is 'Scintillation'. It's unforgettable. Stay away from varieties that have been grown in Oregon—Ohio-grown plants are best.

Blue Holly

Ilex x *meserveae* hybrids

Botanical Pronunciation
EYE-liks MESS-erv-ay

Other Name
Meserve hybrid holly

Bloom Period and Seasonal Color
Glossy evergreen foliage; red or yellow berries

Mature Height x Spread
5 to 6 feet x 3 to 5 feet

The *Ilex* genus gives the homeowner a range of landscape shrubs, both spreading and upright. For years, yew and juniper have been the main choices for the front of the home. Now you can reliably plant broadleaf evergreens as well. Besides looking good all the time, blue hollies are extremely winter hardy, disease resistant, and low maintenance. The foliage on these hollies is quite dark—a blue-green to shiny green that sets off the red berries for a great winter effect. Hollies come in two flavors: male or female. If you want berries, you'll need females, but they can't do it alone. A male holly within the range of a city block will do the trick, but it's best to have a male holly in your neighborhood.

When, Where, and How to Plant

Plant blue holly anytime the ground is not frozen. It does well in full sun to natural shade. It will not perform as well if sited in the summer shade of trees that allow full winter sun when the trees' leaves fall. Blue holly likes acidic soil with good drainage. For those who have alkaline clay soil, acidifiers can be added to keep the plant happy. Dig a hole no deeper than, but twice as wide as, the soil clump. If your soil is heavy clay, add a little organic material to amend it. Break up backfill soil to pieces no larger than golf balls. Water-in well to settle the soil and eliminate air pockets.

Growing Tips

Yellow leaves can be the result of alkaline soil, but you can acidify by fertilizing with an acid-based fertilizer. Do not overwater evergreen hollies, or the green leaves will turn black.

Regional Advice and Care

Blue holly is trouble-free when it comes to bugs and disease. Hand-prune to keep your holly at the desired size and shape.

Companion Planting and Design

These cold-hardy hollies make wonderful foundation plants. Install them close together to form a hedge, or space them apart to grow as individual plants. They work well to close in a patio or low deck. Plant any variety of dwarf spirea in front of blue holly, the foliage of each complements each other. Holly is also a nice background for spirea blooms.

Try These

One of the top blue hollies is 'Blue Maid'; it is a great choice for hedging. The best fruiting partner is, of course, 'Blue Stallion'. 'China Boy' and 'China Girl' is another good pair that has glossy green leaves. There are several varieties that eliminate the need for a pollinator; newer varieties include 'China Duet' (a combo of 'China Boy' and 'China Girl'), a compact upright shrub that can reach 8 feet tall and a 6 feet spread. 'Christmas Jewel' is a small pyramidal tree that grows to 10 feet high, with a spread of 6 feet, making it a perfect specimen tree.

Blue Mist Shrub

Caryopteris x *clandonensis*

Botanical Pronunciation
kair-ee-OP-tur-iss klan-dun-EN-siss

Other Name
Bluebeard

Bloom Period and Seasonal Color
Late July to September; blue blooms

Mature Height x Spread
2 to 3 feet x 3 to 4 feet

This lovely, bright blue-flowering shrub is almost considered an herbaceous perennial rather than a shrub. In Ohio, the plant dies back to the ground each winter. Other plants such as buddleia do the same thing; the term for this is a dieback shrub. This is a benefit because you know your blue mist shrub will never grow bigger than 3 feet × 4 feet. In late summer, blue flowers appear up and down all of the plant stems and last until fall. The leaves are gray-green, adding even more ornamental beauty. Blue mist does best in full sun, but it will provide good flowering even when receiving only a half-day of sun. It is a great, small shrub for late-summer color that lasts into fall.

When, Where, and How to Plant
Container-grown blue mist shrubs can be planted anytime the ground is not frozen. If you don't plant in fall (the best time), plant in spring or early summer to enjoy color the first year. However, some garden stores don't stock this plant until midsummer as the plants prepare to flower. Blue mist shrub prefers full sun to very light shade to maximize blooming. Loose, well-drained soil is ideal. Dig a hole no deeper than, but twice as wide as, the soil clump. Break up the backfill soil to pieces no larger than a golf ball. Loosen any wrapped roots, and backfill the hole. Water-in well.

Growing Tips
Give blue mist an occasional drink of water during hot, dry weather. For example, if there's no rainfall for two weeks, give each plant a 2-gallon bucketful of water. Fertilize with an all-purpose fertilizer once in spring.

Regional Advice and Care
Blue mist shrub resists bugs and disease. The first spring after planting will be scary. "Where's my plant?" you'll ask. Be patient, it will be there; it doesn't show new growth until May. Blue mist shrub is one of the last shrubs to leaf out in spring. In mild winters, your blue mist might not die back to the ground; cut it back to about 1 foot to keep it compact as new growth appears. Spring is the time to cut back all dead branches to the ground. Plants sometimes self-sow; weed out the seedlings as they will be inferior.

Companion Planting and Design
Blue mist shrub is an outstanding addition to any landscape. Plant where you can enjoy this plant from both outside and inside your home. It grows uniformly, making it perfect for a low hedge. It also works well in existing perennial beds to ensure that the beds generate late-summer color. In mixed color beds, plant blue mist with black-eyed Susans and ornamental grasses.

Try These
'Heavenly Blue' produces bright blue flowers that start blooming in late July and last well into September.

Bottlebrush Buckeye

Aesculus parviflora

Botanical Pronunciation
ESS-kew-lus par-vif-FLOR-uh

Bloom Period and Seasonal Color
Late spring to early summer; white; yellow blooms; colorful fall foliage

Mature Height x Spread
8 to 12 feet x 8 to 15 feet

An Ohio book could not be considered complete without including the buckeye. The bottlebrush buckeye is not a tree, but a shrub. Its showy white flowers appear in late May and last four to six weeks. The feathery blooms look like a bottlebrush, hence its common name. This buckeye tends to be wide-spreading with multiple stems, creating an impressive colony. Bright yellow fall leaves add to its landscape value. Look around—I'll bet you'll find a home for at least one, maybe more. This plant is underused. Basically, not many people are aware of it, so many garden centers and nursery stores don't even stock it. There are certain nurseries, though, that will have it in stock. Don't be afraid to order it. *Go Buckeyes!*

When, Where, and How to Plant
Bottlebrush buckeye is best planted in spring, and is available either balled and burlapped or in containers. Container-grown buckeyes can also be planted during summer and fall. It prefers acidic soil, but adapts to alkaline clay. The bottlebrush buckeye is usually listed as needing full sun to part shade, but I have seen it do exceptionally well when planted underneath shade trees with no direct sun at all. If you are planting in clay, add some organic material to the existing soil (about 30 percent organic by volume). Plant according to the tips listed in this chapter's introduction. Keep new plantings moist to encourage strong root growth.

Growing Tips
Bottlebrush buckeye appreciates moist soil, so water it weekly during dry spells. Fertilize in spring with a general landscape fertilizer.

Regional Advice and Care
Bottlebrush buckeye has virtually no problems with disease or insects. Some beetles will pick on a few leaves in early summer, but it's no problem—a few holes won't affect any plants. It will continue to be a great, care-free shrub. You may experience some leaf scorch in hot weather. Prune affected growth back when necessary or cut to the ground to rejuvenate.

Companion Planting and Design
Bottlebrush buckeye shows off well in a mass planting, as a shrub border, or as a one-of-a-kind planting; it also does well as a screening along a 4- to 8-foot-high deck. To make the most of this shrub's potential; plant it where it has room to grow.

Try These
'Rogers' is a form of bottlebrush buckeye chosen for its large flowers. What about the Ohio buckeye? *Aesculus glabra* is the true Ohio buckeye, and the Ohio state tree. It grows 20 to 40 feet in height and width. It can be disease-prone and messy and, although part of our history, it is best relegated to natural settings or large properties. If you want a buckeye tree for your yard, consider the red buckeye *A. × carnea* 'Briotii'. It is a beautiful, disease-resistant, medium-sized tree.

Butterfly Bush

Buddleia davidii

Botanical Pronunciation
BUD-lee-uh duh-VID-ee-eye

Other Name Summer lilac

Bloom Period and Seasonal Color
June to mid-October; blooms in pink, purple,
lavender, red-violet, yellow, white

Mature Height x Spread
4 to 8 feet x 4 to 7 feet (by variety)

Butterfly bush does just what its name suggests: attracts butterflies in summer. It is sometimes referred to as summer lilac because of its long, upright panicles of flowers. It is fast growing, yet it grows to the same size (close to 6 feet tall!) every year. That's because most of each year's growth dies back to within a foot of the ground by the next spring. Butterfly bush boasts sweet-scented flowers sitting on the branch tips. It is usually available in shades of lilac, purple, and pink; there is a yellow variety also. Some varieties have been known to bloom from July into early October. Young children love to watch the butterflies feed off the flowers. Plan a butterfly garden with a butterfly bush this year.

When, Where, and How to Plant

The best selection will be found in spring. Technically, you can plant butterfly bush anytime the ground is not frozen, but plant in spring to early summer to enjoy blooms the first year and give it a chance to establish before its first winter. Butterfly bush grows best in full sun, but will do okay if it receives at least a half-day of sun. Avoid planting in lots of shade because flower production will be disappointing. It grows well in any type of well-drained soil. Follow the planting directions listed in this chapter's introduction. Keep new plants moist to promote healthy root development.

Growing Tips

Once established, butterfly bush is quite drought tolerant. Feed in early spring with garden fertilizer, following the directions.

Regional Advice and Care

There are no important bugs or diseases that bother it. In Ohio, butterfly bush usually dies back to within 1 foot of the ground in winter. When new growth appears near the ground in spring, prune back all the branches to within 1 foot of the ground. After each stem blooms, cut it back halfway to encourage additional blooms. Don't be impatient in spring. Butterfly bush starts showing new growth much later than other shrubs.

Companion Planting and Design

This is a shrub to plant in a spot where kids of all ages can enjoy it from inside or outside the house. If you live in a naturally windy area, plant the shrubs out of the prevailing breeze to encourage butterflies. Butterfly bush makes a colorful accent plant in a bed of mixed perennials. If using standard-sized butterfly bush you can mix with other flowering dwarf shrubs in mixed perennial beds.

Try These

If you want to receive all the fragrance and butterfly appeal of traditional varieties in a small, easy-to-maintain package then get the Lo & Behold series (4 varieties): 'Purple Haze', 'Blue Chip', 'Lilac Chip', and 'Ice Chip'. 'Black Knight with its dark purple blooms is very popular. If you want variety then try the '4th of July' with explosions of color in pink, purple, and white blooms.

Crimson Pygmy Barberry

Berberis thunbergii 'Crimson Pygmy'

Botanical Pronunciation
BER-ber-is thun-BERG-ee-a

Other Name Dwarf red barberry

Bloom Period and Seasonal Color
Red to purple foliage in spring (the more sun, the redder); yellow to orange to red fall color

Mature Height x Spread
1½ to 2 feet x 2½ to 3 feet

Barberry may be thorny, but the pygmies in my landscape are some of my favorites. In fact, I have lined my front walk with them. During the growing season, they have beautiful leaves; the foliage is either maroon ('Crimson Pygmy'), mottled pink ('Rose Glow'), or yellow ('Gold Nugget'). Even in the winter they look great. Add snow, and you have a holiday card. They can take heavy shearing, which will allow you to have a barberry hedge 12 inches high by 10 inches wide. You can even plant a sunny hillside with these, making an outstanding landscape site. To maximize red spring leaf color, plant these shrubs in lots of sun. Another value of barberry is its thorns, which make it a great barrier plant.

When, Where, and How to Plant
Most, if not all, barberries are container-grown. Plant anytime the ground is not frozen. To maximize leaf color, plant barberry in as much sun as possible, at least a half-day. Barberry is self-sustaining; it grows well in what could be described as terrible soil, including clay, as long as it drains well. Consult this chapter's introduction for planting instructions. For hedging, plant on 24-inch centers.

Growing Tips
Barberry is drought tolerant; do not overwater during dry periods. Washed-out looking foliage color with brown leaf tips is a clue of overwatering. In poor soils, fertilize in spring with a general garden fertilizer.

Regional Advice and Care
No bugs or diseases bother these plants. In fact, bunnies don't even like to run through them. All barberries, whether dwarf or standard, will keep getting larger if not pruned. Remember, no tree or shrub stops growing until the day it dies. It's just that some plants can be kept small for years by pruning. Wear gloves; these plants are quite prickly. Prune barberry anytime to the size and shape you desire. Pruning shears are best, but hedge shears are faster as long as you can control the bigger blades.

Companion Planting and Design
Dwarf barberry varieties come with red, pink, or gold leaves. Plant some of each in the same general area, and the color contrast will be fantastic. Pygmy barberry gives leaf color to any landscape during the entire growing season. It excels both as an individual plant and as a dwarf hedging. It also does well as an underplanting.

Try These
In addition to 'Crimson Pygmy', I like 'Bagatelle', very dwarf and has red-purple leaves and great fall color. For a taller hedging plant, 'Atropurpurea' grows larger than a pygmy, reaching about 4 feet. 'Rose Glow' can be kept at 2 to 3 feet and has green and white leaves flushed with a rosy cast. Want yellow foliage instead of purple? 'Golden Nugget' has gold leaves on a compact body just 1 foot tall. Slightly taller 'Bonanza Gold' has golden yellow leaves.

Dwarf Burning Bush

Euonymus alatus 'Compactus'

Botanical Pronunciation you-ON-ih-mus eh-LAY-tus

Other Name Dwarf winged euonymus

Bloom Period and Seasonal Color
Brilliant red fall color; white spring blooms; may
have red berries in fall

Mature Height x Spread 8 to 10 feet x 6 to
10 feet

Dwarf burning bush is a popular plant, not because of its bloom, but because it will fill any spot in the landscape. This plant will grow in full sun to full shade. Burning bush has tiny flowers in spring, but it is best known for its lush, dark green leaves that turn a flaming red in the fall. This bush has ridged, somewhat square twigs that give it a great look in the winter landscape. Burning bush is considered to be a dwarf, not because it grows slowly, but because it will tolerate heavy pruning. Some think this plant has been overused, but if you want a low-maintenance shrub, it is perfect. Sometimes burning bush will have red berries in the fall.

When, Where, and How to Plant
You can buy dwarf burning bush as either a balled-and-burlapped or container-grown plant. It is easily transplanted anytime the ground is not frozen. This plant also spreads underground through the soil; transplant any shoots in early spring to other areas where you want dwarf burning bushes. Choose a location in sun or shade, although sun produces the best fall color. It wants good drainage, but will tolerate heavy clay soil. Follow the general instructions for shrub planting in this chapter's introduction.

Growing Tips
Keep new plantings moist the first year to allow them to establish strong roots. Water weekly if there is no rain during summer. Fertilize in spring, following the directions on the container.

Regional Advice and Care
This is another of my recommended low-maintenance plants. No pests or diseases plague this variety. Prune it as often as necessary to the size and shape you prefer. Your shrub will attain a more attractive form if you avoid shearing and use pruners to thin and shape. You can literally cut the plant back to the ground in spring and *voila*, it's brand-new. This type of pruning causes many new shoots to grow from the soil; leave them in place to add thickness or transplant to other areas.

Companion Planting and Design
Dwarf burning bush fits many landscape situations. It can be used as a specimen plant or grouped for a great hedge. Plant many of them if you want to screen out an unsightly view or to hide the foundation of a home. It's great to use around a basketball backboard to help keep a ball within easy reach when it wants to go out of bounds. Remember, though, it can grow to 10 feet tall and wide, so place it where it has enough room or be prepared to prune to keep it smaller.

Try These
'Compactus' is the most common variety available. 'Chicago Fire' is compact, although it ultimately reaches 8 to 10 feet, with rich red fall color and lots of berries.

Dwarf Falsecypress

Chamaecyparis obtusa
'Nana Gracilis'

Botanical Pronunciation
kam-ee-SIPP-ur-iss ub-TOO-zuh

Other Name Dwarf Hinoki cypress

Bloom Period and Seasonal Color
Dark green evergreen foliage

Mature Height x Spread 6 to 7 feet x 3 to 4 feet

This beautiful, dwarf-growing evergreen is one of the most prized plants in my landscape. Although slow growing, it's worth the wait. 'Nana Gracilis' has dark green needles with new growth that offers just a tinge of light green color, a beautifully rare color that visitors sometimes think is unreal. It is strictly a specimen plant that you will want to place in a prominent viewing area so that it can be appreciated from both inside and outside the home. An area with good drainage and some protection from the prevailing northwest winter winds would be ideal. A native of Japan and China, *Chamaecyparis obtusa* 'Nana Gracilis' brings a little bit of the Orient to the Buckeye State. This variety has many cousins, which I've listed.

When, Where, and How to Plant
Most dwarf falsecypress are container grown. A few grown in the Pacific Northwest are field dug during the months of February and March and sold as balled-and-burlapped plants. Both types can be planted anytime. Plant falsecypress in full sun to a half-day of shade. Make sure your planting site has decent soil (no heavy clay) with good drainage. It does well in non-acidic soil, which is typical for most of Ohio. Dwarf falsecypress needs protection from cold winter winds. Dig your planting hole 50 percent wider than the rootball or soil clump, and no deeper than the depth of the roots. Break up backfill soil into particles no larger than golf balls. Backfill, and water-in thoroughly. Apply a 2-inch layer of mulch.

Growing Tips
Be sure to keep this plant moist, but not wet, during hot, dry summers. Feed with a general-purpose fertilizer in spring, if desired.

Regional Advice and Care
This plant is definitely low maintenance and is troubled by no known bugs or disease. All falsecypress shed inner needles in spring and fall; please don't overreact and think your plant is in trouble. It has a wonderful, natural, upright-growing shape. Don't prune it to be uniform and stiff looking; let it establish its own shape.

Companion Planting and Design
Place falsecypress where you can visually enjoy it year-round. Plant it as a centerpiece in a dwarf conifer bed or rock garden, or use it as the anchor plant in a bed full of annuals and perennials.

Try These
There are many other varieties of falsecypress. If you find one you like, just be sure it's cold hardy enough for Ohio winters. For an impressive and elegant specimen plant, look for the Nootka false-cypress, *Chamaecyparis nootkatensis*. 'Pendula' is a particularly elegant form. The threadleaf false-cypress are plants for that "something different." *C. pisifera* 'Filifera Aurea' produces mounds of thin, golden foliage. 'Golden Mop' is a more compact form—the name says it all.

Dwarf Spirea

Spiraea x bumalda

Botanical Pronunciation
spy-REE-uh bew-MAL-duh

Other Name
Bumald spirea

Bloom Period and Seasonal Color
Late May; red, white, and shades of pink blooms

Mature Height x Spread
2 to 3 feet x 3 to 5 feet (Prune to desired size)

Spirea has a long history in the landscape. In the early fifties, a dwarf variety with rose-pink flowers was beginning to make a name for itself. 'Anthony Waterer' spirea started showing up in garden centers . . . at 3 to 4 feet tall, it was much smaller-growing than the then-popular, but tall and lanky, bridal wreath spirea. Since then, many new varieties of small shrubby spireas have been introduced. Some bloom in white, some pink, and some red, and one—'Shibori'—blooms in all of those colors at the same time. Some have golden leaves, some green, some green-and-red, and some yellow-and-red. All have nice compact shapes, long blooming periods, and great orange-red fall color. Don't overlook these easy-to-grow spireas.

When, Where, and How to Plant

Spireas are grown in containers and can be planted anytime the ground is not frozen. Dwarf spirea does great in any type of soil; just make sure it has good drainage. It blooms best in full sun, but will tolerate a half-day of shade. Dig a hole no deeper than the soil clump and twice as wide. If you have clay soil, break up the existing soil so that no particle is larger than a golf ball. Backfill and water-in well. A 2-inch layer of mulch will keep the soil moist.

Growing Tips

Water your newly planted spirea during dry spells the first year. Once established, it is very drought tolerant. If your plant lacks vigor, consider fertilizing in spring following the instructions on your favorite plant food container.

Regional Advice and Care

Spirea is free of bugs and disease. They have their first—and I mean their *first*—bloom period in late May. After the bloom is finished, take a pair of hedge shears and remove all spent flowers. Wait a month, and it will bloom again. Then remove those spent flowers. Repeat this process all summer, and the flowers won't stop. The pruning will also keep the shrub at a suitable growing size.

Companion Planting and Design

For best landscape effect, always plant three of the same variety. Dwarf spirea makes a great low hedge or an underplanting around a high-branched tree. It also has a nice winter appearance, with bare twigs that say, "Hey, I'm part of this landscape even in winter." Every landscape has room for them.

Try These

'Shibori' is perfect for homeowners who can't make up their mind on color. Each plant is covered with flowers in white, pink, and magenta, creating a festive display. Spireas have become popular for their colored foliage effects. 'Limemound' has foliage that emerges yellow and matures to lime green. 'Golden Princess' has bronzy leaves in spring that change to yellow. There's great red and orange fall color on these shrubs!

Forsythia

Forsythia x *intermedia*

Botanical Pronunciation
for-SYE-thee-uh in-tur-MEE-dee-uh

Other Name Golden bells

Bloom Period and Seasonal Color
March to April; yellow flowers

Mature Height x Spread
8 to 10 feet x 10 to 12 feet

Forsythia is what I call the "Spring Breaker"—when forsythia starts to bloom, spring is in the air. It is not new—it seems like it has been around forever. It may be an oldie, but it sure is a goodie. What would spring be without forsythia? It is an upright-growing shrub; some varieties sweep their branches to the ground. The secret to growing it well is to plant it where it has plenty of room, then put your pruners away and enjoy the show! One forsythia makes a great shrub for spring color, or plant several for a fantastic screening hedge that will block out your neighbor's property—and that's not being mean, either, as both you and your neighbor gain privacy and gorgeous color.

When, Where, and How to Plant
Forsythia plants come from the nursery either balled and burlapped or growing in containers. Plant forsythia anytime the ground is not frozen. A half-day of sun or more is necessary for good bloom color. Forsythia likes good, rich soil, but will adapt to heavy clay soil. Good drainage is a must. Turn to this chapter's introduction for specifics on planting shrubs. For hedge or mass plantings, allow plenty of space between plants; the distance will vary depending on the cultivar.

Growing Tips
Forsythia is low maintenance and drought tolerant. Give it a drink of water if the summer is hot and dry, and there has been no rain for a couple of weeks. Forsythia generally doesn't require fertilization.

Regional Advice and Care
Pests and disease rarely trouble forsythia. A mature shrub will eventually have to be pruned to keep it healthy and inbounds; do this within a month after it blooms. After your forsythia has been planted for eight to ten years, prune one-third of the oldest branches back to about 12 inches from the ground every year for three years. To start an all-new plant instantly, prune back the entire plant to 12 inches from the ground right after it blooms. Avoid shearing your forsythia, which destroys its natural form.

Companion Planting and Design
Forsythia is excellent for massing, informal hedges, or a groundcover on slopes. Just be sure to give it plenty of room so you're not tempted to get out the hedge trimmers. Remember that in most cases forsythia is too big to use as a foundation plant.

Try These
Cold temperatures can blast the flower buds—have you ever seen forsythia blooming just at the bottom below the snowline? If you live in Zone 5, plant cultivars known for their bud hardiness. 'Northern Sun' (8 to 10 feet tall) and 'Meadowlark' (6 to 9 feet) are two of the best. For the amount of bloom color on a single plant, 'Spectabilis' (10 feet) sets the standard for all other selections.

Goldencup St. Johnswort

Hypericum patulum

Botanical Pronunciation
hy-PER-ee-kum PAT-yoo-lum

Other Name Goldencup

Bloom Period and Seasonal Color
Mid-June to August; bright yellow blooms

Mature Height x Spread
3 feet x 3 feet

This is one summer-blooming shrub I really love. The common name I have given this hypericum is "the yellow daffodil bush," because its blooms are the color of yellow daffodils and each looks like a single narcissus. I have a grouping in my front landscape, right outside the picture window in my living room. They bloom some in June, then in all of July and August, and I get to enjoy them from both outside and inside. The fruit will remind you of black olives, and the birds like them too. It can be called semi-evergreen because most of the gray-green leaves remain on the plant in Zone 6. You will find goldencup's persistent bloom a welcome addition to your landscape.

When, Where, and How to Plant
Goldencup is available from the garden store in early spring. You won't be impressed at first because it will look like just a pot of sticks and some leaves, but don't worry. Plant goldencup anytime the ground is not frozen. It flowers best in full sun. It will, however, tolerate a few hours of daily shade. Goldencup appreciates good, loose soil, but will tolerate heavy clay well. Make sure the planting site has good drainage. Since all goldencup plants are grown in containers, remove the soil clump from the pot and loosen any wrapped roots. Dig a hole no deeper than, but twice as wide as, the soil clump. Break up clay particles to the size of golf balls, and water-in well. Space plants 2½ to 3 feet apart. Keep new plantings moist to aid root establishment.

Growing Tips
Because goldencup is shallow-rooted, protect those roots with a 2-inch covering of mulch. Keep the mulch off the stems. This plant is drought tolerant, but appreciates a drink in dry, hot weather. Fertilize in spring, if desired, with a general-purpose or slow-release fertilizer.

Regional Advice and Care
In early spring, prune back all twigs to within 8 inches of the ground. This plant is resistant to insects and disease.

Companion Planting and Design
If you want just one, plant it in your perennial bed. If you have tastes like mine, you'll buy three to five of them, or more. Goldencup looks great in a large sweep or try it as a groundcover. You can also use it in combination with other shrubs, such as blue spirea, juniper, or dwarf barberry. It looks great as an underplanting for a drift of feather reed grass.

Try These
Hypericum frondosum 'Sunburst' has characteristics similar to those of 'Sungold', but it grows a little taller and wider. 'Sunburst' has been a great performer in Ohio, producing yellow flowers, often from June through October. Hypericums are so easy to grow and enjoy; try one.

Juniper

Juniperus cultivars

Botanical Pronunciation
jew-NIP-er-us

Other Name
Red cedar

Bloom Period and Seasonal Color
Evergreen foliage in shades of green, blue, yellow

Mature Height x Spread
5 to 15 feet x 5 to 6 feet (by variety)

Junipers are versatile, hard-working shrubs. They are available for home landscapes as both spreaders and uprights. As spreaders, some junipers grow very low, making them excellent groundcovers (see creeping juniper in the Groundcovers chapter). Others grow to an average height of 4 feet, and work well for foundation plantings or under small flowering trees. Some uprights can become large, pyramidal trees. Many new varieties are soft to the touch, easy to trim, and work well in any landscape. There are thirteen junipers native to the United States. In Ohio we have *Juniperus virginiana*, often called eastern red cedar. The wood of this common variety, which grows along our interstates, is used in making furniture, paneling, and even pencils. A fun fact—the juniper fruit is used to flavor gin.

When, Where, and How to Plant
Plant any juniper whenever the ground is not frozen. Drought-tolerant juniper needs a sunny, well-drained site to thrive—any area where rainwater doesn't stand after ½ inch of rain. Give it at least a half-day of sun. Turn to this chapter's introduction for planting specifics. With varieties that spread over the top of the hole, be sure to backfill completely around the soil clump so there will be no air pockets exposing the roots. Space your plant with its mature size in mind.

Growing Tips
Keep newly planted juniper moist to encourage strong root growth. Avoid overwatering, though, as junipers don't like it wet. Keep them out of the mist of a sprinkler and don't overhead water. In poor soils, mature plants should be fertilized in the spring with a slow-release fertilizer.

Regional Advice and Care
Juniper twig blight can cause branch dieback. The newer varieties listed here are quite resistant to bugs and disease. Problems usually result from planting a juniper in an inappropriate area. Prune infected branches back to healthy growth. Avoid shearing juniper; plant it where it has enough space to accommodate its mature size. Use pruners to remove any straggly or out-of-proportion branches.

Companion Planting and Design
There is no limit to the use of junipers in the home landscape—shrub border, massing, screening, groundcover, and so on. Those used in the Ohio area are Chinese juniper, *Juniperus chinensis*; common juniper, *J. communis*; shore juniper, *J. conferta*; creeping juniper, *J. horizontalis*; eastern red cedar, *J. virginiana*; and singleseed juniper, *J. squamata*.

Try These
When choosing a juniper, first find out the mature height and spread, and compare that to the space in your landscape. Visit your nursery and see what they have. New varieties are constantly being introduced. Here are a few of my favorites: 'Gold Coast' has yellow new growth, and 'Mint Julep' has fountain-like foliage; both are 3 × 4 foot spreaders. For uprights, I suggest 'Robusta Green' and 'Hetzii Columnaris'. They reach about 15 feet tall in the landscape, but can be pruned to keep them smaller.

Korean Boxwood

Buxus microphylla var. *koreana*

Botanical Pronunciation
BUKS-us my-kro-FY-lah

Other Name
Littleleaf boxwood

Bloom Period and Seasonal Color
Evergreen foliage in fresh green

Mature Height x Spread
2 to 4 feet x 3 to 4 feet

For years, homeowners and landscapers alike tried to incorporate common English boxwood into home landscapes in Ohio. But our cold, windy winters wreaked havoc on these tender evergreens, causing the leaves to turn an ugly brown and dieback to occur. What's the point? Then along came Korean boxwood, whose hardiness and compactness allowed homeowners in Ohio to use boxwoods in almost any exposure. Promising hybrids between common box and Korean box are the best yet. These newer boxwoods hold their dark, sometimes glossy, green leaf color year-round and really live up to the term low maintenance. Ask about this latest generation of boxwoods at your local nursery. If you need a number of plants of a cultivar, buy them all at one time to get a matching set.

When, Where, and How to Plant
Plant anytime the ground isn't frozen. Korean boxwood prefers moist, but well-drained soil—not too wet or too dry, please. It tolerates clay soil as long as it has good drainage. Amend heavy clay soil by adding up to 20 percent organic material. Though Korean boxwood can be planted in full to part sun exposures, avoid locations under trees that have summer shade but allow winter sun when the leaves fall, as more leaf burn may occur during a cold winter. Shade is fine as long as it's year-round shade, as on the north side of the home. Follow the planting instructions listed in this chapter's introduction. Space depending on variety.

Growing Tips
Check for moisture during hot, dry periods; water as necessary to keep soil moist. Boxwoods are shallow-rooted, so mulching is important. Maintain a 2-inch mulch layer under each plant. Keep plants hydrated going into winter. Boxwoods can be fertilized in early spring, but take care not to over-fertilize. Follow the fertilizer package instructions.

Regional Advice and Care
Korean boxwoods are low-maintenance plants. Spring aphids can cause some leaf curl, but it is not a serious problem. Following the Growing Tips here will discourage pests. For formal hedges or shaping your plants, it's best to prune boxwood with pruning shears; since they grow slowly, this is not a big chore. It's nice to know that deer don't like boxwood.

Companion Planting and Design
Check with a nursery employee to make sure you get the right variety for your landscape needs. In addition to its fantastic hedging possibilities, hardy boxwood works well as an individual foundation plant, formal accent, or an underplanting for an ornamental tree.

Try These
Look for the hardy, leaf burn-resistant hybrids. Both 'Green Gem' (2 feet tall) and 'Green Velvet' (3 feet) grow like a bright green, round ball. 'Green Mountain', a more vigorous grower, forms a perfect pyramidal upright form and is the best choice for a larger hedge. It's a great substitute for the red-spider-ridden Alberta spruce.

Korean Lilac

Syringa meyeri 'Palibin'

Botanical Pronunciation
si-RING-gah MY-er-eye

Other Name
Manchurian lilac

Bloom Period and Seasonal Color
Mid to late April; purple-lavender blooms;
orange-red fall color

Mature Height x Spread
5 to 6 feet x 5 to 7 feet

For many years, homeowners have bought common lilacs, some of which are called French lilacs, thinking they were buying a shrub. The truth is common lilacs should have been described as trees—that's how big they grow. And if you prune them to keep them short, you cut off all of next year's flowers. Throw in powdery mildew that makes foliage unsightly in summer and the beauty becomes a beast! Finally, some dwarf lilacs have arrived that are truly shrubs. One of the best is *Syringa meyeri* 'Palibin', also called Korean or dwarf Meyer lilac. It has purplish buds that open to fragrant, lavender-pink flowers; a nice compact size; great-looking, disease-free foliage; and fantastic orange-red fall leaf color. Now, that's a lilac you can love.

When, Where, and How to Plant

Plant balled-and-burlapped or container-grown dwarf lilac anytime the ground is not frozen. More sun results in more flowers and better fall leaf color. I have even planted Korean lilac in areas with no sun but good natural light, and it still bloomed and provided fall color. This plant will grow in any type of soil with decent drainage and will produce flowers even as a young plant. Follow the shrub planting directions listed in this chapter's introduction.

Growing Tips

Give your lilacs an occasional drink during hot, dry weather. To be on the safe side, avoid overhead watering that can promote mildew. Mulch to preserve summer moisture. Fertilize in early spring using your favorite slow-release or general garden fertilizer, following the instructions on the container.

Regional Advice and Care

There are no bug or disease problems with Korean lilac. Removing spent flowers—a task often suggested for common lilacs—isn't necessary. If you have time, prune off as many of the finished flowers as possible. This encourages more spot-bloom during the summer.

Companion Planting and Design

This plant works well by itself in the landscape, or use it in a grouping or as a screen. It is the perfect choice for a patio, pathway, or under a window where its sweet fragrance can be appreciated. Plant in front of larger evergreens and the lilac flowers will be more pronounced. Use several different varieties in a mixed shrub bed. Plant with similarly sized shrubs in a border to the extend bloom time of the various shrubs.

Try These

Another shrub called Korean lilac is *Syringa patula* 'Miss Kim'. It is easy to get these plants confused; they are both fantastic dwarf lilacs. 'Miss Kim' has purple buds that open to an icy lavender-blue, with great fragrance, no mildew problems, and often purplish colors in fall. 'Bloomarang Dark Purple' has dark grape-colored buds that open to a purplish plum and continues to bloom until frost. 'Scent and Sensibility' is a dwarf lilac that reblooms with dark pink buds opening into a lilac pink.

Oakleaf Hydrangea

Hydrangea quercifolia

Botanical Pronunciation
hy-DRAIN-juh kwer-se-FOH-lee-uh

Bloom Period and Seasonal Color
Mid-May to July; white blooms; maroon to red
fall color

Mature Height x Spread
5 to 6 feet x 5 to 6 feet

Oakleaf hydrangeas are one of a select group of plants that look good in any season—amazing long-lasting flowers, beautiful foliage, wonderful crimson red-purple fall leaf color, and attractive bark. I *promise* if you plant this shrub, it will become the most asked-about plant in your garden. Oakleaf hydrangea prospers in many landscape situations. It will do well in partial shade to full sun. As its name indicates, it has large, oak-shaped leaves. Starting in mid-May, it produces impressive, cone-shaped, white blooms that size out at 8 inches long and 3 to 4 inches wide. Leave the flowers on the plant because they dry to a pinkish purple that lasts into the fall. I know you can find a spot for this beautiful shrub.

When, Where, and How to Plant

Hydrangea is best planted in spring to maximize the time it has to establish its roots. Select a location in partial to full sun. Hydrangea prefers fairly decent soil that's on the acidic side and has good drainage. It will adapt to clay or alkaline soil. If you have clay, dig a hole no deeper than the soil clump but about three times as wide. Mix some organic material into the existing soil, and break up clay soil particles so that none are larger than a golf ball. Backfill, and water-in well.

Growing Tips

Oakleaf can really look stressed its first year. Try not to overwater or overfertilize when you plant. Be patient, it *will* get a lot better looking. Keep hydrangeas mulched to 2 inches deep, and check for moisture during hot, dry periods. Feed with a soil acidifier every spring.

Regional Advice and Care

No problems with pests or disease with this shrub. Oakleaf hydrangea sets its bloom buds in fall for the next season, so don't prune before they bloom. Always prune away any dead stems as they appear, and don't do any tip-pruning to your hydrangea more than thirty days after it blooms in summer. If any branches fail to leaf out in spring, remove them.

Companion Planting and Design

These plants can get big, and the foliage and flowers are bold. Oakleaf hydrangeas brighten shady or sunny areas, making it great for a group planting and for shrub borders. Only room for one? That'll look great too. Mix with other *Hydrangea* members. The color of various varieties will give you months of color until late fall.

Try These

I couldn't resist listing some of newer *H. macrophylla* varieties. 'Everlasting Revolution Hydrangea' re-blooms, creating a beautiful combination of pinks, blues, maroons, and greens against deeply colored thick foliage. 'Let's Dance Rhapsody' has spectacular blue color. 'Strawberry Sundae' has summer flowers emerging creamy white before turning pink on their way to a beautiful strawberry red.

Rhododendron

Rhododendron species

Botanical Pronunciation
roe-doe-DEN-dron

Bloom Period and Seasonal Color
Spring blooms in all colors

Mature Height x Spread
5 feet x 3 to 5 feet

Rhododendrons have been around in landscapes for 100-plus years. Earlier varieties hated clay soil and very hot summers. In the past, I have personally discouraged homeowners and landscape designers from installing any from this family of plants in the landscape. I used to comment, "They'll never grow in the heavy clay soils of the Tri-State." This large, beautiful, and often fragrant flowers cannot be duplicated by another spring-flowering plant. But plant breeders realized the interest in this plant and have developed more northern hardy cultivars. So now I've had to change my tune about these plants as there are new varieties, which are both dwarf growing and evergreen.

When, Where, and How to Plant
Plant balled-and-burlapped plants as soon as possible after purchasing. Plant container-grown plants in spring or early summer so they establish before winter. An east-facing location works well. Plant these evergreen rhododendrons in cool, moist, acidic, loose, well-drained soil. If your soil needs improvement use one-half existing soil and one-half organic peat. You can add granular sulfur or some other acidifying material prior to planting. Space them about 3 feet apart.

Growing Tips
Rhododendrons are very shallow-rooted. Sufficient soil moisture is critical. Rhododendrons' outstanding flowers are formed during the summer months for the following season's show. If pruning is carried out too late in the summer, it will remove some flower buds. Therefore, pruning these specimens as the flowers fade is the best policy.

Regional Advice and Care
The plants should be fed twice in spring—once before and once after bloom—and in mid-August, with a fertilizer labeled for acid-loving plants. Never fertilize when plants are dry. Apply around the plants' drip line.

Companion Planting and Design
Rhododrens are nice as a focal point in the spring garden or as an understory plant in woodland gardens. See the "Azalea" varieties and plant those in front of rhododendrons.

Try These
'PJM' has large bold foliage and maintains a striking winter color. Robust flowers withstand rain and frost. Sturdy upright stems develop a full lush-looking plant. Its average size will be 8 feet tall and wide. 'Northern Starburst' is a greatly improved cousin of 'PJM'. 'Lakeview Pink Inkarho" works with poor soils! Showy, clear pink flowers in the spring and long, rich green foliage all year long. The mature size will be 5 feet tall and 4 feet wide. 'Abbey's Re-View' is one of the best evergreen rhododendrons for multi-season blooms. The show starts in early spring with an explosion of dark pink flowers and picks up in early fall with another showing. "Abbey's" dark blue green leaves give this rhododendron great year-round interest. Reaching a mounded shape of 6 feet × 6 feet, this rhododendron is perfect for borders or specimen plantings.

Rose-of-Sharon

Hibiscus syriacus

Botanical Pronunciation
high-BISS-kuss seer-ee-AY-kuss

Bloom Period and Seasonal Color
Summer to fall; blue, lavender, and white blooms

Mature Height x Spread
8 feet x 6 to 7 feet

This isn't your grandmother's variety of rose-of-Sharon but a much-improved version. This is a tough adaptable shrub or small tree that flowers in midsummer. You'll want this plant at the end of summer because you'll see rose-of-Sharon putting on a flower show, full of blooms. This show performance starts once most other plants have done their last curtain call. These beauties have hibiscus-type flowers that last well into fall. They even produce brown fruit capsules that persist to add winter interest. Numerous cultivars provide a variety of colors in double or single blooms. There is even a variety or two with bicolor blooms.

When, Where, and How to Plant
Plant container-grown or balled-and-burlapped rose-of-Sharon anytime the ground is not frozen. They do well in full sun to part shade. These plants tolerate a wide range of soil conditions but do best in moist, well-drained soil. They can reach 8 to 12 feet tall and 6 to 10 feet wide at maturity. Space plants 4 to 6 feet apart.

Growing Tips
Rose-of-Sharon adapts to numerous conditions, but it does not tolerate extreme moisture. Water thoroughly whenever the top 4 to 6 inches of soil are crumbly and moist. Mulching helps conserve water and reduce weed problems. Feed in spring with all-purpose plant food.

Regional Advice and Care
Prune established plants yearly to remove dead wood and increase flower size. Prune main branches and shorten side shoots to two or three buds for an impressive flower display. Rose-of-Sharon can be severely damaged or killed in extremely cold winters. New plantings are often slow to leaf out in spring. Give them plenty of time to leaf out before declaring them dead and replacing them. This shrub blooms on new growth so a little spring pruning will go a long way in encouraging heavy blooming.

Companion Planting and Design
Use it as a small specimen or in the shrub border where this feature can be enjoyed. It combines nicely with a wide variety of annuals and perennials. The old-fashioned feel of this plant looks nice against a stone house or mixed with other heirloom plants. Use it in a shrub border with Korean lilacs, butterfly bush, or as a background to a mixed perennial bed.

Try These
'Blue Angel' has large, rich blue flowers. 'Pink Angel' has prominent displays of pink flowers with bright red centers. 'White Angel' has a delicate-looking flower but it is anything but that, because it's tough as nails. 'Fiji' is bursting with flowers come midsummer. The semi-double flowers start a medium pink but open to a softer hue with a streak of reddish purple in the center. 'Bali' is a fancy double, pure white bloom. 'Tahiti' has lavender-pink petals.

Spreading Yew

Taxus cultivars

Botanical Pronunciation
TAKS-us

Other Name
Taxus

Bloom Period and Seasonal Color
Evergreen; some females have red berries

Mature Height x Spread
3 to 6 feet x 6 to 8 feet

Spreading yews have been the most popular plant in home foundation plantings for years. They are durable, attractive, and submit to shearing. Trim to the size and shape you desire your yews to attain. They grow in full sun to full shade. One of the worst exposures you can have for almost any evergreen is summer tree shade that becomes a winter sun site when those trees drop their leaves. But spreading yews can tolerate even those drastic light changes and remain great plants in your landscape. One thing all spreading yews require is good drainage; don't plant them in low areas that collect water after a heavy rain. Some female varieties have red berries in the fall that add to their ornamental beauty.

When, Where, and How to Plant

Plant spreading yews anytime the ground is not frozen. Most yews at your local garden center are balled and burlapped; some are field-potted and available in containers. However taxus is available, it will transplant very easily. Good drainage is a must. Even in clay soil, the planting area must drain after heavy rains; therefore, do not plant under a downspout. Sun or shade, it doesn't matter. This plant does well on the north side of the house where other evergreens might fail or look ugly because of lack of sun. Follow the shrub planting instructions listed in this chapter's introduction.

Growing Tips

Keep newly planted yews moist but don't overwater; yews don't want to be waterlogged. Keep plants mulched. Fertilize with a slow-release fertilizer in spring.

Regional Advice and Care

Yews have few insect or disease problems. Deer, on the other hand, can be a problem. Sprays are available to make your yews less desirable to deer. You can trim spreading yews and keep them as small as 12 × 12 inches, or prune to another desired size. Yews are best trimmed with hand-pruners and allowed to develop a natural form. The berries are poisonous *if* you crack the very small seed in the center of the berry. Lots of nurserymen (as well as birds) have eaten the berries for years.

Companion Planting and Design

Spreading yews make great individual plants or a classic low hedge when allowed to grow together. And, of course, yews are a popular foundation plant. For hedges, plant on 3-foot centers.

Try These

Some of the best spreading yews are cultivars of *Taxus* × *media*, the English-Japanese or Anglojap yew. 'Wardii' is a female with a nice, low-spreading form that grows slowly to 6 feet. A male selection is 'Brownii'. It has a rounded habit that can reach 6 to 9 feet if not pruned. Ask the staff at your favorite nursery to recommend others.

Summersweet

Clethra alnifolia

Botanical Pronunciation
KLEE-thra al-nee-FOH-lee-uh

Other Name
Sweet pepper bush

Bloom Period and Seasonal Color
Late June to August; white, rose, pink blooms;
colorful fall foliage

Mature Height x Spread
3 to 8 feet x 4 to 6 feet

Summersweet is loved for its long-lasting summer flowers, attractive dark green leaves, and wonderful fragrance. It makes a good, narrow-growing shrub border (great for small yards) and an excellent plant for shade and poorly drained areas. Native to the eastern United States, you'll find this plant growing in the wild in dim, marshy locations. This trouble-free plant is a must for homeowners who have problems with drainage. There are many varieties to choose from with rose, pink, or white flowers. They are all great landscape additions and some have yellow to orange fall color. This plant is underused by landscape designers. If you are having professional landscape help and this plant is not suggested, bring it to your designer's attention.

When, Where, and How to Plant

Plant summersweet anytime the ground is not frozen. If you have a choice, choose spring, and you will be able to enjoy its great blooms the very first year. With the exception of deep shade, summersweet will grow in any exposure. It will tolerate poor, slow-draining soil. Most summersweet comes in containers. Dig a hole no deeper than the soil clump and twice as wide. Loosen any roots that are wrapped around the outside of the soil clump. Backfill the hole with the existing soil, making sure no particle of soil is larger than a golf ball. Water-in well to settle the soil. Mulch your plants to conserve moisture.

Growing Tips

Be sure to give summersweet an occasional drink of water during hot, dry weather. In alkaline conditions, consider feeding your shrub with a garden fertilizer for acid-loving plants, following the instructions on the container. Find one you like and read the label.

Regional Advice and Care

Pests and disease aren't a major concern. This plant likes it moist; dry conditions may stress summersweet, leaving it susceptible to spider mites. Do any necessary pruning in spring. Rejuvenate mature summersweet shrubs by cutting back the oldest branches to ground level. This is a suckering shrub, so new young branches will grow to take their place.

Companion Planting and Design

Plant summersweet where you can smell its blossoms and enjoy the hummingbirds that are attracted to it. Make use of its slim shape to form a hedge along your property line or use it in a narrow bed between the house and the sidewalk. The smaller forms can be used as a foundation plant.

Try These

'Hummingbird' is a great plant. It is compact, reaching about 3½ feet and produces lots of fragrant, white flowers. This is a great one by a patio. Look for the newest dwarf form called 'Sixteen Candles'. Several pink forms are available. 'Rosea' has dark pink flowers; 'Pink Spire' has light pink flowers. 'Ruby Spice' is the latest with even darker rosy flowers.

Viburnum 'Alleghany'

Viburnum x *rhytidophylloides* 'Alleghany'

Botanical Pronunciation
vy-BUR-num ri-ti-do-fil-OY-dez

Bloom Period and Seasonal Color
Evergreen foliage; creamy white blooms;
reddish fruit turning black in fall

Mature Height x Spread
8 to 10 feet x 6 to 8 feet

When you think of evergreens, your mind probably wanders to yews, junipers, and blue hollies—now for something different. 'Alleghany' viburnum, a mostly evergreen shrub, has great, dark green leaves with feltlike undersides. In Zone 6, the leaves hold on for most, if not all, of the winter; they may drop in Zone 5 in cold winters, but they will be back. The glossy-veined leaves, a calling card of this plant, appear almost leather-like, which comes from one of this hybrid's parent plants—the leatherleaf viburnum, *V. rhytidophyllum*. 'Alleghany' blooms in mid-April to May and again in September to October with white flower clusters that are 3 to 4 inches in diameter. This dense, rounded shrub also has showy reddish fruit in summer that turns black in fall.

When, Where, and How to Plant

Plant container-grown or balled-and-burlapped 'Alleghany' viburnum anytime the ground is not frozen, but spring offers the most availability. It does well in full sun to full shade. It tolerates summer shade and winter sun, such as that found under deciduous shade trees, though such conditions may cause the leaves to fall off in late November. In southern Ohio, leaves can stay on all winter. Good soil drainage is important. To plant, dig a hole no deeper than the soil clump and twice as wide. Break up the backfill soil to pieces no larger than golf balls. Water-in well. Apply a 2-inch layer of mulch.

Growing Tips

Be sure to water during hot, dry periods, especially if it is growing in the root zones of surrounding trees. Fertilize in spring with a slow-release fertilizer.

Regional Advice and Care

No bugs or diseases bother this plant. This variety is much improved over the original leatherleaf viburnum. It can take heavy pruning; always prune right after spring bloom to avoid affecting next spring's bloom.

Companion Planting and Design

'Alleghany' viburnum has many landscape uses: it makes a great specimen plant; plant several around a foundation as a tall screen; or use it in tree shade where you were thinking of planting a hemlock or white pine. It grows to an average of 8 feet tall, but can be pruned and kept smaller. Combine with other shrubs, such as 'Wine and Roses' weigela or crimson barberries for nice foliage contrast.

Try These

'Willowwood' viburnum is a faster-growing variety, similar to 'Alleghany'. From the flowers to the fruit to the fall leaf color, the deciduous varieties of the viburnum family are a wonderful group of ornamental shrubs. I like *Viburnum* × *juddii* for its sweet spring aroma and 'Shasta' doublefile viburnum (*V. plicatum* var. *tomentosum* 'Shasta') for its large white blooms in spring and black berries in fall. 'Winterthur' has glossy green leaves, white spring flowers, and great fall leaf color. Plant this one in Zone 6 only.

Virginia Sweetspire

Itea virginica 'Henry's Garnet'

Botanical Pronunciation eye-TEE-uh vir-JIN-ih-kuh

Other Name Virginia willow

Bloom Period and Seasonal Color
Early summer; white blooms; burgundy fall color

Mature Height x Spread
3 to 5 feet x 6 feet

If you think I like hypericum, wait until you read how much I like sweetspire 'Henry's Garnet'. Virginia sweetspire is largely unknown to homeowners and many nursery employees, but it is catching on fast with well-informed gardeners. What makes it so good? First, it is easy to grow—shade or sun, wet or dry, even in clay soils. Second, in the early summer when most shrubs are through, it bursts out with fragrant flowers. Next on the list—its rich, deep red fall color (the "garnet" in 'Henry's Garnet'). In fact, in mild Ohio winters, sweetspire holds its beautiful leaves throughout the winter. It's a spreading plant, growing wider than taller. With all this going for it, I'm sure you can find a place for sweetspire in your garden.

When, Where, and How to Plant
You can plant sweetspire anytime the ground is not frozen. Don't wait until fall; if you plant sweetspire in spring, you can enjoy its fragrant flowers the very first year. This plant can adapt to many different soil pH levels. It prefers moist areas and will grow in full sun to shade. If planting in heavy clay, add some organic soil amendments to the existing soil as you backfill. Container-grown sweetspire needs a hole that's no deeper than the depth of the soil clump, and twice as wide. Loosen any roots wrapped around the soil clump. Backfill with existing soil, and water-in well to remove any air pockets. Mulch to conserve moisture.

Growing Tips
Water sweetspire occasionally during hot, dry weather, particularly if it's planted in full sun. Fertilize in spring with a general garden fertilizer, following the package directions.

Regional Advice and Care
Sweetspire is a plant that spreads by sending up new stems from the soil clump. Prune away any unwanted growth anytime you see it. Sweetspire blooms off new growth, so trim it back in early spring to the height you desire. This plant can make more new plants in your landscape if you divide the root clump with a spade in early spring. No worries about pests here.

Companion Planting and Design
Sweetspire makes a great grouping, whether grown as a low hedge or as an underplanting around a flowering tree. Its great winter color makes it a wonderful plant for all seasons. Plant it where you can enjoy the burgundy leaves from inside the house in late fall and winter. Sweetspire's suckering growth habit makes it a good choice for massing, planting on slopes, or for use as an unusual groundcover.

Try These
'Little Henry' is a more compact variety that has 3- to 4-inch flowers on a shorter-growing shrub that reaches about 3 feet. It also has great fall color along with all the other great attributes of 'Henry's Garnet'.

TREES

FOR OHIO

Although all living plants produce oxygen, trees provide a large amount. And a well-placed shade tree on the south or west side of a home can replace a large air-conditioner, cooling your house in summer. When that same tree drops its leaves in fall, it allows the winter sun to help warm the house during the cold months. O.rnamental trees can do the same thing where there isn't room for a large shade tree. Trees provide seasonal color, some give us fall fruit, and they can beautify home landscapes and the whole neighborhood.

Following the Lead of Mother Nature

Many believe spring is the best time to plant a tree (or shrub). After all, spring is when you'll find the best selections. One benefit of spring planting is that it allows you to enjoy the colors of ornamental trees the first year it's planted. And, of course, there is "spring fever," making you aware of all landscaping possibilities. But with the benefits of spring planting come the distinct disadvantages of babysitting a tree all summer, checking water needs weekly.

So what's the alternative? Fall is when Mother Nature drops the majority of her seeds, and fall is when all plants grow most new roots. As the tops of trees stop growing in early fall and prepare for their long winter naps, all that stored food and energy goes to making roots. In all of Ohio, roots continue to grow well into December. When you plant in fall, the weather is getting cooler and rainfall is usually more plentiful. Plus, the roots really put on lots of growth, and your new tree establishes itself very quickly. Another benefit is that you will find great discounts on trees offered for sale in fall. So go ahead, plant in spring and summer if you want, but don't be afraid to plant in fall. Just remember: you can plant a

The trees you plant today, such as these *Quercus alba*, are a legacy for future generations.

tree *anytime* the ground is not frozen. But depending upon the season, you may have to do a bit more maintenance.

How to Plant

Trees are available at your favorite garden centers as balled-and-burlapped (B & B) or as container-grown trees. There is only a short time during which balled-and-burlapped trees can be dug at the nursery, either in late fall (November into December) or late winter (February into early March), before the leaf buds start to open. They are shipped to the retail nursery and heeled-in, covering the ball with aged sawdust or pea gravel. Most field-grown, B & B trees are machine dug with pneumatic spades and placed in metal baskets lined with burlap. The burlap is pinned, and the wire basket is tied to the tree with heavy twine wrapped around the tree trunk.

Dig a hole 1½ times as wide as the rootball and as deep.

One thing to look out for, some trees have not had the excess topsoil removed from the top of their roots. This excess soil accumulates from year to year as the nursery cultivates the topsoil around the trees while they are still in-ground. To check for this problem, place the tree in the planting hole, peel back the burlap on top of the rootball, and use your spade to slice off the soil on top of the ball until you find the top roots. That's the planting depth that you need.

To plant balled-and-burlapped trees, dig a hole half again as wide as the rootball and no deeper. Leave any wire basket that's surrounding the rootball. After placing the tree in the hole, cut away any twine that's wrapped around the trunk. Backfill, breaking up the soil particles so that none is bigger than a golf ball. If you need to slightly amend the soil, add 20 to 30 percent humus or compost to the backfill. Water as you backfill. As the water fills the hole, move your spade or shovel up and down in the water and soil to eliminate any air pockets. Continue to add soil until the hole is filled. This "mudding" will help make sure your new tree is straight (thus, no staking).

After planting, backfill with the same soil you removed from the planting hole.

Container-grown trees are very popular with many nurseries. A newer growing system is being implemented called "pot in pot". Instead of planting trees in the ground, growing them, and then digging them, empty 24-inch diameter pots are placed in the soil. Trees are planted in 20- to 22-inch pots, and that pot is placed inside the sunken empty pot. Irrigation drip systems water each individually planted pot in pot.

Potted trees adapt quickly to their new environment, growing faster than trees planted directly into the nursery soil. These container-grown trees can also be sold anytime during the growing season without any roots ever being cut. Planting container-grown trees is a lot like planting balled-and-burlapped trees. Dig a hole half-again as wide as the soil clump and as deep as the soil clump. Remove the tree from its pot, and loosen any roots that may be wrapped around the outside of the soil clump. Then plant as described for B & B trees.

To Feed or Not to Feed?

When we plant a tree, we can't wait for shade and lots of color. If a little is good, then we figure a lot must be great—right? Because of this tendency to overfeed, many nursery staff agree no fertilizer should be given to newly planted trees for one year. After that, feed trees in late fall (mid-November to mid-December) or in late winter to early spring (mid-February to mid-March). Because of root activity at the time, I prefer the late fall application. Use any general plant food that lists trees among its uses. Follow the directions on the container for how much to use and how to apply it. Do not use tree food spikes, which put too much fertilizer in one spot and none in others.

Completing the Process—Mulching and Staking

Mulching freshly planted trees is important. Mulch rings not only look good, frustrate weeds, and retain moisture, but they also serve to keep the lawn mower from nicking or bruising the trunk. Remember that 2 inches of mulch is enough; just don't put any of those 2 inches on the trunk itself.

Staking trees is unnecessary. Trees do best when *not* secured to wire attached to a stake. To secure your trees, make sure that you backfill all planting holes with the soil you've dug out. Backfill, breaking up all soil particles to the size of golf balls. Water-in well, and as the soil-filled hole is filling with water, take your spade or shovel and work the backfilled soil up and down to settle it. This practice causes the soil clump to become locked in place.

How Big Will That Tree Grow?

No living tree, shrub, or evergreen stops growing until the day it dies. But don't be intimidated by the mature sizes of the trees. A tree purchased at 8 feet might

Know the mature size of the tree you're planting before you install it. Once trees are planted, they are hard to move.

take thirty years to reach its mature height of 40 feet. The average time a family lives in one home is about ten years; thus, many of you will not see the tree you have planted reach its mature height. Still, you don't want to plant a tree that you know will grow 40 feet wide any closer than 25 feet from the house. One other thing: evergreen trees grow much wider at the bottom than they do at the top. Make sure you've got the yard space to give up to this spread. As grandma used to say, "Look up, look down, look all around."

Trees for Special Purposes
It's a good idea to determine the function you want a tree to serve in your landscape, and then select a tree to match. Trees may also be grown as shrubs (depending on pruning or growth habit)—those marked with an asterisk (*) are described in the Shrubs chapter.

Trees for Fast-Growing Screens

Arborvitae	Eastern White Pine	Serviceberry
(certain varieties)	Norway Spruce	White Willow
Canadian Hemlock	Red Maple	

Trees for Formal Shearing

Amur Maple	Columnar Red Maple	Upright Junipers*
Arborvitae	Eastern White Pine	Washington Hawthorn

Deer-Resistant Trees

American Holly	Eastern White Pine	Norway Spruce
Eastern Redbud	Falsecypress*	

NOTE: All shade and flowering trees in the 1-inch to 4-inch trunk caliper size should be protected October through February with a plastic trunk protector to keep buck deer from rubbing their antlers on the trunks of those sized trees; deer can rub the life out of the tree.

Leaving a Legacy

We think of trees as forever, certainly outlasting us here on earth. But trees, like all living things, have a beginning and an end. Trees can have a very long, useful life if the environmental conditions in which they grow are positive. We can't control cold winters, wet springs, or hot dry summers. We can, however, control the planting site, the soil, and the exposure we select for the tree, all the while taking the tree's needs and preferences into consideration.

There are many tree varieties, some more suitable for Ohio planting sites than others. Before deciding what tree you wish to plant, check out the planting site. See how heavy the soil is, and how far from the house, deck, or street your tree will be. Drive around the neighborhood to see what types of trees are growing well. Take all this information with you when you shop, and chances are great that you'll select a tree that everyone will enjoy for many years. It's been said, "The best time to plant a tree was twenty-five years ago; the next best time is today."

Bald Cypress

Taxodium distichum

Botanical Pronunciation
tax-OH-dium DIS-tic-hum

Other Name
Common baldcypress

Bloom Period and Seasonal Color
Deciduous; green needles turn russet brown in fall

Mature Height x Spread
50 to 70 feet x 20 to 30 feet

How about that! A conifer, which we usually think of as evergreen, may not be evergreen at all. Bald cypress has needles, but in the fall they turn orangey brown and drop off. I'll bet that's why they call it *bald* cypress! This stately, upright tree makes a great specimen out in the open yard. It tolerates many site conditions, including clay soil and wet soil. Bald cypress grows quickly, 2 feet per year, and produces great fall color. It even performs well as a street tree. In wet areas, the roots form knobby knees (sections of root that can grow above ground as high as 8 inches) like those seen in a true cypress swamp. The knees form in wet areas so the roots can take in oxygen.

When, Where, and How to Plant
Most bald cypresses are grown in containers. If you find any that are balled-and-burlapped, make sure they were dug in late winter and get at least a one-year guarantee from the nursery. Plant container-grown plants anytime during the growing season. Bald cypress is flexible about its planting site, but it grows best and produces the best fall color in full sun. Consult this chapter's introduction for specifics of planting. In wet areas, elevate 25 percent of the soil clump above the ground and mound-plant. Backfill using existing soil, breaking up soil particles to the size of golf balls. Water-in well. No staking is required.

Growing Tips
Keep the rootballs of newly planted trees moist until established. Once established, bald cypress is drought tolerant. Maintain a 2-inch layer of organic mulch to conserve moisture. See page 186 for input on tree fertilization. In alkaline soils, leaf yellowing may indicate the need to lower the soil pH with an acid-based fertilizer. Read the instructions on the container.

Regional Advice and Care
As with most plants in the tree chapter, bald cypress is low maintenance, unbothered by bugs or disease. Remove dead limbs or do cosmetic pruning anytime it is needed, but don't interfere with the tree's strong central leader. It will continue to grow in a pyramidal shape for the rest of its life.

Companion Planting and Design
Bald cypress does not take up as much ground space as its evergreen relatives (spruce and pine) do. It makes a great screen when planted in a group. You can plant bald cypress within 15 feet of a house to provide shade in summer, while still allowing light in winter. It makes an excellent street tree.

Try These
'Shawnee Brave' is a great street tree with its narrow, upright form. 'Monarch of Illinois' grows much wider, spreading up to 60 feet. Not many people will have enough yard space for this one, in which case the species is the better choice.

Eastern Redbud

Cercis canadensis

Botanical Pronunciation
SER-sis ka-na-DEN-sis

Other Name
American redbud

Bloom Period and Seasonal Color
Deciduous with yellow fall color; April blooms
in purplish pink or white

Mature Height x Spread
20 to 30 feet x 25 to 35 feet

This native tree should have a spot in anyone's landscape. The redbud has flowers that are reddish purple in bud, opening to a rosy pink. The April flowers sit upon individual branches, covering the tree's silhouette with a rosy haze. From the flowers come seedpods that resemble peapods and add to the tree's winter look. The attractive, heart-shaped foliage often turns a nice yellow in the fall. A small tree, reaching 20 to 30 feet, it typically has multiple trunks (clumping) at ground level or a short, single trunk; both create a widespread, rounded form. Redbud is an excellent tree for that sunny area where you were considering planting a flowering dogwood, because it is much hardier. Redbud will also tolerate shade, giving you even more planting options.

When, Where, and How to Plant
Plant container-grown or balled-and-burlapped redbuds anytime the ground is not frozen. An ideal planting site would have moist, well-drained soil. However, this tree will do exceptionally well in any type of soil—clay, sandy, acidic, or alkaline—as long as the planting site has good drainage. Redbuds adapt to sun or shade. The more sun it gets, the more blooms it will produce. Dig a hole as deep as the soil clump, and two to three times as wide. For container-grown trees, loosen any roots wrapped around the soil clump. For trees that are balled and burlapped, peel back the top of the burlap after placing the rootball in the hole. For more planting tips, consult the planting tips in the chapter introduction. No staking is required.

Growing Tips
Keep newly planted trees moist to lessen transplant shock. For the best health of redbud, water your tree deeply when rainfall is below normal. A 2-inch layer of mulch will help conserve moisture. For suggestions on tree fertilization, read page 186 for more details.

Regional Advice and Care
Redbuds are susceptible to a few disease problems—canker and wilt—that can be detrimental. Good cultural conditions will help to prevent problems. A mulch ring is important on redbud to avoid damaging the trunk and creating an opportunity for disease organisms to infect the tree. In higher maintenance areas, you'll want to rake up the pods. Remove any dead or diseased limbs as they appear. As the tree matures, prune off bottom branches to suit your lawn-mowing needs.

Companion Planting and Design
A redbud is an attractive choice for a small front yard. Large, heart-shaped leaves along with the tree's low-branching habit make it a great tree to use as a screen. Redbud is also a nice addition to shady shrub borders and woodland edges.

Try These
'Appalachian Red' has reddish to deep purple flowers. The beautiful 'Forest Pansy' has purple leaves and reddish purple flowers. 'Alba' is cold-hardy and produces white flowers. 'Merlot' is a perfect spring-flowering tree for smaller landscapes, with lustrous, dark purple foliage.

Flowering Crabapple

Malus spp. and cultivars

Botanical Pronunciation MAY-lus

Other Name Flowering crab

Bloom Period and Seasonal Color
Deciduous; spring blooms in red, pink, purple, white; ornamental fruit in fall

Mature Height x Spread
10 to 25 feet x 10 to 20 feet

Crabapples, beloved flowering trees, are popular in home landscapes. However, most of the varieties planted in the 60s and 70s presented problems. Diseases such as apple scab (causing early leaf drop), powdery mildew, and fire blight threatened both the tree's health and appearance, while early fruit drop created a mess and attracted yellow jackets. But many new crabapples (in a range of shapes, sizes, and colors) have been introduced. These disease-resistant cultivars hold their fruit until the birds clean the tree in late winter. Crabapples are one of the showiest ornamental trees that you can have in your landscape. Blossoms are basically red, pink, or white, with single, semi-double, or double forms of flowers. With the right choice you can have all the beauty and none of the headaches.

When, Where, and How to Plant
Plant crabapple anytime the ground is not frozen, but early spring is best if you're shopping for bloom color. Crabapple will be available as a balled-and-burlapped or container-grown tree, depending on size. It tolerates all types of soil, but needs good drainage. It blooms best in full sun, but can give good color in a half-day of sun. Good air circulation helps avoid foliar disease problems. Consult the how to plant section in this chapter for more information on tree planting. Don't overcrowd crabapples; when mass planting, space trees 20 to 25 feet apart.

Growing Tips
Water during its first year, especially during hot, dry weather, to keep the rootball moist. Create a mulch ring with a 2-inch layer of organic mulch. Don't pile mulch on the trunk; give it several inches of clearance. Though fairly drought tolerant, improve your established tree's performance by watering deeply every few weeks during drought. Consult page 186 in this chapter for more information on fertilizing trees.

Regional Advice and Care
Assuming that your selection is a disease-resistant variety, no fungicide needs to be applied during wet seasons. Winter and early spring are good times to prune crabapple as you can clearly see the branches. Prune to shape and remove branches that rub, cross, or grow into the center of the tree. Also remove rapidly growing branches called suckers that form at a tree's base.

Companion Planting and Design
Flowering crabapple produces gorgeous flowers and great-looking fruit. Since there are many selections with different mature sizes, pick a variety to fit your spot. You couldn't ask for a more ornamental and useful tree. They will suit any landscape.

Try These
Selecting a disease-resistant crabapple that fits your available space is important. Consider these: 'Baskatong' (25 feet tall) is an upright oval tree with reddish purple flowers. 'Red Jade' (15 feet) is a weeping variety, with pink buds opening to white; it grows well in limited space and produces great fruit. 'Harvest Gold' (20 feet) has an oval shape, white flowers, and golden fruit.

Flowering Dogwood

Cornus florida

Botanical Pronunciation KOR-nus FLOR-id-uh

Other Name Common dogwood

Bloom Period and Seasonal Color
Deciduous; mid- to late April; blooms in
white, pink

Mature Height x Spread
15 feet x 15 feet

Even though this tree grows wild in the eastern part of the United States, in Ohio it can be considered the most disappointing flowering tree around. I say this because in most of Ohio for the last few years, we've had wet springs and dry summers. Planting dogwoods in open, sunny locations where summer moisture is limited has caused many flowering dogwoods to decline and die. Flowering dogwood likes an acidic, well-drained soil and a location that is in partial, but not total, shade. If you have soil that isn't the best and you want a dogwood, plant *Cornus kousa*, commonly called Chinese dogwood. It blooms later in June, but it will withstand those planting sites that are not suitable for *C. florida*. Both have great fall color.

When, Where, and How to Plant
Balled-and-burlapped and container-grown dogwoods can be planted all season, although spring is preferred. The bigger issue is "when to dig?" Choose a dogwood that has been dug in early spring from an Ohio nursery. For successful growth, this tree needs moist, well-drained, acidic soil that is high in organic matter and a partial shade location. Do *not* plant dogwood in sunny, heavy clay, dry, alkaline, or poorly drained sites. No matter how pretty the flowering dogwood was where you grew up, don't plant one in clay soil. It naturally grows on the front edge of a wooded tree line. Plant yours where large trees protect it from hot afternoon sun. For planting specifics, consult page 185 in this chapter.

Growing Tips
Keep your newly planted dogwood moist, but not waterlogged. Mulch is important both to conserve moisture and to protect the trunk from mower injuries that can lead to pest and disease problems. Create a mulch ring with an organic mulch 2 inches thick. Stressed dogwoods are prone to problems. During dry spells, water thoroughly but don't overwater. Consult page 186 in this chapter for information on fertilizing trees.

Regional Advice and Care
There won't be much of a problem with bugs or disease unless you have planted in a poor location. If so, these trees can suffer from mildew, anthracnose, and borers. Prune trees to remove dead branches as necessary.

Companion Planting and Design
Dogwoods offer great fall leaf color, berries, and beautiful blooms. But if dogwood won't work on your site, there are many other flowering trees to choose from, such as redbud.

Try These
When planting flowering dogwood, look for trees grown from northern seed stock. Ask your nursery for the hardiest selections. 'Cherokee Chief' has deep pink, almost red flowers. 'Cloud 9' is a beautiful small tree that blooms heavily when it's young. If you would like to try one of the Chinese dogwoods, *C. kousa* 'Summer Stars' is one of the best. The Rutgers series is another great choice.

Heritage® River Birch

Betula nigra 'Cully'

Botanical Pronunciation BET-you-luh NYE-gruh

Other Name 'Cully' heritage birch

Bloom Period and Seasonal Color
Deciduous with showy, pale brown, exfoliating bark; yellow fall color

Mature Height x Spread
30 to 50 feet x 30 to 50 feet

There are many species of birch. The white-barked ones seem to be the prettiest, but a healthy brown bark birch grows best. All birches love cool summers and good, loamy soil, so you may wonder how *any* birch made it into *Ohio Getting Started Garden Guide*. It is true that white birches don't live very long here; they grow under constant stress, and soon the birch borer finds them and finishes them off. River birch is the best birch for the Midwest and tolerates Ohio's soil much better. In fact, it even thrives here. Heritage® river birch is an attractive, vigorous, river birch with pinkish tan bark. Heritage® has good yellow fall color and often grows with multiple trunks, displaying even more of its beautiful bark.

When, Where, and How to Plant
River birch trees are available as small, container-grown plants and large balled-and-burlapped specimens. Plant Heritage® river birch anytime the ground is not frozen. River birch loves full sun to part shade and slightly acidic soil. This tree does well in dry to moist soil, but needs soil acidity to keep the leaves dark green instead of yellow-green. If you have mostly alkaline soil, which is common in Ohio, acidify it. Check out page 185 in this chapter for the specifics on tree planting. No staking is needed.

Growing Tips
Keep your newly planted tree moist to encourage healthy root growth. Create a mulch ring with a 2-inch layer of organic mulch, being careful to keep the mulch away from the trunk. In extended drought periods, where rainfall is less than normal, give your birch a thorough watering. As stated, this tree struggles in high pH soil. If your tree is chlorotic, apply a fertilizer for acid-loving plants. Read page 186 in this chapter for more on fertilization.

Regional Advice and Care
Remember, river birch resists the problems that plague the white bark birches. There are few bugs or diseases that bother this plant. Prune any crossing branches that interfere with the tree's natural habit. You may also wish to remove a few of the lower limbs to expose more of the attractive bark. Don't let early leaf drop concern you—it is typical with birches. Avoid locations near a swimming pool where the falling leaves create a nasty maintenance problem.

Companion Planting and Design
The peeling bark of river birch and its fall leaf color add beauty to any landscape. Heritage® birch trees are available with single or multiple trunks. Both types make for a great landscape specimen. It is also great as a yard tree or as a corner tree for a two-story house.

Try These
Betula nigra, the straight species of river birch, has bright cinnamon-brown, peeling bark. Both the species of river birch and Heritage® are great trees in Ohio.

Japanese Maple

Acer palmatum

Botanical Pronunciation
AY-sur pal-MAY-tum

Bloom Period and Seasonal Color
Deciduous foliage in green, red, or variegated green-and-white; outstanding fall color

Mature Height x Spread
4 to 20 feet x 15 to 25 feet

Looking for a one-of-a-kind specimen? Or a beautiful patio tree? Consider the Japanese maple. What a *wonderful* group of plants. Japanese maples offer dramatic branching habits, attractive foliage in different colors, and a range of shapes and sizes from weeping to upright. These trees are stunners. Japanese maples, depending on the variety, have either crimson-red leaves, green leaves, green leaves with a tinge of red, or variegated green-and-white leaves. As a rule, their fall color is spectacular. Know though that shopping for these maples can be confusing. Different selections grow at different rates, and prices will reflect this. You might find two plants of similar size with vastly different price tags. Ask nursery personnel about the growth qualities of the maple before making your choice.

When, Where, and How to Plant
Balled-and-burlapped and container-grown Japanese maples can be planted anytime the ground is not frozen. This is a tree you should buy from a qualified source. Choose locations with full sun to partial shade; in fact, some shade is beneficial. Rich, well-drained, slightly acidic soil is preferred, but these maples are rather tolerant, just avoid heavy clay and hot, dry locations. Make sure you know your maple's ultimate size before selecting a spot. Page 185 in this chapter gives directions on planting trees.

Growing Tips
Take care that your newly planted Japanese maple isn't allowed to dry out. A 2-inch layer of mulch will cool the root zone and conserve moisture. In drought periods, when rainfall is less than average, give your Japanese maple a deep soaking every few weeks until regular rainfall resumes. Refer to page 186 for fertilizing tips.

Regional Advice and Care
This group of plants is free of bugs and disease. Don't be concerned if you notice small pinholes on some of the leaves during summer. These are called "sun spots" and are caused by water droplets on the leaves situated in hot sun. You can trim or prune a Japanese maple anytime, although pruning is rarely necessary. *Never* use a hedge shear or chainsaw. Use handpruners instead, and prune unwanted branches entirely. Remove any dead branches or prune to expose more of the beautiful branching habit.

Companion Planting and Design
Japanese maples make wonderful accent trees or a one-of-a-kind specimen plants. The larger-growing varieties can shade a patio, and all will add great leaf color to accent any landscape.

Try These
'Bloodgood' (15 to 20 feet high and wide) is a great choice for its reddish purple leaf color and red fall color. It is known for retaining its foliage color all season. A great tree for shade, 'Viridis' (6 to 8 feet tall), also called 'Viride', has a cascading habit and light green, serrated, almost fernlike leaves. These fine-leaf forms are sometimes called "threadleaf maple." 'Crimson Queen' is a great weeping dwarf with bright red leaves.

Kentucky Coffeetree

Gymnocladus dioicus

Botanical Pronunciation
jim-NOCK-luh-dus dye-oh-EE-kuss

Other Name Espresso coffeetree

Bloom Period and Seasonal Color
Late May to early June, male and female flowers are a greenish white

Mature Height x Spread
60 to 75 feet x 40 to 50 feet

This is a tree that usually grows 60 to 75 feet in height, spreading to 40 to 50 feet. It *can* grow to 90 feet as the national champion is 90 feet tall × 89 feet wide, in West Liberty, KY. Kentucky coffeetree has an interesting bark pattern, and is one of the latest trees to leaf out in the spring, usually emerging about May 5 to May 20 in Ohio. New leaves are tinged pinkish to purplish, gradually changing to dark green, almost dark bluish green in summer. The fall color is a weak yellow on some trees while others have bright yellow and are very showy. Female flowers bloom in panicles of white. Males are pretty, too, with males and females each having a very fragrant rose aroma.

When, Where, and How to Plant
Plant anytime the ground is not frozen. Transplant balled-and-burlapped or container-grown specimens into amended soil, rich in soil conditioners, for the best growth. However, it's adaptable to a wide range of soil conditions such as limestone clay, drought, and city conditions. Plant in full sun. For more planting tips consult the planting section in this chapter on page 185.

Growing Tips
Usually develops vertically ascending branches which form a narrow column. Bare limbed and clumsy looking in the winter but they have unique growing habit. Certainly no two trees look alike, some with very irregular branching others with weeping lower branching. It's slow to medium growing, reaching 12 to 14 feet after 10 years.

Regional Advice and Care
Kentucky coffeetree is not prone to any serious diseases or insects. Prune in winter or early spring, as needed.

Companion Planting and Design
This is a choice tree for parks, golf courses, and other large areas (estate homes). This tree has interesting characteristics especially the bold winter habit and handsome bark. It is absolutely beautiful and results in a bunch of "What is it?" questions both from landscapers and homeowners. Plant this tree at least 40 feet from the house, and do not plant under power lines. Kentucky coffeetree gives you the opportunity to have a tree that's very hardy and another choice for a tree collection in your landscape.

Try These
'Stately Manor' grows narrow and upright making it a good street tree. 'Prairie Titan®' is a good male selection, and 'Variegata' has pinkish to purplish new growth and its variegation is very handsome.

Lacebark Elm

Ulmus parvifolia

Botanical Pronunciation UL-mus par-vi-FO-lee-uh

Other Name Chinese elm

Bloom Period and Seasonal Color
August flower fruit September yellowish and reddish purple in fall

Mature Height x Spread
40 to 50 feet x 40 to 50 feet

This is an excellent, tough, durable tree for just about any situation. Do not confuse it with the inferior Siberian elm, which sometimes is labeled and offered as lacebark elm. Make sure the variety you choose is indeed lacebark elm. Some of the great gardens of the world consider lacebark elm as a superior tree and the entire nursery industry should be alerted to this tree as well. Disney World in Orlando, Florida, has used this tree extensively throughout the grounds and the lacebark elms have never heard a bad word from any of Disney's horticulturists.

When, Where, and How to Plant
You can plant lacebark elm (along with any other tree or shrub) anytime the ground is not frozen. Most plants now are grown in containers so no roots are ever disturbed. If your lacebark is nursery field grown, make sure that it gets dug during the dormant season, November through March. Plant lacebark elm where it has room to grow, such as a site 20 feet or beyond the home itself. Dig a hole one-half size bigger than the diameter of the root clump. Break up any backfill soil so no particle is bigger than a golf ball. Water-in well to settle the soil. Repeat watering as needed.

Growing Tips
Like any tree, lacebark appreciates a fertilizer application to its roots in late fall. Although very drought tolerant, a drink of water during hot, dry weather is welcomed also. Its best growth is achieved in moist, well-drained soil.

Regional Advice and Care
This is a very low-maintenance tree. Very heat and drought tolerant, this tree will provide some of our most beautiful shade trees in the years ahead. Here are some of its pluses: it shows considerable resistance to Dutch elm disease, it's easily transplanted, and it's adaptable to extremes of pH and soil. Its excellent urban soil tolerance makes it a fantastic street or boulevard tree.

Companion Planting and Design
This is a great tree to plant 20 to 30 feet away from the house on the west or south side of your home for summer shade and winter sun to help with your energy bill. For a mix of trees, plant with some of the maples and oaks listed in this chapter.

Try These
I like 'Athena® Elm', 'Bosque™', 'Burgundy', and 'Central Park Splendor™'. All of these varieties make for a very desirable street tree or patio or deck planting for some shade.

Norway Spruce

Picea abies

Botanical Pronunciation
PYE-see-uh AY-beez

Bloom Period and Seasonal Color
Evergreen with dark green needles

Mature Height x Spread
30 to 60 feet x 20 to 30 feet

Mike Dirr, the guru of woody plants, wrote in his book *Manual of Woody Landscape Plants* (my bible, by the way) that Norway spruce is much overplanted. Well, Mike, whose family comes from Cincinnati, has been spending most of his time out of state. Norway spruce is a stately, pyramidal evergreen that performs better than white pine in most parts of Ohio. Many homeowners who have white pine in their landscape may wish that they had Norway spruce instead. A Norway spruce makes an impressive specimen, or plant a row of them for a great tall screen and windbreak. You will find the entire spruce group to be very landscape friendly. The gorgeous Colorado blue spruce, *Picea pungens* var. *glauca*, adds lots of color to the home landscape.

When, Where, and How to Plant
Look for balled-and-burlapped spruce trees from spring to fall. After purchasing, plant right away; don't leave it sitting out of the ground any longer than necessary. Norway spruce prefers full sun to a half-day of sun; it tends to grow weakly in lots of shade. It performs best in sandy, acidic, well-drained soils, but will tolerate heavy clay or somewhat alkaline soil as long as the planting site has good drainage. Remember, it might be a little tree today, but in twenty years it will be 20 feet wide. Don't plant it close to sidewalks, drives, or homes. Check out the "how to plant" section in this chapter for specifics on planting. For a windbreak, space trees 18 to 20 feet apart.

Growing Tips
Keep newly established trees moist, especially going into fall; evergreens lose moisture in winter too. After planting, layer 2 inches of organic mulch around it, keeping the mulch away from the trunk. Though generally tough, drought stress can make trees susceptible to pests or disease. If rainfall is below normal, give your tree a thorough soaking every few weeks. For a discussion of tree fertilization, consult page 186 in this chapter.

Regional Advice and Care
Norway spruce is susceptible to a few bugs, but if you keep your trees mulched and watered during drought, they should stay healthy. To slow down the overall growth of your spruce, shear off new growth during its "new growth stage" in late spring. This will also make your spruce much fuller.

Companion Planting and Design
Norway spruce is great as a windscreen and gives privacy year-round. It produces cones and provides shelter to wildlife. Norway spruce makes an excellent backdrop for early flowering trees, such as redbud or serviceberry.

Try These
Serbian spruce, *Picea omorika* (50 to 60 feet tall), is another wonderful, dark-needled spruce with a narrow pyramidal habit. And of course, there is the Colorado blue spruce; my favorite is 'Hoopsii'. It is smaller (5 to 6 feet tall), round to pyramidal, with great blue color.

Ornamental Pear

Pyrus calleryana

Botanical Pronunciation
PYE-rus kal-ler-ee-AY-nah

Other Name
Bradford pear

Bloom Period and Seasonal Color
Deciduous with red fall color; early to late April; blooms in white

Mature Height x Spread
30 to 50 feet x 15 to 20 feet

Ornamental pears are among the most popular flowering trees sold at garden centers because of their glossy green leaves, white spring flowers, tremendous fall color, and fast growth rate. First introduced to me in the '60s, callery pears (the most common of which is the 'Bradford' pear) impressed me as beautiful, easy-to-grow, oval-shaped trees. Twenty years later, the industry discovered that 'Bradford' pears grew narrow-crotched, lateral branches that caused the trees to split during high winds. Well, now there's good news. New varieties are available that, so far, have shown tremendous improvement over the old 'Bradford'. Ornamental pear makes a great street tree, tolerating some not-so-great planting locations. The last tree to turn color, callery pear stands out in the late fall landscape.

When, Where, and How to Plant
You can plant balled-and-burlapped or container-grown callery pear trees anytime the ground is not frozen. This tree will perform best in full sun, but will also grow well on the east or west side of your home (in half-day shade). Ornamental pear does well in all types of Ohio soil as long as the planting location is well drained. This tree is urban-tolerant. Don't site it too closely to other trees where its overall shape could be negatively affected. Read the "how to plant" secton in this chapter for specifics on planting a tree. Do not stake.

Growing Tips
Keep newly planted trees moist until established to lessen transplant shock. Create a mulch ring

2 inches deep with organic mulch. Keep mulch several inches away from the trunk. Mature trees are drought tolerant. See page 186 in this chapter for specifics on fertilizing.

Regional Advice and Care
There are no pest and disease problems with the pear varieties listed here. Fireblight can be a concern with some pears. To lessen the possibility of winter storm damage, prune the canopy of your pear to open it up. Every few years in late winter or early spring, remove some of the vertical branches that create narrow crotch angles with the main trunk. Choose improved cultivars to avoid this task.

Companion Planting and Design
The fast-growing ornamental pear is best used as a street or lawn tree. Though all have great spring blooms, different varieties grow to different widths. Be sure to find out how wide your selection will get. Some consider the flower fragrance unpleasant.

Try These
My current favorite is 'Cleveland Select', also sometimes called 'Chanticleer'. This pear grows to about 35 feet, flowers profusely, and has great fall color. Its more narrow form (about 15 feet wide) allows it to be used in smaller spaces. I also like 'Aristocrat' and 'Redspire'. Avoid the old 'Bradford' and plant the improved 'New Bradford'. Check with your local nursery staff for more information about the latest selections.

Red Maple

Acer rubrum

Botanical Pronunciation
AY-sir ROO-brum

Other Name
Scarlet maple

Bloom Period and Seasonal Color
Deciduous, red, orange, yellow fall color; early spring "blooms" in red

Mature Height x Spread
40 to 80 feet x 30 to 40 feet

Red maple is one of the most popular shade trees in Ohio. The basic *Acer rubrum* is a seedling-grown tree that might or might not have red fall color; it may have yellow-green, yellow, or orange. That can be very disappointing to the homeowner who thinks he or she is buying a tree with red autumn color. After all, isn't that why they call it a *red* maple? So, to be sure you get the flaming red fall color you're looking for, choose named varieties. These new maples are very attractive, growing in an upright, pyramidal shape and are the best choice for a home landscape. Red maples have red flowers before they leaf out in early spring. From these flowers come the characteristic "helicopter" seeds.

When, Where, and How to Plant
Red maples can be planted anytime the ground is not frozen. They will be available in smaller sizes growing in containers; larger specimens are available as balled-and-burlapped trees. Buy from reputable dealers. They grow well in shadier sites under other trees, but maples located in full sun produce the best fall color. Red maples prefer fertile, moist soil, but they will tolerate a wide range of conditions. Plant at least 20 feet from the house.

Growing Tips
Maple trees will show stress during drought. Please water them when Mother Nature does not. Always check the soil around newly transplanted maples with a trowel during dry, hot weather, digging down 5 to 6 inches. If the soil is dry, you need to water.

Mulch your trees with a 2-inch layer of organic mulch; replenish as needed. Remember not to pile mulch around the trunk; leave a few inches of space. Fertilize in late fall with a granular all-plant food.

Regional Advice and Care
Red maples are rarely troubled by pests or disease. When the seeds (helicopters) start to fall in the spring, use a seed germination preventer in your planting beds so you don't wind up with numerous baby maple trees. Mowing will eliminate any seedlings that start to grow in lawn areas.

Companion Planting and Design
Red maples are an excellent shade tree for a lawn specimen with memorable fall color. They are a good choice in locations where the soil stays moist. However, like many maples, they produce a lot of surface roots that can interfere with growing lawn grass in heavy soils.

Try These
Choose maples with a track record of performing well in Ohio. I recommend 'Red Sunset' and 'October Glory'; both have fantastic fall color. Look for 'Autumn Blaze', a hybrid between silver maple and red maple. This fast-growing selection has excellent late fall color, drought tolerance, and low seed production—making it a superior choice.

Red Oak

Quercus rubra

Botanical Pronunciation
KWURK-us ROO-bruh

Bloom Period and Seasonal Color
Deciduous; red fall color

Mature Height x Spread
60 to 80 feet x 60 to 75 feet

R ed oak is a very misunderstood tree. Most people think all oaks are slow growing. While this may be true of some oaks, it is definitely not true of red oak. Red oak can grow up to 2 feet per year once it has gotten established in its planting site, and it can get quite large because of its long lifespan. When planted in a good location, it can easily live over 100 years and grow to 80 feet tall. Red oak is best planted as a yard tree rather than as a street tree. The fall leaf color of red oak is just as its name suggests; it has green leaves during the growing season that turn to shades of russet red in the fall.

When, Where, and How to Plant
Red oaks are available as balled-and-burlapped trees, but in general, more trees are being grown in pots. Oak trees are available in containers with up to a 2½-inch trunk. Spring or fall is the preferred time for planting. When selecting your oak, choose one that has a trunk diameter of 3 inches or less to lessen transplant shock. Plant red oak in full sun with lots of room to grow, no closer than 25 feet from the house. Red oak prefers loose, well-drained, slightly acidic soil; however, as long as the site has good drainage, it will adapt to alkaline clay soils. Read the "how to plant" section in this chapter for specifics on planting.

Growing Tips
Red oak is drought tolerant once established, but keep your new tree roots moist to lessen transplant shock. Mulch with a 2-inch layer of organic mulch. Take care to leave several inches around the tree trunk free of mulch. For information on fertilizing trees, read page 186 in this chapter.

Regional Advice and Care
There are no serious bug or disease problems that bother red oaks. Oaks have the type of tree bark that deer *love* to use to remove their antler fuzz. Protect young trees (up to 4-inch trunk caliper) with tree wrap in fall; remove the wrap in spring. All oak trees dislike having their roots disturbed. If you are building on a lot that has oak trees, keep the bulldozer and trencher away from the root zone or the tree could be seriously damaged.

Companion Planting and Design
If you have the space, planting an oak is a great service to future generations. Red oak is a handsome, fast-growing tree for any larger landscape. Give it plenty of room and it is sure to develop into an impressive specimen.

Try These
Take note of these other oak species. White oak, *Quercus alba*, and swamp white oak, *Q. bicolor*, form impressive specimens. Willow oak, *Q. phellos*, has a unique, fine texture provided by its willowlike leaves. Willow oak is less hardy and unsuitable for northern Ohio.

Serviceberry

Amelanchier arborea

Botanical Pronunciation
am-ul-LANK-ee-ur are-BORE-ee-uh

Other Name
Juneberry

Bloom Period and Seasonal Color
Deciduous, yellow, orange, red fall color; April flowers in white

Mature Height x Spread
15 to 25 feet x 10 to 15 feet

Even though this tree is unfamiliar to many people, it is one of the great small flowering trees of the future. Serviceberry has it all—beautiful white spring flowers, attractive habit (with single or multiple trunks), smooth gray bark, purplish black fruits, and wonderful fall color. Fall color can differ from year to year, but you can always expect shades from yellow, to orange, to red. Sometimes all the colors appear on the same tree during the same fall. The edible fruits are slightly sweet and very tasty—just ask the birds. Tree expert Mike Dirr ranks serviceberry as one of his tops for making pies. He states that the ripe fruit from serviceberry is even tastier than highbush blueberries. Try it yourself and let me know what you think.

When, Where, and How to Plant
Plant balled-and-burlapped or container-grown serviceberry trees in spring or fall for the best results. You can have success planting container-grown plants anytime the ground is not frozen. Serviceberry grows best in full sun to a half-day of shade. It will tolerate more shade, but too much could affect the amount of bloom (hence the amount of fruit) and the fall color. Serviceberry prefers acidic soil, but it will adjust to less-than-perfect soil. Make sure the planting site has good drainage.

Growing Tips
Keep your newly planted tree moist until established. Mulch serviceberry with a 2-inch layer of organic mulch. Don't pile the mulch around the trunk. Be sure to water occasionally during summer droughts when it's hot and dry and the soil feels dry under the mulch. Fertilize yearly in late fall with tree and shrub food.

Regional Advice and Care
Most of the new varieties remain free of any bugs or disease. To shape your serviceberry, prune anytime. If you want to enjoy the fruits, you will have to fight the birds to get your portion.

Companion Planting and Design
Use serviceberry in any number of landscape situations in Ohio—shrub borders, entrance gardens, woodland edges, and patio plantings. A single-stemmed sort would make a nice street tree. *Amelanchier arborea* is an upright-growing tree with some plants having multiple trunks and others that have a single trunk. Some species of *Amelanchier* have a suckering, shrubby habit; select from the ones I recommend.

Try These
Several superior serviceberry selections exist that are hybrids; these are often referred to as cultivars of *A. × grandiflora*. One to look for is 'Autumn Brilliance'. This superior cold-hardy selection has showy flowers, brilliant fall color, and lots of fruit. It reaches about 20 to 25 feet. 'Princess Diana' is another cold-hardy *grandiflora* that has large fruit and great red fall leaf color. 'Lamarki' is cold hardy; it grows like a small tree or a shrub with multiple stems or trunks.

Silver Linden

Tilia tomentosa

Botanical Pronunciation
TILL-ee-uh toe-men-TOE-suh

Bloom Period and Seasonal Color
Deciduous, yellow fall color; late June to early July blooms in creamy white

Mature Height x Spread
50 to 70 feet x 30 to 40 feet

Silver linden, a great ornamental shade tree, is underused. Because growth rate regulates price and because lindens are slower growing, the price per size of tree will be higher than others. But read on. This tree does a lot more than many other shade trees. To begin with, it has showy fragrant flowers in early summer. Next, its shiny, dark green leaves have a silvery cast on the undersides. Add wind and you have a beautiful sight. Also, expect golden yellow fall color. Silver linden makes a superior street tree because it tolerates heat and drought. Some linden varieties attract Japanese beetles, but not the silver linden. You might have to call around to a few garden centers to locate silver linden, but you'll thank me later.

When, Where, and How to Plant
You will find most lindens at the nursery as balled-and-burlapped trees. You might find very young trees in containers. Both types can be planted anytime the ground is not frozen. Easy to transplant, silver linden—like all lindens—would prefer moist, well-drained, good soil (wouldn't all trees!). The nice thing about silver linden is that it will adapt well to different types of alkaline and acidic soil, and it tolerates polluted conditions. Choose a location in full sun to half-day shade. For planting specifics, read the "how to plant" section in this chapter.

Growing Tips
Be sure to keep the root zone of your newly planted tree moist. Even though silver linden is drought resistant for the first few years after it is planted,

give it a deep soaking of water during dry spells when rainfall is less than average. A 2-inch layer of mulch applied in a ring will help protect against water loss. For advice about fertilizing trees, read page 186 in this chapter.

Regional Advice and Care
In general, lindens attract several pests, such as Japanese beetles and aphids; however, silver linden seems to be less attractive to insects. Disease is of little concern. This tree grows very shapely on its own with little or no pruning on your part.

Companion Planting and Design
Silver linden has fragrant flowers, showy foliage, good fall color, and beautiful bark. You couldn't find a more impressive shade tree for a larger landscape. It also makes an attractive and unusual street tree.

Try These
'Sterling Silver' makes a great street tree with its broad, pyramidal shape. It has gorgeous, deep green leaves with silver undersides. 'Green Mountain' is very similar to 'Sterling Silver', but it has an improved and more rapidly growing form. Littleleaf linden, *Tilia cordata*, is another linden to consider for your landscape. 'Greenspire' (40 to 50 feet tall) is a popular street tree. This pretty, urban-tolerant tree has a uniform pyramidal habit, fragrant flowers, and glossy foliage.

Sweetbay Magnolia

Magnolia virginiana

Botanical Pronunciation
mag-NO-lee-uh ver-jin-ee-AY-nuh

Other Name Laurel magnolia

Bloom Period and Seasonal Color
Evergreen; May and June creamy white blooms

Mature Height x Spread
15 to 25 feet x 20 feet

Sweetbay magnolia is a tree that should be in every landscape. This magnolia blooms in June, so its flowers are never threatened by spring frost like many others. You and your neighbors will know when sweetbay is in bloom. The creamy white flowers look and smell like gardenias—not overwhelming, just wonderful. Now, as for the tree itself, the leaves are a shiny green on the top side and silvery underneath. In the wind, that makes a beautiful contrast. This tree will grow under many circumstances. Sweetbay magnolia will tolerate heavy clay soil, will grow in sun or shade, and will sustain itself in extremely dry to somewhat wet areas. A small tree, sweetbay magnolia makes a superb patio tree.

When, Where, and How to Plant
Magnolias as a family are slow to generate new roots after transplanting. You will see more growth the first year from balled-and-burlapped trees that are planted in spring. You can successfully plant any magnolia (balled-and-burlapped or container-grown) anytime, though you'll need to give these plants extra care. While it will tolerate a wet location, sweetbay also appreciates good drainage along with decent soil. Sun or shade is fine. This is definitely a tree adaptable to many locations. To plant, follow the tree planting directions on in this chapter in the "how to plant" section.

Growing Tips
As with all new trees, keep the root zone moist the first season. Apply a 2-inch layer of organic mulch around your tree, keeping the mulch away from the trunk. For advice on fertilizing trees, read the fertilizing section on page 186. In high pH soils, sweetbay benefits from a fertilizer for acid-loving plants. You will know if the soil is too alkaline by the yellowish green color of the leaves.

Regional Advice and Care
Sweetbay is easy to care for. It has no problems with bugs or disease. Prune your tree after it blooms to get the shape and size you want. All magnolias form their bloom buds in the fall. Avoid pruning after July 15 so that you don't cut off the following year's blooms.

Companion Planting and Design
There are many ways to use this versatile small tree. Plant sweetbay off the corner of a house, out in the yard as a specimen tree, or group several together to screen out an unpleasant view. You can prune this tree to confine it to most areas of the landscape.

Try These
'Henry Hicks' is more reliably evergreen. Another favorite magnolia for Ohio gardens is the star magnolia, *Magnolia stellata*. Like sweetbay, it is a smaller (5 to 15 feet), almost shrubby plant. It's an early bloomer though, so its starry white flowers will occasionally be destroyed by frost. Avoid warm southern exposures that will encourage earlier bloom. 'Royal Star' is a great selection.

Thornless Honeylocust

Gleditsia triacanthos var. *inermis*

Botanical Pronunciation
gluh-DIT-see-uh try-uh-KAN-thus

Other Name Common thornless honeylocust

Bloom Period and Seasonal Color
Deciduous; yellow fall color

Mature Height x Spread
40 to 60 feet x 40 to 60 feet

Some plant experts think this tree is overused. On the contrary, it is its cousin, the black locust, that lines the interstates of Ohio. The thornless honeylocust is a wonderful plant for home landscapes. Perhaps its best assets are its leaves. Their fine-textured canopy provides filtered shade that allows grass to grow right up to the trunk, and when the yellow leaves drop off in fall, they are small enough that no raking or gutter cleaning is necessary. However, the large seedpods of honeylocust are a nuisance, so plant seedless selections. Honeylocust is a fast grower (as much as 2 feet or more per year); it tolerates all types of soil as long as the drainage is good; and it grows well in urban locations. Honeylocust produces good, yellow fall color.

When, Where, and How to Plant

Smaller sizes of honeylocust are available in containers; larger trees are balled and burlapped. Plant either type in spring or summer. Stay away from field-grown trees that are freshly dug in the fall. Plant trees that have been dug in late winter anytime the ground is not frozen. Choose locations in full sun for the best results. Honeylocust prefers rich, moist, well-drained soil, but it will prosper in average to heavy clay soil, as well. Dig a hole no deeper than and two to three times as wide as the soil clump. Backfill with existing soil, breaking up all soil to the size of golf balls. Water-in well. See page 185 for more tips on planting trees. No staking is required.

Growing Tips

Keep newly planted trees moist the first few years, after that your tree will be drought tolerant. Mulch with a 2-inch layer of organic mulch, keeping the mulch several inches away from the trunk. Advice on fertilizing trees can be found on page 186 in this chapter.

Regional Advice and Care

Honeylocusts can attract webworms, which build a nest in the branches and eat the leaves. Use a bamboo pole or a strong water jet to break up the nests. The tree's leathery pods are a nuisance to rake up and also lead to self-sown trees. Make sure you purchase a seedless cultivar. When trees are young, prune anytime to shape as you desire.

Companion Planting and Design

Honeylocusts provide great, filtered shade without inhibiting other vegetation from growing underneath. This quality makes them a wonderful lawn or patio tree. Their adaptability and salt tolerance make them a good choice for a street tree. Give honeylocust some yard space; don't plant it within 20 feet of the house so the branches won't grow toward the house.

Try These

One of the best is 'Shademaster', a vigorous, vase-shaped tree with deep green leaves. 'Skyline' is another great choice noted for its yellow fall color. 'Sunburst' is remarkable for its golden yellow leaves throughout the growing season.

Weeping Cherry

Prunus subhirtella var. *pendula*

Botanical Pronunciation
PROO-nus sub-hur-TELL-uh

Other Name
Higan cherry

Bloom Period and Seasonal Color
April; pink blooms

Mature Height x Spread
12 to 25 feet x 6 to 30 feet

Drifts of pink-flowered 'Kwanzan' cherry and white-flowered 'Yoshino' cherry trees prompt the cherry blossom festival in Washington, D.C., each spring. It's a beautiful vision, but in Ohio there is a problem with this type of cherry: it is short-lived. In our climate you can expect these trees to live only eight to eighteen years—not long for a tree. A better choice is Japanese weeping cherry; it lives much longer, with an average lifespan in Ohio of thirty to forty years. Weeping cherry is a broad-growing tree with long, weeping branches and pink (or sometimes white) single or semi-double flowers. It's worth growing for its beautiful silhouette alone. Give this tree lots of room, and it will become a gorgeous specimen tree in your landscape.

When, Where, and How to Plant

Most weeping cherry trees are planted in spring. That's when we see these beautiful trees in bloom, and we just simply have to have one. Actually, you can plant these trees anytime the ground is not frozen. They are available as balled-and-burlapped or container-grown trees. Weeping cherry likes lots of sun, a half-day or more. Well-drained soil is a must. (If you have heavy clay soil, consider planting a weeping crabapple tree instead.) Do not plant a weeping cherry within 15 feet of the house, walkway, or drive. Follow the instructions for tree planting in this chapter on page 185.

Growing Tips

Keep newly planted cherries moist to aid root development and lessen transplant shock. Cherries tend to be shallow rooted, so mulch to conserve moisture and reduce weeds. Create a mulch ring 2 inches deep, keeping it away from the tree trunk. To determine if your tree needs fertilization, read page 186.

Regional Advice and Care

Other than a few bug holes in some leaves, weeping cherries have no real problems with insects or disease. Trim off excess weeping growth anytime. The most popular way to grow weeping cherries is by top-grafting the weeping form to a seedling cherry understock. Sometimes, growth off the understock (called suckers or water sprouts) will produce vertical twigs that destroy the weeping form. If this occurs, remove the upright growth.

Companion Planting and Design

Weeping cherry continues to accent the landscape even after it blooms because of its beautiful habit. Ornamental year-round, it is the perfect specimen tree. Young trees look beautiful at holiday time if dressed with miniature lights.

Try These

A great cherry for a small- to medium-sized landscape is 'Snow Fountains®'. It reaches about 10 to 12 feet tall, but only 6 feet wide. It covers its weeping branches with white flowers and has orange-yellow fall color. This tree, introduced by Lake County Nursery of Perry, Ohio, is usually listed as a selection of weeping cherry, although it is probably a hybrid.

Weeping Willow

Salix alba

Botanical Pronunciation
SAY-licks AL-buh

Other Name
Golden weeping willow

Bloom Period and Seasonal Color
Deciduous, bright golden spring foliage

Mature Height x Spread
Up to 75 feet x 75 feet

I wasn't sure I was going to include the weeping willow in this book because there are so many that are misplanted and misunderstood. Then I thought, "Denny, maybe that's *why* it should be included." Weeping willow has a graceful rounded form and delicate pendulous branches. You have probably noticed its bright golden color in the early spring landscape. Traditionally, you will find weeping willow near a pond; however, if you have lots of yard space and good soil drainage, weeping willow will make a nice addition. Compared to the other, larger-growing shade trees listed in this chapter, willow—even under the best growing conditions—is shorter-lived. Willow nomenclature can be confusing; *Salix alba* 'Niobe' is also called the golden weeping willow.

When, Where, and How to Plant
Willows are easy to transplant and can be planted anytime during the growing season. Most are nursery-grown in containers. Weeping willows need lots of room. If planted in good conditions, they will grow 50 to 75 feet tall and 50 to 75 feet wide. Plant in full sun in a spot with average to fertile moist soil; avoid heavy clay. Willows have invasive roots that wreak havoc on sidewalks, sewer lines, and septic systems, so site them carefully. Also, they are weak-wooded and prone to breakage, so choose a location away from buildings. Read page 185 for planting tips.

Growing Tips
Keep your new willow moist, although you most likely have chosen a moist spot. Willow thrives with moisture, but do not plant in areas that are constantly holding water; it is not a wet vac. A 2-inch layer of organic mulch will help conserve moisture. In periods of drought, when rainfall is less than average, give your tree a deep soaking. For information fertilizing trees, read page 186.

Regional Advice and Care
Happy willows don't present any serious pest or disease problems. Trim dead wood anytime it appears. Pruning to develop a strong branching habit is advisable. Keep in mind that willows grow large; if you try to dwarf them by pruning, you'll soon realize you have the wrong plant in the wrong place. Willows are messy trees and often drop leaves, twigs, and branches. You'll inevitably spend some time cleaning up.

Companion Planting and Design
Weeping willow makes a graceful specimen tree in a big landscape setting and looks picturesque by a pond. Willow needs a space of its own; its surface roots will always out-compete other plant species. This is a beautiful plant, but site it carefully to avoid problems.

Try These
Another beautiful willow is the golden corkscrew willow, *Salix* 'Golden Curls'. This tree has twisted, ornamental, orange-yellow stems that are great for winter interest and useful for flower arranging. It is smaller, reaching about 30 feet.

'Winter King' Hawthorn

Crataegus viridis 'Winter King'

Botanical Pronunciation
kruh-TEE-gus VEER-ih-diss

Bloom Period and Seasonal Color
Deciduous, orange-red fall color; mid- to late spring white blooms; colorful fall berries

Mature Height x Spread
20 to 30 feet x 20 to 30 feet

'Winter King' is the most attractive hawthorn, and it has year-round appeal. In the spring, this tree has masses of beautiful, lacy, white flowers. The flowers form loads of green berries that turn to a beautiful orange-red in fall. A picture of the 'Winter King' with fruit and snow cover would make a beautiful holiday card. The fruit remains on the tree until the birds feast on it in early winter. The silver-tinted bark in the winter and red-to-purple fall color make for additional landscape appeal. Unlike many hawthorns, this tree generally remains free of disease problems. Its rounded habit and smaller size make 'Winter King' a great tree for a small yard. Birds love the berries, and you will love its great landscape color.

When, Where, and How to Plant
Balled-and-burlapped trees, which are dug during late winter before bud-break, are best planted in spring. Container-grown trees are always ready for planting; plant anytime the ground is not frozen. Any hawthorn requires at least a half-day of sun, but full sun is preferred. 'Winter King' is urban-tolerant and will grow well in virtually any well-drained soil. To plant, dig a hole no deeper than the rootball and two to three times as wide. For more planting details, consult page 185.

Growing Tips
Keep newly planted hawthorn moist until it's established; after that it will be drought tolerant. During hot or dry periods the first year, let the hose run slowly for 15 minutes near the trunk and then check the surrounding soil to see if there is moisture around the rootball. Mulch your tree with a 2-inch layer of organic mulch, keeping it away from the trunk. For information on fertilizing trees, refer to page 186.

Regional Advice and Care
This tree is low maintenance. 'Winter King' is free of serious pest and disease problems. Prune in late winter to thin the crown and remove any crossing branches. These trees are usually grafted; remove any vertical growth (suckers) that appears at the base of the tree below the graft union. Take care when pruning to avoid getting stuck by thorns; fortunately 'Winter King' has fewer thorns than many other hawthorns.

Companion Planting and Design
Consider using this tree as part of a corner foundation planting or as a specimen. It could be used as a tall hedge or barrier plant. An evergreen backdrop will really set off the berries. Because of its thorns, do not plant it near a sidewalk or children's play area. This tree provides a natural bird sanctuary during the winter.

Try These
Though 'Winter King' is definitely the best, you might want to try a selection of English hawthorn, *Crataegus laevigata*, called 'Crimson Cloud'. It has large, red flowers with a starry white centers and red fruits. Also, it's resistant to leaf blight.

Zelkova

Zelkova serrata

Botanical Pronunciation zel-KO-va ser-RA-ta

Other Name Japanese zelkova

Bloom Period and Seasonal Color
Non-showy flowers in April; dark green leaves in summer turn to yellow-orange-brown in fall (depending on summer heat)

Mature Height x Spread
50 to 60 feet x 30 to 40 feet

This is a very handsome tree because of good, healthy looking foliage, very interesting habit of growth, and very attractive bark. Zelkova is well-suited for lawns, residential streets, parks, and large areas that could use a tree or two. Years ago elms were all dying from Dutch elm disease. Zelkova was considered as a replacement for the American elm but this is no longer true due to all the great and beautiful specimens at the various arboretums across the Midwest. This tree even performs well in soil where a high pH soil is the norm.

When, Where, and How to Plant
Zelkova transplants easily if it's balled and burlapped when field grown and the tree was pre-dug during early spring before bud break. This tree prefers moist, deep soil. It's pH adaptable, and once established it becomes very wind and drought tolerant. Consult the "how to plant" section in this chapter for the specifics on tree planting. Plant according to my instructions and no staking is needed. This tree is also excellent as a street tree between your street and your sidewalk.

Growing Tips
Keep all your shade trees from summer stress by playing Mother Nature and give all trees timely waterings during summer's hot, dry weather. Fertilize with granular plant food in November to December.

Regional Advice and Care
It's susceptible to some of the few problems that beset the elm; however, zelkova is resistant to Dutch elm disease. These trees are much cleaner that the elms and shows good resistance to Japanese beetles. As a small young tree, zelkova is a low-branched, vase-shaped tree. As trees mature the vase shape will remain with many ascending branches. Zelkova's fruit is a small kidney bean-shaped drupe about ¼ inch across, ripening in the fall.

Companion Planting and Design
Use as a centerpiece on the front lawn. Plant on 25-foot centers in front of your home or as boulevard trees that won't create a mess when situated between your street and sidewalk. It's very neighborhood friendly.

Try These
'Autumn Glow' has deep purple fall color. 'Halka' is fast growing. 'Green Vase' is also fast growing, up to 2 feet per year. 'Spring Grove' has dark green foliage and great red fall color. 'Village Green' is another fast-growing variety, up to 3 feet per year.

TURFGRASSES

FOR OHIO

Grass is the number one plant (if you are counting actual plants!) in our landscapes. If we talk about drive-by appearances, we judge the beauty of many a home by the appearance of its lawn. I've often said that if a lawn looks green from the street, it's perfectly okay. How often have you said, "My neighbor doesn't do half the yard work I do, and his lawn looks better than mine!"? Well, that's because you're not picking up your neighbor's newspaper every morning. Every morning you walk out on your lawn and say, "Look, I have this weed, this brown 3-inch spot, and oh, what's that?" We become lawn fanatics. We view our neighbor's yard from afar, where his lawn looks better. Want to feel better? Go pick up your neighbor's paper, and you will see the same things or worse in his lawn than in your own.

There's no denying the lovely picture a well-maintained lawn can make.

What's in the Seed I'm Buying?

All grass seed sold in Ohio is tested by the Ohio Department of Agriculture. All seed has to have a label with information gathered by people working in a lab. They count the seed and other matter by hand and test it for germination. Always check the label, especially when comparing prices. The label should tell you the following:

- **Variety:** the correct name(s) of the grass seed you're buying; no common names, such as "Super Blend," are allowed.
- **Seed purity:** the percentage of pure grass seed that you're buying; this should always be above 95 percent.
- **Other crop seed:** the percentage by weight of unlisted grass seed varieties that are in your seed; this percentage should always be 1 percent or less.
- **Inert matter:** the non-seed count or other non-seed material that you are buying; it should be 1 percent or less.

- **Weed seed:** the percentage of bad, weed-causing seed that's in your seed. It should be less than ½ percent. (Just 1 percent of weed seed can amount to *one million* chickweed seeds.)
- **Noxious weeds:** should read "none found." Never buy grass seed with noxious weed seed in it.
- **Lot number:** the number that was assigned to a particular crop of seed that came from the same harvest and the same growing field.
- **Germination:** the percentage of the seed you're buying that you can expect to grow; it should be 80 to 90 percent.
- **Origin:** the state where the seed was harvested.
- **Test date:** the date that the seed from your particular lot was tested. Grass seed should be viable for 2½ years after the testing date shown if it is kept cool and dry.

Not all grass seed is equal. Grass seed is sold by the pound, but the price per pound should not be the determining factor in buying decisions. The number of seeds in an actual pound of grass seed varies with the type of seed you're buying. Example: Kentucky bluegrass has approximately one million seeds to a pound, while turf-type rye and turf fescue have 200,000 seeds to a pound. That means bluegrass will cover five times the soil area as the other two. Buy grass seed by the coverage, not by the pound.

Lawn Food: What the Numbers Mean

There is a dizzying assortment of lawn fertilizers available at local garden stores. First, it's important to know that all established grass needs one pound of nitrogen for every 1,000 square feet of lawn per application. You will see three numbers on a bag of fertilizer (sometimes called the analysis). These show the amounts by weight of the nitrogen (N), phosphorus (P), and potassium (K), always in that order. A 50-pound bag of fertilizer with an analysis of 10-6-4 contains 10 percent nitrogen, 6 percent phosphorus, and 4 percent potassium and covers 5,000 square feet. You may see an 18-pound bag of lawn food whose analysis is 20-4-6 and whose directions say it covers 5,000 square feet. Well, let's do some math. If we take 20 percent of

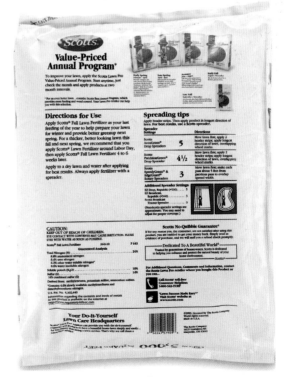

The label on a bag of fertilizer contains a great deal of useful information, but you need to know how it applies to your lawn before you make your purchase.

18 pounds (multiply by .20), we come up with 3.6 pounds of nitrogen per 5,000 square feet. Not enough. You might find a 50-pound bag of 10-6-4 fertilizer that will cover 5,000 square feet of lawn. Using the same math, 10 percent of 50 pounds is 5 pounds of nitrogen per 5,000 square feet, which is the right amount. Just looking at the numbers on the bag without factoring in the coverage information might have you believe that 20 percent is more than 10 percent, which isn't always the case with fertilizers.

When Is the Best Time to Sow Grass Seed?

Fall seeding (mid-August to the end of September) is best. During this period, soil temperatures are high, which promotes quick germination. Annual weeds have already germinated and are less likely to be a concern. Watering may be necessary if natural rains are not available.

Dormant seeding (January 1 to March 15) is second best. Soils are usually freezing and thawing, which works the seed into the soil for great seed-to-soil contact. Remove any fallen leaves or other debris that prevents seed from making seed-to-soil contact. Naturally, seed will not germinate until soil temperatures reach at least 55 degrees Fahrenheit, but having seed in the soil can give desirable grasses a headstart before spring-germinating weed seeds erupt.

Spring seeding (March 15 to June 15) is third best. Germination can occur, but weed competition will be at its highest. Ignore broadleaf weeds until desirable grasses mature (or have been mowed two to three times). At that time, treat weeds with a selective broadleaf weed control, following label directions.

Summer seeding (June 15 to August 15) is fourth best. With irrigation, germination will be fast during these months, but high day and night temperatures may result in diseases, such as damping-off, pythium, and brown patch. Crabgrass is also likely to be present. Add to these negatives the fact that tender, young grass seedlings literally cook under the summer sun.

Late-fall seeding (mid-October to January 1) is the least desirable. Seed will likely germinate, but it will not have enough time to develop

Use a hand spreader to spread grass seed thickly and evenly over the entire area, slightly overlapping the edges of the grass that isn't covered with soil. When you're done seeding, the ground should look like it lightly snowed.

an adequate root system to protect it from heaving and thawing. In most cases, this seeding will result in seedlings being "popped" out of the ground and just drying out (desiccating).

Successful Lawn Seeding Step-by-Step

Grass thrives when properly planted in the right location. Many of us think grass seed will grow if we simply throw it on the lawn and walk away. For winter seeding, this is mostly true. But for fall or spring seeding—it's just not so. Here are step-by-step ways to successfully seed your lawn.

Spot-Seeding Bare Spots

1. Take a steel rake and loosen the soil.
2. Apply seed with an applicator or by hand at the rate of four to five seeds per inch. Freeze grass seed overnight for faster germination (this isn't necessary for winter seeding).
3. Dampen daily until seed germinates. Water as much as if you're watering the dust off a ball field. Do this daily. (A light application of straw is optional.)
4. After germination, deep-water the new grass weekly (an equivalent of 1 inch of water minus any rainfall). Water all at one session, or divide it into no more than two watering sessions per week.
5. Mow as soon as the new grass reaches 2¼ inches or more, to a height of 2 inches. Raise the mower ½ inch after four cuttings of the new grass.

Seeding New Lawns or Reseeding an Existing Lawn—the Don'ts

1. *Don't* rototill the soil. This causes the soil to settle unevenly and wakes up *thousands* of weed seeds that will compete with the new grass (and it's a lot of unnecessary work).
2. *Don't* apply topsoil unless you spread it to a depth of 4 to 6 inches over the entire area. Use topsoil to fill in low areas. Settle the new topsoil with irrigation before seeding. Re-loosen the topsoil with a steel rake to break up the crust. Then apply seed.
3. *Don't* even read any further unless you can keep new seed dampened daily until germination (assuming no rain on a given day). Try the winter seed method if this seems like too much trouble!

Now for the Dos—Please Read Carefully

1. *Do* kill all existing vegetation in the area to be reseeded. Weeds and other vegetation should be watered well before the application of the herbicide (healthy weeds die faster). In late summer (early August), allow 3 to 4 weeks before retreating, as some weeds re-grow after initial treatment. Old lawns should be between 2 to 3 inches tall when treating; this is especially true with nut sedge.

2. *Do* rent a seed-slitter or verti-slicer. Set the blade to cut a ½-inch slit. Run the machine east to west and north to south (a checkerboard pattern). Most machines come with a seed box. If so, set the seeder to drop 4 to 5 seeds per inch of soil. For turf fescue and turf rye, make another couple of passes northeast to southwest and southeast to northwest.

3. *Do* freeze seed overnight. It can stay frozen until you're ready to apply it. (This is not necessary with winter seeding.)

4. *Do* fertilize with a starter-type fertilizer, such as a 9-18-18. *Do not* mix seed and fertilizer together in the same applicator hopper; apply fertilizer first.

5. *Do* lightly water grass seed daily (assuming rainless days) to keep seed moist until germination. Then water once weekly with the equivalent of 1 inch of water (including rain). Water during hot, dry weather. If it rains, subtract that amount from the 1 inch. In order to tell how much you are watering, place a straight-sided glass in the area of the sprinkler and when an inch of water appears in the glass, move the sprinkler and the glass.

6. *Do* mow grass as soon as it's 3 inches. Mow new grass to 2 inches and mow often. The more mowings, the quicker new grass matures. You will get a few new broadleaf weeds. *Do not* apply a broadleaf weedkiller until you've mowed at least three times. Raise the mower to a 3-inch cutting height after three cuttings.

7. *Do* use good grass seed. Don't mess everything up with so-called bargain seeds. Check the seed label for purity, weed seed content, and inert ingredients.

Lawn Notes

1. The best feeding times for all types of lawns are early September and again in November, both times with a high-nitrogen fertilizer. (Feedings should be 1 pound of actual nitrogen per square foot.) The only other time to fertilize is in early spring at a rate of ½ pound nitrogen per square foot.

2. Leave grass clippings to feed the lawn. An exception is the tall clippings due to rainy periods. Collect those that would clump and smother grass plants or wait until the clumps dry and mow again, or spread them out over the lawn using a leaf blower.

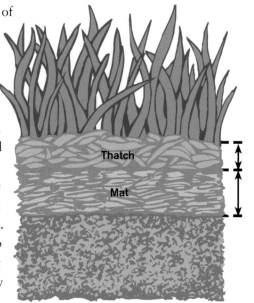

Thatch is a layer of organic matter, dead and living shoots, stems, and roots. It is not caused by grass clippings.

3. Grass clippings do not cause thatch. Thatch is caused by the natural growing habits of bluegrass and creeping fescues. So what to do about clippings? Just leave them. That's right. A full season of grass clippings returned is the equivalent of one full feeding. If the grass gets extra-long between mowings due to rain, mow the lawn after the wet clumps dry to blow the grass clippings uniformly over the lawn or blow the excess grass clippings with a leaf blower to disburse.

4. Choose grass varieties that fit your maintenance schedule. For example, bluegrass is high maintenance, perennial grass is medium to high maintenance, and turf-type fescue is low maintenance.

5. Winter seeding is a great if you can't seed in fall. In early February to early March, remove fallen leaves and twigs from the areas to be reseeded; this will help ensure

Vertical mowers can open up the turf, allowing greater penetration of water and nutrients.

that seeds make good seed-to-soil contact. Apply seed to those areas (four to five per inch) and go back inside and watch TV. Freezing and thawing create a natural seedbed. The seed will germinate in spring when the soil warms to the proper germination temperature.

6. For spring and fall seedings, straw helps hold moisture around the seed, but straw does not *replace* the moisture. You have to water daily. If you use straw, a bale should cover 2,000 square feet. This is a very light application. If done this way, no straw removal will be necessary, as it'll decompose and not inhibit new grass as it starts to grow.

7. Do I feed first or seed first? When putting down lawn food and grass seed the same day, always fertilize first so you avoid walking on grass seed anymore than necessary.

8. Sharpen the lawnmower blade at least twice a season. Have it done by a professional so the blade remains balanced (weighs the same on both sides of the center hole). Grass does *not* like to be cut. It's designed to grow to maturity and then produce seed. We mow to keep our lawns looking neat, but every time we mow, we injure the blade tissue, which is a water and nutrient reservoir. When we cut our grass with a dull blade, moisture and nutrients escape. A sharp mower blade allows cut grass blades to reseal immediately.

Mow as high as possible, setting your mower as needed.

Ten Tips and Hints to Conserve Water

One acre of grass gives off 2,400 gallons of water every hot, summer day. This has the cooling effect of a 140,000-pound air conditioner, a 70-ton machine. Here are ten ways to conserve water on established lawns during hot, dry weather and save money on your water bill, as well.

1. Mow as infrequently as possible. Mowing stresses grass and it will use more water.
2. Mow higher than normal. Larger leaf surfaces hold plant liquids and shade the root zone. Never remove more than one-third of a leaf blade in one mowing. Longer blades usually mean deeper, more efficient roots.
3. Water and mow in the early evening or morning. Less wind and heat reduces stress on the plant and allows greater penetration and less runoff.
4. Water for deep penetration. Stop watering when puddles or runoffs occur; allow water to penetrate into the soil before restarting. Light, infrequent sprinkling actually brings roots to the surface and does more harm than good.
5. Spot water. Drier areas near buildings and on slopes require more water than flat areas where water doesn't run off.
6. Aerify or verti-cut turf. Increased penetration of water and air will place the water where it can be used by grass.
7. Test soil moisture with a probe or screwdriver. Water *only* when the soil is dry or the probe is difficult to push into the ground.
8. Match fertilizer to plant requirements. Extension agents can recommend the timing and amounts of fertilizer needed by each grass variety. This reduces waste and mowing needs and diminishes overly succulent, water-wasting growth.
9. Increase disease and insect control with care. Drought-stressed turf is more susceptible to pest problems, but too much pesticide will increase plant stress.
10. Accept a little-less-than-lush lawn. Grass naturally goes dormant during drought, but it will readily regenerate when water becomes available. Reduce traffic on those areas if possible.

What Grass Is Best for Shade?

A seven-year study on grass cultivars grown in tree shade in Columbus, Ohio, tested thirty grass varieties. At the end of seven years, with the grasses being tested under sugar maples and sycamores, the scores were as follows (100 percent being the best):

- Turf Fescue 84 percent
- Fine Fescue 50 percent
- Kentucky Bluegrass 32 percent
- Perennial Rye 9 percent

The final results showed that turf fescue did the best; fine fescue was a distant second, followed by Kentucky bluegrass and perennial rye. Turf fescue actually became thicker, while all the others lost as much as 70 percent of their original grass cover.

Insects and Disease

Bluegrass lawns are wonderful for attracting chinch bugs, grubs, and other insects. Grubs do not cause spring damage to lawns, but new grubs returning into the soil in the fall can be quite damaging. Two lower-toxic products have been introduced to get the grubs and other harmful lawn insects without killing the good guys, such as earthworms. Apply these products (with the active ingredients Merit and Mach 2) from May 15 to August 15. Please read the instructions.

Turf disease is more difficult to control. Environmental conditions along with natural drought stress and other negative factors can cause many diseases that, for the most part, only do temporary damage. You will find more turf disease problems with bluegrass and turf-rye than with turf fescue. When in doubt, take a 12-by-12-inch sample that has both good grass and bad grass on it to your garden center or Cooperative Extension Office for an analysis.

Broadleaf Weed Control

Springtime equals weed time for a lot of lawns. Unwanted weeds start to appear in mid- to late spring. Chickweed (which doesn't become visually apparent until March) and henbit are the first to appear, closely followed by dandelions, then plantain, wild violets, ground ivy, clover, and so on. All seed, including weed seed, germinate at different soil temperatures. That's why chickweed appears in March, and spurge and purslane appear in June and July.

There are many selective (meaning they will not harm grass) broadleaf weed controls on the market. However, there is only one type that will get all the broadleaf weeds, from the easy-to-control ones like dandelions to the tough-to-kill ones like wild violets and ground ivy. That product (sold under different brand names) contains a chemical called Trimec®, which is a combination of three different weed killers. Trimec-based products are available as a liquid concentrate, a granular form by itself, or mixed with lawn food. I recommend the liquid concentrate as it's more cost-effective and allows you to just treat the weeds. There is another product that has all these benefits plus the herbicide carfentrazone, which kills weeds even with temperatures in the lower 40s. All others need outdoor temperatures of 65 degrees or more.

Caution: Remember, weeds die from light contact, not by drowning. Just wet the leaves of your various weeds and move on. Any weed control should be on the plant for twelve hours before rain. Don't mow afterward for twenty-four hours. When using a granular product, apply it early in the day when the dew is present or if later, lightly water the lawn before applying. Do not reseed treated areas for thirty days.

Weeds Can Be Summer Friends

The majority of weeds will appear in spring. If you treat large areas of weeds and kill them, you will be left with large bare spots. Remember you have to wait thirty days to reseed. If you kill in late April, that means you can't reseed until late May, a very difficult time to seed and expect good results. Those spring weeds can be summer friends, being green from the street and from inside your home. If you have lots of weeds, give serious consideration to lawn renovation in fall. The best control for any lawn weed is a nice, thick stand of turf that doesn't allow any room for windblown weed seed to land and grow in your lawn.

Is Crabgrass Making You Crabby?

Crabgrass is an annual grass that returns annually from seed produced the previous year. Other annual weed grasses, such as goose grass and dallasgrass, can be present too. Annual grasses need warm soil to trigger germination. In Ohio, crabgrass usually starts to germinate the end of May in Zone 6 and mid-June in Zone 5. There are many pre-emergent crabgrass control products. The vast majority of these products control weed seed germination for ninety days after application. Wet springs can reduce the effectiveness to sixty days, so be careful not to apply too soon in the spring.

There is a herbicide available that has Prodiamine® as the active ingredient. Prodiamine® lasts up to six months, not only killing crabgrass seed as it tries to germinate, but also any weed seed—eliminating lots of trouble before you ever see it. Prodiamine® is formulated that even with six month control, you can still reseed in fall. There are also post-emergent herbicides that allow you to spray existing crabgrass and other weeds selectively during summer.

Nut Sedge Driving You Nuts?

That fast-growing, light yellow-green plant in your lawn that you call a grass is actually a sedge plant, called nut sedge. It's so-named because shortly after germinating from seed, it starts forming little corms on its roots that resemble nuts, thus the name. It *appears* easy to pull, but the more you pull, the more you get because the nuts break off the roots, making lots more plants. Until recently, there was nothing selective over the counter that would control the sedge. There are several products out there that say they do, but they don't. A new chemical is now available to you to completely control the nut sedge. This nut sedge killer contains halosulfuron and is very effective. Follow the directions completely for definitive control of nut sedge.

Fine-Leaf Fescues—*Festuca* cultivars

Fine-leaf fescues are fine-bladed varieties that grow in sun or shade. The two most popular types are chewings fescue—a clump form—and creeping red fescue, which spreads through underground rhizomes. Like bluegrass, creeping red fescue makes its own thatch with those rhizomes. Fine-leaf fescues are more drought and shade tolerant than bluegrass. They grow better in northern Ohio than in the central and southern parts. For those of you in the north: If your lawn has a combination of sunny and shady areas, mix your fine-leaf fescue with a variety or two or even three of Kentucky bluegrass. That way, each grass variety will dominate in that portion of your lawn that is best-suited for it.

Growing and Care
The best time to plant is fall, between mid-August and the end of September. The second-best time is winter, spring is third, summer is fourth, and late fall is the worst. Plant creeping red and chewings fescues in natural shade cast by a permanent structure or tree shade. These varieties tolerate shady and dry sites better than perennial rye or bluegrass. Fine-leaf fescue grows in all types of soil, but it grows best in soil that's not heavy clay. Fertilize with a high-first-number (nitrogen) lawn food in September and again in November. Give fescue a light feeding of lawn food in mid- to late May. Fine-leaf fescues are vigorous growers in spring and fall. They'll grow and stay greener with supplemental watering in late summer, when Mother Nature gets chintzy with rain. Even though it is somewhat drought tolerant, make sure fine-leaf fescue receives 1 inch of water weekly in hot, dry weather. When using a seed mix of fine-leaf fescue and bluegrass, mow both types at 2½ inches in spring and fall, and 3 inches during summer. If you are seeding straight varieties of fine-leaf fescue, reduce those cutting heights by ½ inch. Wet springs can cause some fungus diseases, none of which is fatal. Improved varieties of creeping red fescue include Pennlawn and Dawson, both known for shade tolerance. Banner and Checker are good varieties of chewings fescue.

Kentucky Bluegrass—*Poa* cultivars

For years, Kentucky bluegrass was *the* grass of choice. But for it to look lush and green, it had to be fertilized four or five times a year. There were not a lot of other choices. Now we know that bluegrass doesn't do well under certain environmental conditions. To begin with, it needs the decent soil most likely found in northern Ohio. It doesn't tolerate southern and central Ohio's summer heat, and it stresses during the dry periods of the growing season. Weakened by stress, bluegrass becomes vulnerable to insects and disease. Kentucky bluegrass is still the grass of choice in northern Ohio—for now. But, for the rest of you, check out the turf fescues that tolerate the conditions in the rest of the state.

Growing and Care
The best time to plant is during fall, between mid-August and the end of September. The second-best time is winter, spring is third, and summer is fourth. Bluegrass does best in full sun, although it tolerates up to a half-day of shade. If planting in partial shade, add creeping red fescue to your seed mix. Bluegrass

continued on age 218

does not do well in heavy clay; use turf fescue instead. Kentucky bluegrass can become dormant (brown) during summer heat and drought. Provide at least ¼-inch of water weekly during this period, minus any rainfall. That will keep the roots alive until the weather cools and ample rainfall occurs, then bluegrass will turn green and grow again. Mow to a height of 2 to 2½ inches in spring and fall. Raise the mower ½ inch for summer (to 3 inches). Thatch is the number one problem—not the clippings, but the rhizome's growth habit. Control thatch by aerating twice a year. Watch constantly for soil insects and disease; timing is everything. Check weekly during cool, wet periods in spring and again during July, August, and September. If areas of your bluegrass lawn turn brown, seek professional help. My favorite is—turf fescue (ha!). The best-looking lawn on any Ohio street is a turf fescue.

Perennial Rye—*Lolium* cultivars

Perennial rye is a clump-forming turf grass that quickly germinates and begins growing. It is most often mixed with bluegrass or fine-textured fescue to get your newly seeded area off to a fast start. New varieties of perennial rye are much improved, yet one problem still exists—they are susceptible to turf disease when the weather doesn't cooperate. Newer varieties are more resistant, but not as resistant as the turf fescues. You can plant perennial rye in sun or in shady areas with good natural light. When mixing with bluegrass, never have more than 20 percent rye to 80 percent bluegrass. With the newer turf-type rye varieties, you will get best results by mixing together two or three of the better varieties.

Growing and Care

The best time to plant is fall, between mid-August and the end of September. The second best is winter, then spring, and then summer. Perennial turf-type rye grows best in full sun. The more shade, the more problems you can have. Turf-type rye prefers moist areas; it does not fare well in heavy clay soils. It also doesn't do well in soil types that dry out quickly. Always use a lawn food with a seed-starter formula to help new grass seedlings establish faster. Make sure turf-type rye receives 1 inch of water per week during the hot summer months. Fertilize rye in mid-spring and twice in the fall—in early September and in early to late November. Mow turf-type rye to 2½ to 3 inches in spring and fall, and raise the mower ½ inch for summer. You need to watch for disease problems, which usually occur during cool, rainy periods. Treat weeds anytime they appear. Rust is the number-one problem, but brown patch and dollar spot disease also affect perennial rye. Improved varieties include 'Pennant', 'All Star', 'Citation II', and 'Fiesta II'. 'Fiesta II' and 'Citation II' are reported to have better shade tolerance than other turf-type rye grasses.

Turf-Type Tall Fescue—*Festuca* cultivars

I am sold on turf-type fescues. This grass is a relative of the grass that grows in the median strips of interstates and on many sports fields. It will be the grass for central and southern Ohio. The first cultivars were introduced about thirty years ago, and seed hybridization has improved turf fescue so much that the newest cultivars have the texture of bluegrass. Add to that the deep-root characteristics of coarse fescue and the shade tolerance of fine-leaf fescue, and you have a good-looking, drought-, disease-, and insect-resistant grass. Not bad for one of the newest kids on the seed block. If you decide to plant this grass, you really should get rid of all the others before making the switch.

Growing and Care
The best time to plant is in fall, between mid-August and the end of September. Winter is second best, then spring, and then summer. Plant in sun or shade. This grass is drought tolerant in sun and is also shade tolerant. Turf-type fescue does well in all Ohio soil types. Turf-type fescue is drought tolerant, so there's not much to worry about during dry periods. Turf-type fescue will do just fine with two applications of lawn food. One application at the rate of 1 pound of nitrogen per 1,000 square feet in September, and 1½ pounds of nitrogen per 1000 square feet in November. The November feeding will provide spring nutrients. If your lawn winterburns, apply ½ pound of nitrogen per 1,000 square feet in mid-May. Mow turf-type fescue at 2½ to 3 inches in spring and fall, and raise the cutting height by ½ inch for summer. Because of this grass's vast, deep root system, grubs aren't much of a problem. Turf-type fescues contain endophytes, a natural ingredient that top-feeding insects, such as billbugs, do not like. Brown patch is the only disease problem I've seen, and it isn't terminal. 'Crewcut', 'Crossfire II', 'Plantation', and 'Rebel III' are some of the newest varieties. To find out which ones will grow best in your particular lawn, check with your local garden store.

A Final Word of Advice

Lots of products are available to ease your job of maintaining a good-looking lawn. These products will work to your expectations and will be environmentally friendly if you read the label and follow the instructions! And remember guys, more is not better.

Lawns can be very challenging, but don't become a "lawn nut." In this chapter, I have listed several varieties of lawn grass. Read carefully and find the one that fits your growing situation, from soil type to exposure to ease of growing. Don't argue with yourself, hoping to get the grass you thought you wanted and finding it doesn't fit your growing environment. Study and understand the information in this introduction before reading about individual grass varieties. You'll be glad you did.

VINES

FOR OHIO

Vines hold a very special place in a well-designed landscape. I say "well designed" because some homeowners who design their own landscapes are either fearful of vines or just simply don't understand them. Many might not even know about them. Well, I'm going to break the ice between you and vines.

How to Hold On . . . Or Not to Hold On

Different vines have different ways of clinging. Some vines have their own methods for attaching themselves to a structure; others need assistance to remain upright. In this chapter, I will explain what each vine needs or doesn't need to stay upright.

In addition to being decorative, vines can cool a house if they're planted on the west- or south-facing side of a home.

220 • *Ohio Getting Started Garden Guide*

Vines do not grow vertically into thin air. Whether a vine is self-clinging or not, a structure is needed. That structure could be the side of your house, a wooden or plastic trellis, or an arbor. It could be soft jute twine attached to something at both ends. It could even be a chain-link fence that you know could use some landscape help. All vines will make a groundcover if they are not furnished with support. When some plants can't stand up, they lie down and, in the case of vines, they cover the ground. Unsupported vines will continue to grow in a very horizontal way. There may be situations in which you would prefer to have a vine grow as a groundcover.

I'm the Boss!

Yes, you are the boss. Control the height and spread of vines by pruning. Do that pruning anytime a particular vine starts growing out of the boundaries you have given it. Remember, annual vines die in late fall. Cut back all of their old growth to the ground whenever you're in the mood.

A Big No-No

Never plant self-attaching vines to painted wood or the siding on your home. These vines hold moisture and can cause quick deterioration of painted wood; they can cause permanent stains on siding. If the wall is brick, stone, or stucco, go ahead and plant the vines. If you currently have vines self-attached to your home and you decide you don't want them anymore, you can pull the vines off. However, you will notice that the tentacles left behind will be hard-fastened to the wall. Rent a power sprayer and spray the remaining tentacles until they come off. If some still remain attached, use a wire brush or some other means to remove the stubborn ones. To completely kill the existing vines, cut the main stems at the group and apply a vine and stump killer product to the end parts left in the ground.

Multi-Dimensional

Vines serve many purposes. For starters, properly placed vines growing against the home on the south or west side is like adding room air-conditioners to the windows with those exposures. Using vines that drop their leaves in the fall allows winter sun to help warm the home on cold winter days. Vines by their nature are vertical. They take up very little yard space. So if you have a small yard, you can still have a big impact using vines. A vine can also be a beautiful, blooming shade provider for an outdoor gathering area. Lattice over a deck or patio can be made into a Garden of Eden by planting vines to cover it. And what looks more inviting in a yard than an arbor covered with blooming vines? Even without flowers, the leaves add landscape beauty.

Boston Ivy

Parthenocissus tricuspidata

Botanical Pronunciation
par-then-oh-KISS-us try-kusp-ee-DAY-tuh

Bloom Period and Seasonal Color
Deciduous glossy green foliage turning
red in fall

Mature Length
30 to 70 feet

It's called Boston ivy, so what's it doing in Chicago on the outfield walls of Wrigley Field? What it's doing is thriving and, in some cases, hiding the ball from the outfielder! This wonderful vine has beautiful, three-lobed, glossy green leaves during the growing season that turn scarlet red before dropping in the fall. The vine is self-clinging and can effectively hide an ugly wall. It also does one heck of an air-conditioning and heating job. Plant Boston ivy against the west or south side of a house where it will shade that wall during the summer. After beautiful fall color, the leaves will drop off, allowing that same wall to receive the warmth of the winter sun. (Your utility company will not be happy, though!)

When, Where, and How to Plant
Plant Boston ivy anytime the ground is not frozen. You will get the best fall color if Boston ivy gets sun; it's nice to know, though, that it does well in all exposures. Boston ivy tolerates a wide range of soil types, but needs good drainage. To plant, dig the hole no deeper than the soil clump but twice as wide. Plant the soil clump as close to its "wall to climb" as possible. Loosen any wrapped roots, and backfill using the existing soil, first breaking up all backfill soil to the size of golf balls. Water-in well.

Growing Tips
Water new vines to keep the soil moist until plants are established, after that your plants will be drought tolerant. Mulch your vine with a 2-inch layer of organic mulch. You won't need to fertilize Boston ivy.

Regional Advice and Care
There are no major bugs or diseases to bother Boston ivy. Don't be afraid to prune to keep it contained. You will want to keep this plant away from windows, screened porches, and ventilation vents. Don't let it engulf your home! Remember that anywhere it goes it leaves behind its adhesive disks, which are difficult to remove should you decide you no longer want the vine.

Companion Planting and Design
Boston ivy makes a wonderful screen. If you don't have a natural wall for it to grow against, use an arbor or trellis to give you privacy. If you decide to grow it on the wall of your house, know that its aerial roots and the adhesive disks will cause the gradual deterioration of painted wood surfaces. No, the vine will not harm masonry; that's an old wives tale. It's been on the wall at Wrigley for eighty years, and the wall is still standing.

Try These
'Fenway Park'—now that's in Boston! This variety has green foliage that starts off yellow in spring and ends with great red fall color. 'Green Showers' has large, fresh green leaves and a burgundy fall color.

Clematis

Clematis spp. and hybrids

Botanical Pronunciation
KLEM-uh-tiss

Bloom Period and Seasonal Color
Late spring to summer or fall; white, red, pink, purple, and bicolor blooms

Mature Length
8 to 20 feet

What a beautiful vine! The flowers are just gorgeous, and they bloom in many colors, from white, blue, and purple to yellow and deep red. You will see them on lampposts, on mailbox posts, even growing against tree trunks or scrambling over shrubs. Clematis is one of the most popular vines. Once you see this vine in bloom, you will understand why. There are many types of clematis, including showy large-flowered hybrids, smaller-flowered hybrids, and species clematis that have smaller flowers but in such tremendous numbers you won't care about size. This is especially true with fall clematis, *Clematis paniculata*. It has thousands of small white flowers in August and into September. Clematis is not a self-clinger; provide a trellis, structure, or even another plant for your vine to climb.

When, Where, and How to Plant
Plant clematis in spring. Choose a location with good, well-drained soil. Avoid heavy clay. The best situation is where the top of the clematis is in sun and the base of the plant is shaded by other plants, keeping the root zone cool. Annuals or perennials can be planted around the base to achieve this. To plant, dig a hole no deeper than the soil clump, but up to three times as wide. Remove your plant from the container carefully. Some clematis are planted 1 to 2 inches deeper than the soil level in the container; follow any specific directions that come with your plant. Backfill with existing soil and water-in well. Provide a support for the clematis to climb.

Growing Tips
Mulch with 2 inches of organic mulch, but don't pile mulch around the stems. Keep soil of newly planted clematis moist, but don't overwater. Water established plants regularly; your plant wants to be *moist*—not wet or dry. It can be slow to get going and may not bloom for the first year or two; be patient. Fertilize in spring with a well-balanced garden fertilizer and again after flowering.

Regional Advice and Care
Pests and disease are not generally a problem. Clematis is often pruned to remove dead wood and sometimes to control growth. Clematis blooms on new growth or old growth, depending on the type. In general, those that bloom on new growth can be pruned, as the buds swell in spring, down to about 1 foot from the ground. Seek specific pruning information about your plant.

Companion Planting and Design
Clematis is lovely on wooden fences, posts, trellises, or pergolas.

Try These
There are so many types it is hard to recommend just a few. For beginners, *C.* × *jackmanii* is easy to grow and produces tons of velvety purple flowers. It's a nice one to grow together with a climbing rose. My favorite of the large-flowered types is 'Nelly Moser'. Its huge, mauve-pink flowers are striped with deeper pink.

Climbing Hydrangea

Hydrangea anomala ssp. *petiolaris*

Botanical Pronunciation
hy-DRAIN-juh ah-NOM-uh-luh

Bloom Period and Seasonal Color
June to early July; blooms in fragrant white

Mature Length
60 to 80 feet

You will soon understand why climbing hydrangea is my favorite vine. It would be yours, too, unless you've either never heard of it, or you've never seen it growing. A great choice for a brick or stone wall, chimney, or trellis, this vine covers itself with clusters of white flowers in early summer. The snowball-like flowers have an appealing fragrance. Even when not in bloom, its glossy, dark green leaves are attractive. Although the fall color is variable, after the leaves drop, the cinnamon-colored shaggy bark is appealing. Climbing hydrangea is slow to get going, but as it matures it will become a first-class specimen. Take a look around your landscape. You must have a spot for this *spectacular* aristocrat of vines.

When, Where, and How to Plant

Spring and early fall are the preferred times for planting. Hydrangeas will flower best in full sun to part shade. It will grow in total shade, but it won't bloom as heavily. Choose a location with rich, moist, but well-drained soil shielded from strong northwest winds. Dig a hole as deep as the soil clump and two to three times as wide. If you're working with clay soil, mix in several shovelfuls of organic material. Avoid disturbing the root system. Break up all backfill soil to the size of golf balls. Backfill, and water-in well. Create a reservoir around the plant to direct moisture to the roots by mounding soil in a ring.

Growing Tips

Climbing hydrangeas are slow to start growing after they are transplanted. Be patient. Keep the rootball moist, but don't overwater. These plants will certainly kick in by the third year and start to put forth some serious growth. Don't overfertilize new plants. After your vine is established, fertilize in spring with a slow-release fertilizer. Mulch with a 2-inch layer of organic mulch to conserve moisture. Keep mulch away from the stems.

Regional Advice and Care

There are no known bugs or diseases that threaten climbing hydrangea. The vine attaches through the use of aerial rootlets. You may need to give your vine some help to get it going. Use a small wooden trellis to direct your plant to a wall or tie the branches gently onto a support structure. After many years, your plants will become heavy and large. Removing some of the vine to lighten the load will help prevent it from becoming detached.

Companion Planting and Design

This attractive woody vine is primarily a specimen plant for brick and stone walls or for an arbor or other freestanding structure. Climbing hydrangea will not give you quick cover. After a few years, though, you will have a remarkable focal point for your landscape.

Try These

Plant the species; there are not any selections of climbing hydrangea.

Mandevilla

Mandevilla x *amabilis*

Botanical Pronunciation
man-de-VILL-uh a-MAH-bih-liss

Bloom Period and Seasonal Color
Late spring to fall; blooms in light pink, dark pink, white

Mature Length 15 to 20 feet

Mandevilla is a tropical vine. That translates into a plant that will not survive the winter here in Ohio. So what's it doing in this book? Well, let me tell you. Plant your mandevilla, pot and all, into the ground close to the structure it's to grow on. Why go to this trouble? No other vine, in this chapter or otherwise, will bloom as much as mandevilla. Won't you have to plant a new one every year? Not if you bring your plant inside and treat it like any other indoor tropical plant over the winter. Next spring, in late May, take it back outside for another summer of beautiful trumpet-shaped flowers. It is not much work for a whole lot of flowers. Give it a try!

When, Where, and How to Plant
Wait to plant mandevilla until the danger of frost is over in your area of Ohio. Mandevilla will grow in full sun to a half-day of sun. If your plant is in a 1-gallon container, repot it into a 5-gallon container using a soilless mix. Dig a hole that is big enough to contain this pot close to the vine support. Next, sink the plant—pot and all—into the hole. When planted, the top edge of the pot should be level with the top of your soil.

Growing Tips
Mandevilla needs good drainage. If you are growing it in a pot sunk into the ground, it won't dry out very fast. Water when the soil in the pot is dry, but take care not to overwater. If you are unsure, dig down using a narrow trowel to see if the soil is dry. Fertilize every three weeks with your favorite water-soluble plant fertilizer following the package's instructions.

Regional Advice and Care
Pests and disease are rarely a problem. Mandevilla *does* need a structure to grow on. You can use arbors, trellis, latticework, or even soft jute twine. Prune back unwanted growth as necessary. In mid-September cut the vine back to 18 inches and lift the pot out of the ground. Inside your home, treat it like any other houseplant. Give it bright light and water when dry, taking care not to overwater. In late May, replant your mandevilla outside in the garden.

Companion Planting and Design
For a little bit of work—taking your mandevilla outside each spring, then reversing the procedure in early fall—you will get a beautiful, tropical-looking plant perfect for decks and patios. Train it up a trellis or pergola for a striking result.

Try These
The most well-known selection is 'Alice du Pont'; it has ice pink flowers with a darker pink throat. If you prefer white, 'Monte'—also called Summer Snow®—has gorgeous white flowers with a pink and yellow throat.

Moonflower

Ipomoea alba

Botanical Pronunciation
ip-oh-MEE-a AL-ba

Bloom Period and Seasonal Color
Midsummer to fall; blooms in white

Mature Length
To 15 feet

Moonflower, a first cousin to morning glory, grows readily from seed, and you can get many plants for the price of a seed packet. Moonflower begins to bloom in midsummer with gorgeous, fragrant flowers that measure up to 6 inches across. As its name implies, the flowers open at sundown (you will see blooms earlier in the day if the sky is cloudy). The blooms unfurl in about a minute; you can almost watch the flowers open. It's a wonderful plant for an area where you spend time on a summer evening. Moonflower is a good selection for hiding unsightly structures—such as an old chainlink fence—but this vine is so special, you may want to give it an ornamental trellis of its own.

When, Where, and How to Plant

To grow your moonflower from seed, soak the seed for 24 hours prior to planting for the best results. Wait until mid-May or early June to plant the seed directly in the ground. Choose a sunny location with at least a half-day of sun and average, well-drained soil. Moonflower likes it hot. To plant seed outside, loosen the soil to a depth of 6 inches. Place three seeds about 2 inches apart and about 1 inch deep. Water-in and be patient. It can take up to two weeks for the seed to germinate. To start seeds inside, plant three seeds in a 3-inch peat pot filled with a soil mix. If more than one seed sprouts, cut off the weaker plants. Plant the entire peat pot into the ground, keeping the seedling at the same depth it was in the pot.

Growing Tips

Moonflower doesn't need to be "mothered." In fact, many homeowners cause serious harm to this vine by being too kind. It doesn't need to be fertilized, and it should be watered only during hot, dry summers if the leaves are drooping. If you are growing your plants in a container with a soilless mix, fertilize with a water-soluble fertilizer several times during the summer. Always follow the instructions on the container.

Regional Advice and Care

Provide a structure for your moonflower to grow up on. You can prune unwanted growth anytime. Pests and disease are rarely, if ever, a problem for moonflower.

Companion Planting and Design

Plant near a deck or patio where you sit at night so that you can enjoy the evening blooms. If you want more color, mix moonflower with morning glory.

Try These

If you enjoy growing annual vines from seed, try another relative of moonflower, *Ipomoea quamoclit*, the cypress vine. This climber has finely divided foliage and brilliant red flowers. It will vine on the same structure and interweave itself with the moonflower, making a beautiful show of color that will bloom in the daytime, giving the effect of round-the-clock color.

Morning Glory

Ipomoea purpurea

Botanical Pronunciation
ip-oh-MEE-a pur-PUR-ee-uh

Bloom Period and Seasonal Color
Mid-August to fall; blooms in blue, red, white, or bicolor

Mature Length
8 to 10 feet

This rapidly growing annual vine is one of the oldest known plants used in the garden. Morning glory can be traced back to the early settlers who moved in, built homes, and wanted some summer color. Like its cousin the moonflower, it should be planted from seed—and yes, be patient, because it won't start blooming until late summer. That's really not a bad time, though, because Ohio gardens are looking a little tired by mid-August. But at that time, morning glory vines are just beginning to bloom—and bloom and bloom. They do so in colors of blue, violet, white, and pink. Fast-growing morning glory will screen lots of ugly sights. It does a great job of concealing that chainlink fence that you want covered by full-looking flowers and foliage every summer.

When, Where, and How to Plant
Plant morning glory from seed. To aid germination, soak seeds for 24 hours before planting. Place the seeds directly into the ground around the middle of May to mid-June. Choose a sunny to half-sunny location. Morning glory will tolerate any type of soil as long as there's good drainage. To plant seeds, loosen the soil about 6 inches deep and place three seeds ½ inch deep and 3 inches apart. It will take up to four weeks for the seeds to germinate. You can also sow your seeds inside in 3-inch peat pots three to four weeks before the last frost date. To plant seedlings in peat pots, plant the entire pot, keeping the seedling at the same soil level as it was in its pot. If necessary, peel away any part of the pot that extends above soil level.

Growing Tips
In drought periods, when rainfall is less than normal (3 to 4 inches a month), provide some water for morning glory. A 2-inch layer of organic mulch helps conserve moisture. Do not fertilize as this causes too many leaves and not enough color from the flowers.

Regional Advice and Care
Morning glory is easy to care for. Pests and disease won't be a problem, and deadheading is not necessary. Provide a fence, trellis, wires, or other support for your morning glory to climb.

Companion Planting and Design
Morning glory is the perfect summer remedy for ugly, rusty chainlink fences. It is charming when grown on fences, porches, and trellises as well as in hanging baskets, containers, and wall planters. Just be sure to plant quicker-blooming annuals with it for full-season color.

Try These
'Heavenly Blue' has 3- to 4-inch, beautiful sky blue flowers. 'Pearly Gates' has large white flowers. An All-America Selection, 'Scarlett O'Hara' has blooms in deep red. Combine all three for a mix of colors. Remember all morning glories are annuals, but they're easy to plant and they're worth it.

Silver Lace Vine

Polygonum aubertii

Botanical Pronunciation
pol-LIG-go-num aw-ber-TE-i

Other Name Fleece flower

Bloom Period and Seasonal Color
July to September; white to greenish
white flowers

Mature Length
Virtually unlimited; trim to maintain desired
size and shape

Silver lace vine does not care what kind of soil it grows in, so for many Ohio gardeners—who have basically rotten soil—this could be the vine for *you*. Silver lace vine grows in sunny to shady locations. It is easily transplantable, and it rapidly spreads by means of underground stems. Silver lace vine needs a support—a trellis, lattice, or arbor—to grow on. It grows quickly; if it dares to grow out-of-bounds, trim off the excess anytime. Silver lace vine produces small flowers, but there are so many blooms clinging close together, you will get lots of color in July, August, and much of September. Because of its rapid growth, there may be a few weeks between blooms. Be patient; more flowers are coming.

When, Where, and How to Plant
You can plant silver lace vine anytime the ground is not frozen. It will grow in sun to shade, but you will get more blooms with more sun. This vine will grow in any kind of soil type, but it does not like poorly draining soil that holds water after a rain. In rich soils, its growth may be too rampant. To plant, dig a hole no deeper than the soil clump but twice as wide. Loosen any roots that are wrapped around the clump. Backfill with existing soil, breaking up all backfill soil to pieces no bigger than golf balls.

Growing Tips
Silver lace vine is easy to grow and needs no special coddling. Water new plants to help them get established, after that you can mostly put the hose away. Water established plants once a week if no significant rain falls. No fertilization is necessary; it grows well even in poor soil.

Regional Advice and Care
There are no bad bugs or diseases that attack this vigorous vine. It makes a good quick cover, but prune anytime to keep it within the area you've allotted it. If desired, cut your vine back severely each spring to keep its growth in check. It can grow 10 to 20 feet in a single season. If necessary, control its spread with a non-selective herbicide. Since this vine grows from underground stems, you can get more plants by digging up a section of the vine to plant elsewhere.

Companion Planting and Design
Silver lace vine isn't a specimen vine like clematis or climbing hydrangea. The best use of this vine is where you need quick cover, particularly where the soil is too poor or too dry to grow other vines. This plant can be messy and weedy, so keep it away from formal gardens. Use it where its exuberant growth is welcome.

Try These
I know of no selections of silver lace vine, so plant the species.

Trumpet Vine

Campsis radicans

Botanical Pronunciation
KAMP-sis RAD-ee-kans

Other Name
Trumpet creeper

Bloom Period and Seasonal Color
June to July; red, orange, yellow blooms

Mature Length
10 to 25 feet

Here is a vine *anyone* can grow! Fast growing—often downright rampant—trumpet vine will engulf a lattice, trellis, fence, or arbor. Its common name comes from its trumpet-shaped, orange-red flowers that appear in June and July. Want hummingbirds? They love trumpet vine and will find yours if they're in the neighborhood. Trumpet vine attaches by aerial roots that hold the vine to its support. Soil types are not important, as trumpet vine will tolerate most. Take advantage of its rambunctious nature by using it to cover a sturdy fence, but keep it away from your house where it can create a problem. This vine can be a garden thug; be prepared to prune to keep it in-bounds. The structure for this vine should be at least 4 inches thick.

When, Where, and How to Plant

Plant container-grown trumpet vine anytime the ground is not frozen; the best selections are available from May to early June. Trumpet vine performs best in full sun, but it will do fine in a half-day of sun. This vine will tolerate all types of soil conditions as long as water doesn't stand after a rain. To plant your vine, dig a hole as deep as the soil clump but twice as wide. Plant so that it is at the same level it was in the container. Use existing soil to backfill, breaking up all backfill soil to the size of golf balls. Water-in well.

Growing Tips

Keep the root zone of your newly planted trumpet vine moist to help it get established. Though generally drought tolerant, in times of severe drought, water your trumpet vine to keep it healthy. Mulch with a 2-inch layer of organic mulch, keeping it several inches away from the stems. No fertilizer is necessary or advised.

Regional Advice and Care

Pests and disease won't trouble this vigorous grower. However, you will need to control its rampant growth. Don't let this plant get any bigger than the space you've allowed. Prune back unwanted growth anytime. After three to five years, start pruning back some of the oldest growth to within 12 inches of the ground—do this in early spring. Trumpet vine suckers at the roots; these can be dug and planted elsewhere.

Companion Planting and Design

Fast-growing trumpet vine makes a wonderful screen plant for hiding an undesirable view. Grow it on sturdy structures or stone walls. Don't plant it adjacent to your home or garage where it can create problems. Although a native, it can be invasive and shouldn't be planted near sensitive natural areas.

Try These

'Flava' has large, bright yellow flowers; it is, in my opinion, the best of the trumpet vines. 'Crimson Trumpet' has velvety, deep red blooms. Keep your eye out for new selections of trumpet vine; many new ones are entering the marketplace.

Virginia Creeper

Parthenocissus quinquefolia

Botanical Pronunciation
par-then-oh-KISS-us kwin-kway-FOH-lee-uh

Other Name
Woodbine

Bloom Period and Seasonal Color
Deciduous glossy green foliage turns crimson in fall

Mature Length
30 to 70 feet

Is that poison ivy growing in my landscape? No, it's Virginia creeper. It has glossy green, five-part leaves that emerge as a bright bronzy red and give you a spectacular fall color show with purplish red leaves. This deciduous vine grows fast and is self-clinging—meaning it needs no support. It tolerates extreme cold, windy conditions, sun, shade, and just about any type of soil. It will also grow up a tree, which does not hurt the tree, or it can be used as a rambling groundcover. Like its cousin Boston ivy, it is good for growing on the southern or western walls of the house. When it drops its leaves, it exposes your house to the winter sun, saving on utility bills. Birds love the berries of this native vine.

When, Where, and How to Plant
Plant Virginia creeper from containers anytime the ground is not frozen. The best selections will be available in spring. Virginia creeper grows well in sun or shade. It grows well in any soil type as long as there is decent drainage. To plant, dig a hole no deeper than the soil clump and twice as wide. Loosen any roots that are wrapped around the clump. Keep the plant at the same level it was growing in its pot. Always backfill with the existing soil, breaking up all backfill soil to the size of golf balls. Water-in well. For use as a groundcover, space plants 2½ to 3 feet apart.

Growing Tips
Keep the root zone of new vines moist to promote healthy root growth. Watering will only be necessary during severe drought periods. Mulch with a 2-inch layer of organic mulch to conserve moisture. You won't need to apply fertilizer.

Regional Advice and Care
No bugs or diseases bother this vine. In its young stages, guide this vine so that it grows where you want it. Don't let your ivy have a free rein. Trim away or pull down all unwanted growth, especially around windows, doors, and ventilation vents or anywhere it overgrows its bounds. This plant can be weedy; don't be surprised to see seedlings coming up in other parts of your landscape.

Companion Planting and Design
Self-attaching Virginia creeper is a tough, low-maintenance vine that will cover walls, trellises, and the ground. The aerial roots and tendrils of Virginia creeper will not cause the deterioration of masonry or brickwork. However, even after removing the vine, its adhesive disks will remain and are difficult to remove; plan accordingly.

Try These
'Engelmannii' has smaller leaves that grow denser than those of the species. 'Dark Green Ice' has shiny leaves that tend to have a more yellowish fall color. See Boston ivy, another species of *Parthenocissus*.

Wisteria

Wisteria floribunda

Botanical Pronunciation
wis-TEER-ee-uh flor-ih-BUN-duh

Other Name
Japanese Wisteria

Bloom Period and Seasonal Color
April to May; lavender-blue, rose-purple, white blooms

Mature Length
30 to 50 feet

Fragrant wisteria cascading from an arbor is a vision pursued by many; however, one of the questions I am most often asked is, "Why won't my wisteria bloom?" Disappointment can be the name of the wisteria game. Here are a few suggestions: Avoid cold-exposed areas where the flowering buds—formed in the fall—can freeze. Choose named selections grown from cuttings of wisteria; plants grown from seed can take up to twelve years to produce flowers. Don't overfertilize; high nitrogen leads to lush foliage and no flowers. Even with the uncertainty of flowers, wisteria is an excellent vine for a sturdy structure. The only difference between a wisteria vine and a wisteria tree is the way it is trained; either "end result" can come from the same plant.

When, Where, and How to Plant
Plant wisteria vine anytime the ground is not frozen, although spring is the best. Choose a location in sun to part shade. Wisteria blooms best where it has protection from the prevailing northwest wind in winter. The vines grow in all types of soil, including those with a high pH, as long as the soil is well drained. Plant wisteria as close to its climbing structure as possible. Dig the hole twice as wide as and no deeper than the soil clump. Loosen any roots that are wrapped around the clump. Chop up the backfill to the size of golf balls. Backfill with existing soil, and water-in well.

Growing Tips
Keep the root zone of a newly planted wisteria vine moist to lessen transplant shock. Water older plants only during drought. Mulch with a 2-inch layer of organic mulch. Too much nitrogen promotes foliage at the expense of flowers. If you fertilize, use a formula low in nitrogen.

Regional Advice and Care
No bug or disease problems will hassle wisteria. These vines become very woody after only a few years, and they need a strong support structure to climb. Tie the stems gently to the support to guide your vine where you want it to grow. Prune from summer to fall to keep it within bounds. Don't be afraid to cut your vine back; if desired, you can cut back each stem to three or four buds in spring. To "shock" a non-blooming wisteria into flowering, try making a circular cut 1 foot from the main trunk all around the plant using a spade.

Companion Planting and Design
Fast-growing wisteria provides lots of shade when used on sturdy wooden structures built over patios and decks. Keep it away from your home where its strong stems can damage windows and gutters.

Try These
I like 'Violacea Plena' for its dramatic, double, violet-blue flowers on 10- to 12-inch racemes. 'Texas Purple', with its long clusters of purple flowers, is known to bloom at a young age.

How Plants Prepare for Winter

All summer, with the long hours of sunlight and a good supply of water, plants are busy growing, as well as making and storing food. But what about winter? The days are much shorter so there is less sunlight, and water is harder to get. How do plants survive? Never fear, plants have many different ways of getting through those harsh days of winter.

Annuals and Perennials

Some plants, including many garden flowers, are *annuals*, which means they complete their life cycle in one growing season. They die when winter comes, but their seeds remain, ready to sprout again in the spring. *Perennials* live for more than two years. This category includes trees and shrubs, as well as herbaceous plants with soft, fleshy stems. When winter comes, the woody parts of trees and shrubs can survive the cold. The aboveground parts of herbaceous plants (leaves and stalks) will die off, but the underground parts (roots and bulbs) will remain alive. In winter, perennial plants rest and live off stored food until spring.

Deciduous or Evergreen

As plants grow, they shed older leaves and grow new ones. This is important because leaves can become damaged over time by insects, disease, and weather. The shedding and replacement of leaves continues all the time. In addition, *deciduous trees*—such as maples, oaks, and elms—shed all their leaves in fall in preparation for winter. *Evergreen trees*, however, keep most of their leaves during winter. They have special leaves that are resistant to cold and moisture loss. Some, such as pine and fir trees, have long, thin needles. Others, such as holly, have broad leaves with tough, waxy surfaces. On very cold, dry days, these leaves sometimes curl up to reduce their exposed surface. Evergreens may continue to photosynthesize during the winter as long as they get enough water, but the reactions occur more slowly at colder temperatures.

Where Do Those Leaf Colors Come From?

During summer, leaves make more glucose than the plant needs for energy and growth. This excess is turned into starch and stored until needed. As the days get shorter in autumn, plants begin to shut down their food production. And for deciduous trees and shrubs, something special begins to happen. There are many changes that occur in the leaves of deciduous trees before they finally fall from the branch. Each leaf has actually been preparing for autumn since it first started to grow in spring. At the base of each leaf is a special layer of cells called the abscission, or separation, layer. All summer, the small tubes that pass through this layer carry water into the leaf and food back to the tree. In the fall, the cells of the abscission layer begin to swell and form a corklike material, reducing and then finally cutting off the flow between leaf and tree. Glucose and waste products are trapped in the leaf. Without fresh water to renew it, chlorophyll begins to disappear. Other colors, which have been there all along, then become visible.

Orange colors come from carotene (KAR-uh-teen) and the yellows from xanthophyll (ZAN-thuh-fil). These are common pigments, also found in flowers and foods, such as carrots, bananas, and egg yolks. The exact role these pigments play in leaves is not known, but scientists think they may somehow be involved in photosynthesis. Bright red and purple colors come from anthocyanin (an-thuh-SI-uh-nuhn) pigments. These are also common in plants such as beets, red apples, and purple grapes, and in flowers such as violets and hyacinths. These pigments form in autumn from the trapped glucose. Different combinations of these pigments account for the wide range of colors each fall. Brown colors, however, come from tannin, a bitter waste product. As the bottom cells in the abscission layer form a seal between the leaf and the tree, the cells at the top of the abscission layer begin to disintegrate. They form a tear-line, and eventually the leaf is blown away or simply falls from the tree.

One important question remains: What causes some trees to have only so-so fall color, while other trees of the same species are simply spectacular? The answer lies in the weather. The brightest colors are seen when late summer is dry, and autumn has bright sunny days and cool (low 40s Fahrenheit) nights. This weather combination causes trees to make lots of anthocyanin pigments—and, thus, beautifully bright fall colors. A fall with cloudy days and warm nights, however, will bring drab colors, and an early frost will quickly end any fall display. The best place in the world for viewing fall colors is probably the Eastern United States. That is because of the climate and the wide variety of deciduous trees. So this fall, as you gaze out at the amazing hues of the fall colors, give a little thought to the even more amazing process that creates those colors.

RESOURCES

Ohio State University Extension Service

Ohio State University Extension Service is a wonderful resource for all Ohio gardeners. They continually offer current, research-based information through classes, workshops, newspaper articles, and master gardener programs. They also provide a weekly B.Y.G.L. (Buckeye Yard and Garden onLine) newsletter to hundreds of us in the industry. The bulletin sheets are available on the Internet at **http://bygl.osu.edu/** and cover hundreds of topics from bugs to disease to many "how-to" tips on growing plants in Ohio. These printed sheets are also available at your county extension office. Bulletins are a good local resource for gardeners and landscape professionals alike. Always feel free to contact your local County Extension office for a list of publications, soil test information, and other resources available in your county.

Use the Ohio State University Extension Service's websites to find information pertaining to trees, shrubs, or any plants that are grown in Ohio. This is a service that is paid for with your tax dollars, so feel free to use it and use it often. The people on the other end are very knowledgeable, helpful, and just great to deal with. They would love to help you. Check them out at:

http://www.ag.ohio-state.edu/   http://bygl.osu.edu/
http://buckeyegardening.com   http://plantfacts.osu.edu/

Bibliography

Cox, Jeff, *Perennial All-Stars*, Emmaus, PA: Rodale Press, 1988.
Dirr, Michael A., *Manual of Woody Landscape Plants*, Champaign, IL: Stipes Publishing, 1998.

Other Resources

Bailey Nurseries, 1325 Bailey Rd., St. Paul, MN 55119
Ball Seed Co., 622 Town Road, West Chicago, IL 60185-2688
Buckeye Resources, Inc., P.O. Box 519, South Charleston, OH 45368
Conard-Pyle Co., 372 Rose Hill Road, West Grove, PA 19390-0904
Diefenbacher Greenhouses, 11443 Colerain Ave., Cincinnati, OH 45252
Fortmeyer and Sons Greenhouse Co., 5311 S. Sectionline Rd., Delaware, OH 43015
Monrovia Nursery, 18331 E. Foothill Blvd., Azusa, CA 91702-2638
Ohio Nursery and Landscape Association, 72 Dorchester St., Westerville, OH 43081-3350
OSU Extension Adm., 3 Agriculture Adm. Bldg., 2120 Fyffe Rd., Columbus, OH 43210-1084
Proven Winners North America, 426 W. Second St., Rochester, MI 48307
Seeds Ohio, LLC, 127 Jackson, P.O. Box 49, West Jefferson, OH 43162
Willoway Nurseries, Inc., 4534 Center Road, Avon, OH 44011
McKeown, Chris; Wood, James (Woody); Routt, Greg; Scott, Debbie; Lerch, Diana; Denny McKeown Inc., Cincinnati, OH 45242

INDEX

PHOTO CREDITS

MEET DENNY MCKEOWN

Denny McKeown is a respected, popular, and highly regarded gardening expert who has been in the nursery business for more than 50 years, many of them spent as an executive with Natorp's. In the early 1990s, McKeown founded The Bloomin' Garden Centre, a year-round retail garden business that he operates with his son, Chris. Another business, Denny McKeown Landscape, is a full-service landscape design company featuring design and installation for residential and commercial properties.

McKeown has reached gardeners via radio, television, and print. He was the long-time host of the popular radio call-in program, "The Denny McKeown Gardening Show," heard across Ohio on various radio stations every Saturday morning. McKeown has also appeared regularly on the nationally broadcast Scripps-Howard program "DIY" sharing garden tips. McKeown has also appeared on garden segments for WCPO-TV and then WKRC TV both in Cincinnati, Ohio, for 24 years.

In addition to co-authoring the *Month-by-Month Gardening in Ohio: Revised Edition*, McKeown is the author of *Month-by-Month Gardening in Ohio, The Gardening Book for Ohio: Revised Edition, The Gardening Book for Ohio, My Ohio Garden: A Gardener's Journal, Kentucky Gardener's Guide*, and *My Kentucky Garden: A Gardener's Journal*, all for Cool Springs Press.

McKeown currently has a weekly gardening newspaper column for the Saturday home section of the *Cincinnati Enquirer*. He also writes a weekly multi-page newsletter for his website of very timely tips of what's happening in your landscape fifty-two weeks a year, including new trees, shrubs, annuals, new general garden products available along with information on bugs and other potential problems. You can get your free monthly newsletter by providing your e-mail address to www.bloomingarden.com.

McKeown has received numerous awards and honors. The author served as President of The Garden Centers of America and was awarded its highest honor, The Jack Schneider Award. The American Nursery and Landscape Association presented McKeown with The Garden Communicator Award, which is given to the person who has done the most to promote gardening and planting across America.

McKeown lives in Cincinnati with his wife, Patricia, where he enjoys his children, Molly and Christopher, and his grandchildren Maddie, Ryan, Caroline, and Courtney.